HEAD START

HEAD START

The Inside Story of America's Most Successful Educational Experiment

EDWARD ZIGLER
SUSAN MUENCHOW

BasicBooks
A Division of HarperCollins*Publishers*

Library of Congress Cataloging-in-Publication Data

Zigler, Edward.
　　Head Start: the inside story of America's most successful educa-
tional experiment/Edward Zigler, Susan Muenchow.
　　　　p.　cm.
　　Includes bibliographical references (p.　) and index.
　　ISBN 0–465–03316–4
　　1. Project Head Start (U.S.)—History.　2. Zigler, Edward, 1930–
—Views on education.　3. Education, Preschool—United States.
I. Muenchow, Susan.　II. Title.
LC4091.Z54　　1992
372.21'0973—dc20　　　　　　　　　　　　　　　　　91–59015
　　　　　　　　　　　　　　　　　　　　　　　　　　　　　　CIP

Designed by Ellen Levine

　　93　94　95　SWD/RRD　9　8　7　6　5　4　3

*This book is dedicated to
Sargent Shriver, Robert Cooke,
Julius Richmond, and Jule Sugarman,
the brilliant individuals
who made Head Start happen*

Contents

Preface

THIS BOOK IS A COLLABORATIVE EFFORT. EDWARD ZIGLER'S PROFESsional life has been intimately involved with Head Start for 27 years. From his participation on the Planning Committee for Head Start in 1965 to his role as the first director of the Office of Child Development in the early 1970s, he helped shape the program's development directly. Together with Jeanette Valentine, Zigler edited the archival history of Head Start presented in the book *Project Head Start: A Legacy of the War on Poverty*, which was published in 1979. Zigler was also selected by President Carter to chair a committee review of Head Start on the occasion of the program's 15th anniversary in 1980. From his first paper on Head Start in the late 1960s until the present, Zigler has continued to participate in numerous research and evaluation projects on the program. In addition, Zigler has served as an adviser to several administrations on Head Start's direction.

Susan Muenchow also has a long history of involvement with Head Start and other early childhood programs. A former reporter for *The Christian Science Monitor*, she has published numerous articles on early childhood issues in both academic journals and such popular periodicals as *Parents* magazine. While serving as public education coordinator and a research associate on the faculty of the Bush Center in Child Development and Social Policy at

Yale, she wrote the report *Head Start in the 1980s: Review and Recommendations* for the committee selected by President Carter. As a child advocate and state administrator in Florida, Muenchow has promoted collaboration among the state's three major providers of early education services—Head Start, Subsidized Child Care, and the Prekindergarten Early Intervention program.

This book weaves together Zigler's personal experiences in Head Start with Muenchow's historical and field research, including interviews of more than two hundred persons associated with Head Start (national figures, federal administrators, early childhood experts, and Head Start parents and staff). The first nine chapters tell the story of Head Start through Zigler's experience interspersed with Muenchow's discoveries. The last chapter offers the authors' joint recommendations for Head Start's future.

The book also includes a series of sketches or "snapshots" of the people behind Head Start, including parents, staff and national leaders. These vignettes, set off in italics, are intended to reveal the ideas behind Head Start, and how they have played out at the local level in programs across America.

And finally, a note about the book's subtitle. We frequently make the point that Head Start is much more than an educational program, and that much of its success can be attributed to its comprehensive health and family support services. However, Head Start is the nation's most important *educational* experiment when education is defined in the broad sense to include the upbringing of children, and not in the narrow sense of academic instruction. We firmly believe that education for young children, in this broader sense, has become a national imperative.

Acknowledgments

THIS BOOK COULD NOT HAVE BEEN WRITTEN WITHOUT THE HELP OF the people we interviewed. It is impossible to list here the names of more than two hundred individuals who shared their insights with us during the nearly two years that the manuscript was in preparation. In fact, the nation's enthusiasm for Head Start is evident in the large number of people who, once they heard about this project, were not only willing but eager to share their Head Start experiences with us.

The following persons deserve a special word of thanks. Edmund Gordon shared not only his time but also a manuscript he began many years ago on the history of Head Start. Saul Rosoff provided countless hours of essential background information. Joan Lombardi provided excellent suggestions throughout the project, and also reviewed the manuscript thoroughly. Helen Blank, Don Bolce, Raymond C. Collins, Harley Frankel, Peggy Pizzo, and Marilyn Segal also were extremely helpful.

We also want to express our gratitude to the directors of five Head Start programs that we visited extensively during the preparation of this book: Ophelia E. Brown, director of Head Start, Youth and Family Development, Community Action Agency of Metro-Dade County, Florida; Fran Collins, director of Head Start, Cambridge, Massachussetts; Muriel Hamilton-Lee, director of Head

Start under the School Board of New Haven, Connecticut; Willette Hatcher, director of Head Start under the School Board of Broward County, Florida; and Nancy Spears, director of Head Start under the Human Relations Council of Lee County, Alabama. These Head Start directors and their staffs literally opened their programs to us so we could take a fresh look at how Head Start is functioning at the local level today. The staff and teachers in these programs represent some of the most dedicated individuals we have ever met. The Head Start children and their parents provided the inspiration to complete the book.

Several persons read the manuscript and provided thoughtful suggestions. In particular we thank Jim Levine, our agent, who encouraged us to pursue the project; Sarah Greene for her helpful review of the manuscript; Sally Styfco for her skillful editing; and Charles Muenchow, who patiently read and critiqued numerous drafts of the manuscript. Bernice Zigler not only reviewed numerous Chapters, but also collected news articles over the years to provide some of the documentation for the book. Most especially, we thank Jo Ann Miller, our editor at Basic Books, for setting us on the right track and for redirecting the project at a crucial stage in its preparation.

Finally, the preparation of this book was facilitated by support from the Spunk Fund, the A. L. Mailman Foundation, and the Smith Richardson Foundation. A special word of thanks is extended to Marianne Gerschel, for her insights about Head Start.

1

High Hopes

"WHY DID HEAD START SUCCEED?" A REPORTER ASKED ME RE-
cently. "And why did the rest of the War on Poverty fail?"
I paused a moment, reflecting on the fact that there are
more children caught up in the most debilitating forms of poverty
today than there were a quarter of a century ago, when Head Start
began. Just a few blocks from my office at Yale there are children
as neglected as war orphans, preschool children who wander
around outside abandoned storefronts, their very lives at risk.

Unlike many social critics, however, I do not think the War on
Poverty failed, but rather that it was prematurely halted. The one
campaign in that war that was allowed to continue, namely Head
Start, has been a success. Head Start is far from perfect, and the reality has often not measured up to the possibility. But there was
something about Head Start that was able to bring together diverse
people for the sake of the children, and, more than 25 years later, it
still has the capacity to inspire people as far apart politically as
Jesse Jackson and Orrin Hatch.

High hopes made Head Start possible. Some of the hopes of the
mid-1960s were naive; some led to inflated promises that no social
program could possibly deliver. But we need to recapture the hope,
to believe once more that it is possible to set the next generation of
American children and families on a course toward a better life.

Head Start, the most important social and educational experiment of the second half of the twentieth century, continues to thrive and to offer direction for the future.

Although Head Start came to play a pivotal role in my life, I was not one of the original anti-poverty warriors. At the time the War on Poverty was declared, I was more involved in research on mental retardation than in issues of social policy. Yet Head Start swept down, lifting me and other social scientists out of the relatively private world of university research and dropping us, for a time, into the political arena. I eventually returned to my office in a neo-Gothic tower at Yale, but my experience with Head Start changed my life and influenced virtually all of my subsequent work.

The War on Poverty: Not Just in Name

The use of the term "War on Poverty" was more than a catchy metaphor; it conveyed the hope that it was possible, once and for all, to eliminate poverty from America's cities and streets. The rhetoric of war also suggested the sense of urgency necessary to defeat a well-entrenched enemy, and the level of resources the Johnson administration was willing to commit to the battle, at least initially.

In the Economic Opportunity Act of 1964, Congress opened the War on Poverty on several fronts: the Job Corps, to provide education and training for employment; the Community Action Program (CAP), to mobilize the poor themselves to fight poverty; and VISTA, a domestic Peace Corps. Within these broad parameters Congress gave the Office of Economic Opportunity (OEO) the equivalent of wartime emergency powers—a degree of flexibility that would be unimaginable today. By contemporary standards, congressional requirements for program accountability were virtually nonexistent. If the campaign against poverty was going badly on one front, the president could simply broaden it on another without bothering to seek formal approval.

Indeed, Head Start owes its very existence to the disappointing early record of the Community Action Program, which focused primarily on efforts to organize and employ poor adults. Congress had allocated $300 million for the first-year CAP. By midyear, OEO had spent only $26 million of that appropriation. Additional grant requests had been received, but it was unlikely that more than half the allocated funds would be used by the end of fiscal year 1965.

Sargent Shriver, OEO director and President Johnson's chief general in the War on Poverty, simply couldn't find many cities willing to take on the CAP battle. During the fall of 1964, when OEO was funding its first CAP grants, New York City officials were involved in a battle with Mobilization for Youth, one of the CAP prototypes. The New York agency had been charged with Communist infiltration, mishandling of funds, stirring up the poor, and undermining the authority of local government.[1] With this kind of advance publicity, mayors were forewarned that CAP dollars were one kind of federal money they might want to do without.

As any government agency leader knows, it is almost as bad to have a surplus in a federal budget category as it is to have a deficit. If you don't spend the dollars Congress allocates, you are certain to get fewer dollars the next time around.

Confronted with the possibility of a Community Action Program surplus, Shriver asked himself, What do I do with this money that can't be properly spent?[2] Sargent Shriver, it is important to understand, is an activist. Impatient with people who merely study problems instead of solving them, he thinks the only excuse for government is constructive action. So he asked OEO's research division to look into the total problem of poverty and to come back with not just a report, but also with recommendations for how to put the surplus to good use.

When Shriver looked at the pie chart that the group prepared, showing the distribution of poverty in the United States, he almost fell off his chair. The chart informed him that nearly half of the nation's 30 million poor people were children, and most were under the age of 12. "It was clear that it was foolish to talk about a 'total war against poverty,' the phraseology the president was using," said Shriver, "if you were doing nothing about children."

Worried about the backlash against the first Community Action

Program efforts, Shriver also knew that poor children were far more appealing victims than their parents. No one could accuse preschool children of being lazy or responsible for their own financial miseries. A War on Poverty that would benefit children, regardless of their race or ethnicity, was a war most Americans would want to fight.

FORWARD—TO A BRIGHTER AMERICA

While a budget surplus provided the opportunity to create Head Start, it was Sargent Shriver who had the vision to launch the program. His idea for Head Start stemmed from a desire to improve the intellectual capacity and school performance of poor children.

Shriver's interest was not entirely political. Both he and his wife, Eunice Kennedy Shriver, had been involved in early intervention projects for retarded children, particularly those who were also economically disadvantaged. Eunice Shriver had a retarded sister, and her parents, Joseph and Rose Kennedy, had established the Joseph P. Kennedy, Jr. Foundation to work on problems related to mental retardation. Eunice Shriver had also served as a consultant to a task force of the President's Panel on Mental Retardation in 1962, which offered the first proposal for a public compensatory preschool program. After President Kennedy's death in 1963, she had worked hard to implement the panel's recommendations.[3]

As Shriver was thinking about how he could use the Community Action Program surplus for children, he recalled a Kennedy Foundation project he had visited near Nashville, Tennessee. Conducted by Susan Gray, a psychologist at George Peabody Teachers College (now part of Vanderbilt University), the Early Training Project served some 60 black preschool children who were at risk of educational failure. It was designed, according to Gray, to offset "progressive retardation."[4] The program gave the children an intensive period of stimulation experiences, primarily aimed at developing their intellectual capacity as well as their attitudes toward school.

What struck Shriver most was Gray's finding that it was actually

4

possible to raise the IQs of mentally handicapped children—say, from 65 to 70 or 80. "Being of an era when we thought you were born with an IQ just as you are born with blue eyes," said Shriver, "that fact really impressed me and stuck in my head."

Shriver thought that if intensive efforts were able to raise the IQs of retarded children, a similar program might achieve comparable results with young people who were of normal intelligence, but who were poor and unlikely to do well in school.

The children in Susan Gray's Early Training Project in Murfreesboro, Tennessee, all came from families way below the poverty line. Their average IQ at the time the program started in 1962 was in the mid-80s, and a substantial portion were in the mildly retarded range.

The children attended 10-week summer sessions for three years prior to entering school. Each group of 20 children had four teachers, who were undergraduate or graduate students interested in acquiring more experience with young children.

The program used the same materials as a traditional nursery school, but in a manner designed to stimulate attitudes and aptitudes necessary for later school success. For example, the children loved to ride tricycles, but were only allowed to do so if they asked for them properly and identified the particular tricycle they wished to ride. Later on, the teachers set up the tricycles in a miniature traffic situation. The children learned to respond to traffic signs and to play traffic officer. Teachers in Gray's program also read to the children several times a day, and encouraged them to dramatize stories such as "Little Red Riding Hood" or "The Three Little Pigs."

To build a bridge from the progress made from one summer session to the next, the program included weekly home visits during the rest of the year. The home visitors, black women in their forties with considerable teaching experience with young children, worked not just with the children, but also with their mothers. The idea was to help the parents carry on in their homes some of the activities the children had learned in the program.[5]

Shriver's interest in creating Head Start also sprang from his experience as president of the Chicago School Board. Keeping in mind that the city closed the schools during the summer, and that most of the teachers were unemployed during that time, Shriver hoped to solve three problems with one program: to make efficient use of tax-supported school facilities; to provide summer jobs for teachers; and to find a way to introduce poor preschool children to the school environment during the summer before their first year of school.

Shriver's idea was essentially intended to prepare poor children for first grade by helping them overcome any fears they might have of school—both about the place and the activities they would encounter there. Most of these children had never been in a school building, and they didn't know anybody who worked there. In addition, many of their parents associated school with personal failure. As a result, the inside of a school, Shriver reasoned, "must be as intimidating to these disadvantaged children as the inside of a bank to a pauper." No wonder that both the children and their parents tended to view the first day of school not with anticipation, but rather with a sense of foreboding.

In Shriver's view, then, the whole concept behind Head Start was elementary: "Everybody has been in some kind of a foot race, where one group, by reason of a handicap, is given a head start," he said. "It was a facile phrase, and it actually did represent what we were trying to give these kids—a running head start."

Shriver tried out his idea of a preschool program designed to make poor children smarter on a broad range of scientists and experts in children's services. Like a general gathering intelligence before a major invasion, he consulted the directors of model preschool programs sponsored by private foundations, child psychologists who were studying early intervention, and his family pediatrician and Kennedy Foundation science adviser, Dr. Robert Cooke. All of these experts urged him to proceed.

Origins of a Comprehensive Program

In the fall of 1964, Shriver asked his friend Cooke to spend some time at OEO thinking about a program for poor children.[6] Cooke had been the chief instigator behind the creation of the National Institute of Child Health and Human Development during the Kennedy administration. Like the Shrivers, Cooke had a personal as well as professional interest in mental retardation. Chairman of the Department of Pediatrics at Johns Hopkins and a researcher into the biomedical causes of retardation, Cooke himself had two severely retarded children with genetic disorders. He was concerned about the deplorable treatment of retarded people in institutions. Too often, in his opinion, these institutions looked like human zoos. He was also bothered by the general status of health care among poor children. Immunization rates were abysmally low, and there was very little in the way of screening for correctable problems such as hearing and visual impairments. Finally, Cooke was one of a growing number of medical experts concerned that poor nutrition was responsible not only for chronic ill health, but for many birth defects as well.

Cooke's involvement, probably more than any other individual's, guaranteed that Head Start would have a component devoted to children's health. "When I started out," said Cooke, "there was no name, there was no model, with the exception of some preschool programs established by the Ford Foundation in some of the inner cities, and the early intervention model of Susan Gray."[7] Until Cooke got involved, Shriver's idea had been for an educational program and little more.

Shriver's OEO staff also deserves credit for expanding the notion of the preschool program beyond a strictly academic approach. In October 1964, Shriver gathered his senior advisers in the War on Poverty to etch out a plan. They were headquartered in a dilapidated old building with the unlikely name the "New" Colonial Hotel. It was not exactly an auspicious site for a high-profile, White House initiative. But it symbolized the true spirit of the effort: that this was not going to be bureaucracy as usual.

The staff actually had little to go on. The Economic Opportunity Act contained only one line authorizing, but not mandating, a preschool program. An interesting suggestion came from Richard Boone, director of OEO's Division of Policy and Development and the person most often credited with the phrase "maximum feasible participation of the poor" in the War on Poverty legislation. Boone thought that the preschool effort, like other CAP projects, should help empower the poor by employing them in various roles in the program. In December 1964, Boone drafted an important memo to Shriver suggesting that Head Start have medical screening and nutrition components, and that one-quarter of the staff hired in the program be paraprofessionals, primarily parents of the children enrolled.[8]

With all these ideas circulating, it is now impossible to determine who actually came up with the name Head Start. Some speculate it was a veteran Department of Labor official, Judah Drob;[9] others credit Holmes Brown, a Republican businessman whom Shriver hired to serve as OEO's Director of Public Affairs.[10] Or it may even have been Shriver himself, the consummate salesperson/politician. The nation is indebted to whomever it was. It is hard to imagine that any of the other names considered—"the Kiddy Corps" and "Project Success" among them—would have had the popular appeal or staying power of "Head Start."

In December 1964 Cooke was asked to chair a Head Start Planning Committee. "My contribution was getting the right people," said Cooke. The comprehensive scope of Head Start was determined by the committee's very composition. Only two of the members were early childhood educators. The rest of the committee was comprised of four physicians, a professor of nursing, an associate dean of social work, a nun who was a college president, a dean of a college of education, a clinical psychologist, and two research psychologists—including, to my surprise, me.

Avoiding the IQ Trap

I was 34 years old, an associate professor of psychology at Yale, and not very well known outside the academic world. I was just beginning to acquire a reputation for research on mental retardation, with a secondary focus in clinical psychology. One morning I was sitting in my small, cluttered office preparing lecture notes for a class in abnormal psychology when I got a call from Washington, D.C. It was Bob Cooke, whom I had met on a panel at the University of Minnesota, asking me if I would like to serve on a national planning committee for a preschool program for poor children.

I knew child development theory, and I had watched with interest the development of a preschool program for poor children in New Haven sponsored by the Ford Foundation. But aside from an informal observation of a model program, my expertise was primarily in areas pretty far from early childhood education and the social consequences of poverty.

The roots of Head Start in New Haven, Connecticut, date back to the spring of 1963, when the Ford Foundation sponsored a ten-week trial program for 15 four-year-old children living in an inner-city neighborhood.

Jeannette Galambos Stone, the early childhood educator hired for the New Haven program, had taught in a parent cooperative preschool for middle-class children in Washington, D.C. Early childhood education was just starting to become fashionable. Indeed, just before moving to New Haven when her husband joined the Yale faculty, Stone had been considered for a job at the White House to set up a nursery school for Caroline Kennedy. "Shouldn't the children be learning French or ballet?" asked Mrs. Kennedy's staff while observing Stone engage preschoolers in messier but more age-appropriate activities like finger-painting.

Instead of going to work in the White House, Stone was

soon walking the poorest streets of New Haven with
Grayce Dowdy, a social worker. Together they combed the
city's housing projects looking for four-year-old children
to participate in the preschool. Of the first class of 15 chil-
dren, not a single child had any previous immunizations.

I accepted Cooke's invitation to serve on the committee with great pleasure—and some reservations. I was concerned that a committee including several experts in mental retardation might appear to be drawing an analogy between poverty and retardation. As a child, I had been poor, helping my immigrant father sell produce from a horse-drawn wagon in Kansas City during the Depression, so I just didn't buy the implication that being poor meant being stupid. I believed that poor children suffered from a lack of money, not a lack of intelligence.

I also did not share the then-popular vision that an early intervention program could permanently raise children's IQs. In fact, I was probably one of the few psychologists during that period who was skeptical of the whole idea that it was possible to raise IQs dramatically. I thought that instead of trying to improve children's intellectual capacities, we would be better off trying to improve their motivation to use whatever intelligence they had. The distinction may not seem very great, but it had implications not only for the design of programs, but also for how they would be evaluated. My selection for the Head Start Planning Committee was, therefore, somewhat surprising. Shriver's initial attraction to preschool programs for poor children stemmed from his observation of the IQ gains among children in Susan Gray's program. And here I was trying to discourage the whole emphasis on IQ points.

Mine was not a popular view in the 1960s, the golden age of cognitive psychology. The optimism of John Kennedy's campaign theme song, "High Hopes," was infectious. It seemed that the whole country was captured by an environmental mystique; it was as if the biological law of human variability had been repealed, and all that was known about genetics was being denied.

In its simplest form, the environmental mystique held that intelligence—memory, concept formation, the formal structures of thought—was an environmental product. The implication was that if you supplied the right environmental nutrients, especially in the early years of a child's life, you could not only accelerate intellectual growth but also permanently increase mental capacity.

Prior to this period of "naive environmentalism," as the behavioral psychologist Sandra Scarr later dubbed it, the prevailing view had been that biology was destiny. Since the basic nature of children's development was thought to be biologically set, there seemed to be little point in trying to alter it. But in the 1960s, when the pendulum swung from predeterminism to environmentalism, development came to be considered almost infinitely open to the manipulation of experts.

The enthusiasm for improving intelligence was spurred by animal research, which seemed to indicate a link between early experiences and later ability. For example, one experiment showed that animals raised in the dark couldn't run a maze very well as adults. In other words, early perceptual or environmental deprivation seemed to create a permanent deficit in later problem-solving ability in laboratory animals. Many thinkers made a quick leap from sensory deprivation in animals to cultural deprivation as a cause of weak intellectual functioning among poor children.

One problem with this analogy is that many poor children, living in large families in crowded homes and cities, suffer more from sensory overload than from sensory deprivation. The precise nature of the deprivation that supposedly led some poor children to have lower intelligence than their middle-class peers was never adequately explained. Another problem is that the percentage of retarded people is only slightly higher among the poor than among the total population. More important, the range of intelligence is equally great among poor children and the more affluent. All in all, no one made a convincing case that the basic problem of poor children was a cognitive deficit.

Intelligence and Experience,[11] a 1961 book by Joseph McVicker Hunt, a professor of psychology at the University of Illinois, served as the credo—almost the Bible—for the naive environmentalists. Hunt believed that a child's mind was like a field waiting to be cultivated, and that the key to an IQ harvest was the proper stimulation.[12] So strong was Hunt's faith in the benefits of varied stimulation that he used it as a argument for "multiple mothering."[13] He even thought that television, by providing a variety of new role models, might make children smarter—an idea that I'm sure he would retract if he were alive today.[14] Hunt was even specific about how great a harvest the right environmental nutrients could reap—from 30 to 70 points.

Hunt's work had the merit of providing a rationale for experimenting with programs to enhance young children's development. In the post-*Sputnik* era, Americans welcomed any theory that promised to make this nation's children more intelligent. But in focusing on IQ, the most stable of all psychological measures, Hunt was on shaky ground. Even at the time, for every study indicating that early intervention had positive effects on intellectual capacity, there was another one indicating no such effect. Forty to 60 percent of studies conducted prior to 1965 indicated that compensatory education did not change IQ, and those that showed that it did generally showed only small effects.[15]

Another guiding principle of cognitive psychology in the 1960s was that intervention programs are most effective if administered during a critical time frame—by conventional wisdom, the earlier the better. This "critical period" concept was popularized in Benjamin Bloom's influential work *Stability and Change in Human Characteristics*. Bloom, a University of Chicago psychologist, argued that the human organism is most sensitive to environmental inputs during periods of rapid growth, which certainly occur during the early years. From correlations between IQ test scores obtained at different ages, Bloom noted that IQ scores at about age four account for half of the variance of adult IQ scores. Hence, there emerged what became a cliché of the 1960s: half of the child's learning is over by the age of four.

This is illogical on the face of it. Since no one knows when all learning is over, how could anyone possibly know when half of it is over? Applying Bloom's logic to the fact that the correlation between parents' and children's IQs is about the same as that between a person's four-year-old and later scores, one could just as

12

well claim that half of a child's learning is over before he or she is even born.

Once the media began to popularize these environmentalist theories, caution was thrown to the winds. *Reader's Digest* published an interview with Dr. Hunt, heralded by a blurb on the cover that read, "How to Raise Your Child's IQ by 20 points." *Harper's Magazine* publicized Dr. O. K. Moore's "talking typewriter," a machine that supposedly allowed three-year-olds to teach themselves to read.[16] *Life* did a cover story on the work of Dr. Burton White, which proclaimed the importance of putting a mobile over an infant's crib.[17] That article cited the "finding" that infants lucky enough to have had mobiles scored higher on certain developmental tasks than did infants deprived of these contraptions. Ignored was the fact that there was no relationship whatsoever between measures of these early developmental abilities and later intelligence scores.

So much press attention was given to the proposition that you could enhance cognitive growth simply by hanging a mobile over a baby's crib that, for many years afterward, concerned parents would approach me for advice, wanting to know how to compensate for the fact that their children, now school-aged, had suffered from "mobile deprivation" during infancy.

I still chuckle recalling the middle-aged woman who approached me after I had completed a lecture. "Oh, Dr. Zigler," she said. "I feel so guilty that I did not give my son the proper toys and stimulation when he was a baby."

Assuming that the boy must be retarded, I asked gently, "And how is your son now?"

"Oh, he's a junior at Cornell, and he just made Phi Beta Kappa!" she replied.

In short, during the period when Shriver was envisioning Head Start, the nation was preoccupied with intelligence. Scientists and lay people alike were displaying an almost magical faith in the power to increase mental capacity. I was simply not a believer. I even participated in several heated debates with Joe Hunt, who was much older than I and highly respected as the leader of the environmentalist camp. The debates usually took place on university campuses, but they were advertised somewhat like competitions between rival evangelists. The debates were animated, though Joe and I did remain friends. I recall how, just before one of our sessions, Joe took me aside and tried to exercise a little popular psychology on me. "Go easy on me, Ed," he pretended to beg.

The Power of Motivation

Given my pessimism regarding the notion that preschool programs could make lasting improvements in children's IQs, why was I selected for the Head Start Planning Committee at all? The answer is that there is a sense in which I, too, was a "naive environmentalist"—and still am. I believed then, as I do now, in the power of the environment to affect the *motivation* of any individual, retarded or normal, to make the most of his or her life's chances. I was conducting studies that showed how motivation and personality variables affected retarded children's everyday performance.

I pointed out, for instance, at a panel discussion at the University of Minnesota, that one could not really use IQ scores to predict which mentally retarded people would be able to function outside an institution. Among people whose IQs ranged from approximately 40 to 80, for example, IQ bore surprisingly little relationship to their adaptation to the work place or the military service.[18] Among the large group of moderately retarded persons who had no organic defect, I found that many behavior patterns resulted as much from motivational and emotional problems as from cognitive deficits.[19] The experience of repeated failures, for example, leads moderately retarded people to distrust their own solutions to problems even when they have the "right" answer, and to look to others for clues as to how to proceed. My research had shown that by giving them a few successes, their performance improved, even though their IQ scores did not.

The discussion of motivation apparently made an impression on another member of the panel, Bob Cooke, who was talking about the biomedical aspects of mental retardation. Cooke believed that a big problem for poor children was that they experienced too few successes in their lives. He felt that, as a result, poor children's motivation to try was diminished. It was my perspective on how to give success experiences to disadvantaged children that Cooke wanted me to share with the Planning Committee.[20]

The Revolutionary Idea of Parent Involvement

If it was revolutionary to focus on motivation instead of IQ in the mid-sixties, it was probably even more radical to insist that it was crucial for parents to be involved in their children's programs. At the time some experts actually recommended the separation of parent and child as an antidote to environmental deprivation. Psychiatrist Bruno Bettelheim, for example, thought the best model was the kibbutz, where children could be reared largely apart from their parents. Even years after Head Start's creation, Bettelheim questioned whether we weren't "re-creating in the centers exactly the home background from which we want to remove these children if we ask their mothers to work there."[21] Similarly, the President's Panel on Mental Retardation in 1962 had suggested that mothers be taught by social workers in one setting, while their young children were educated separately.[22]

Against this background, Cooke's selection of Cornell research psychologist Urie Bronfenbrenner as a Planning Committee member was another surprise. But it proved to be one of the most important decisions in the history of Head Start. Cooke had come to know Bronfenbrenner during their involvement in various Kennedy Foundation activities as well as on the National Advisory Council for the National Institute of Child Health and Human Development. Taking a radically different tack from Bettelheim, Bronfenbrenner was starting to develop his now widely accepted ecological approach to child development—the idea that you can't take children from their homes for only a few hours a week and expect to work miracles. To have any lasting impact, the children's day-to-day environment—particularly their families, but also their neighborhoods and communities—must foster similar goals. Bronfenbrenner insisted that, to be effective, any program for children, whether they were rich or poor, would have to involve the child's parents. Clearly, he was not coming at this principle from a Community Action Program standpoint, where it was vital to offer jobs to poor parents as an economic empowerment strategy, but the two rationales were complementary. The Planning Committee took Bronfenbrenner's advice to heart, and parental involvement became one of the hallmarks of Head Start.

Bronfenbrenner's notion of parent involvement and the ecological model of child development emerged from two sources—his own childhood and his cross-cultural research. Born in Moscow, he emigrated to the United States in 1923. His father, a physician, took a job as director of an institution for the "feeble-minded" in Letchworth Village, New York.

From time to time, Bronfenbrenner's father would anguish over the commitment to the institution of a person who was not retarded. Sadly, after a few weeks there, these people of normal intelligence would begin to mimic the mannerisms of the rest of the residents. When one of these patients came to work in the Bronfenbrenners' household, however, she gradually resumed a "normal" life. To young Urie, it was an important lesson in how family and community expectations influence human behavior.

After such an upbringing, Bronfenbrenner decided to become a psychologist. During the course of cross-cultural studies in western and eastern Europe, he was struck by the observation that Russian parents, both fathers and mothers, seemed to spend more time with their children than did American parents. When he was asked to present his findings at a National Institute for Child Health and Human Development meeting in 1964, a woman named Florence Mahoney commented, "Why, the president ought to hear about this."

A few weeks later the White House called, and

16

Bronfenbrenner and his wife were soon presenting their observations on Russian childrearing complete with slides to Lady Bird and her daughters. The Johnsons were impressed, especially by the pictures of Russian preschools. One of the Johnson daughters asked, "Why couldn't we do something like this?" [23]

Healthy Start: The Precursor to Equal Opportunity

While Bob Cooke's own background virtually guaranteed that Head Start would include a health component, he gives primary credit for that element of the program to another Planning Committee member, his friend Edward Davens. A pediatrician, Davens had served on the Prevention Task Force of the President's Panel on Mental Retardation in 1962. He had a master's degree in public health and was at the time Commissioner of Public Health in Maryland. He advocated that the program have nutritional and health aspects by stressing the importance of immunizations and other preventive measures. His thoughts moved Head Start further in the direction of a comprehensive child development program, rather than just an educational service.

Every Head Start Planning Committee member made a strong contribution to the program's conception. However, I have singled out the spokespeople for physical health and parental involvement because it was their ideas that made Head Start unique.

"Creative Recombination"

Once selected, the Planning Committee had only six weeks to come up with a program proposal. During that time, the committee met eight times in Washington and New York; we were constantly on our way to or from these meetings, trying to meet what seemed like impossible deadlines. There were 14 of us, and, for the most part, we hardly knew each other. However, strangers quickly became colleagues, and many life-long friendships developed.

Helping us function as a team was Jule Sugarman, who served as the committee's executive secretary. A former State Department administrator who had recently moved to OEO, Sugarman assisted Cooke in preparing numerous drafts of what was to become "Recommendations for a Head Start Program by a Panel of Experts," the so-called Cooke memorandum of February 19, 1965.[24]

During our meetings, Shriver generally kept a low profile. He gave us a pep talk at the beginning, but he did not dictate what the program should be. He did not even try to influence the committee by giving us the memorandum his senior staff prepared earlier, listing possible components of the program. I know that I, at least, never saw that memorandum. According to Sugarman, "It simply wasn't among the documents we had. The Community Action Program staff must have been moving on a separate but parallel track."[25]

No one on the committee came to the table fixed on a specific idea. Rather, there was real team spirit. One person's suggestion would build on another's. The result of this process was what Cooke called a "creative recombination." Likewise, no one element of the planning document was unique, yet when individual elements were put together, the result was extraordinary. Never before had a program with such comprehensive scope been designed for children. Health, motivation, and parent involvement evolved as strong themes throughout the document. In one of the opening paragraphs of its recommendations, the Planning Committee literally underlined its commitment to a comprehensive program: "*It is clear that successful programs of this type must be comprehensive, involving activities generally associated with the fields of health, social services, and education.*"

Far from limiting Head Start to an educational program, then, the committee placed "improving the child's physical health" first in a list of seven program objectives. The planning document actually includes more specifics on the health component than it does on early childhood education. Children were to receive pediatric and neurologic physical measurements; an assessment of nutrition, vision, hearing, and speech; and selected tests for tuberculosis, anemia, and kidney disease. While never designed to substitute for regular medical care, Head Start would help children get necessary immunizations and follow-up treatment, if needed. They also received dental examinations.

The wisdom of Head Start's emphasis on health seems all the more striking today, when many states are still establishing preschool programs for disadvantaged children that focus on education in a vacuum, as if the mind and body have nothing to do with one another. Although these programs generally require immunizations, most do not provide the health screening and follow-up treatment that are so integral to Head Start.

"Success experiences" was another important theme in the Planning Committee document. One of Head Start's seven program objectives was "to establish patterns and expectations of success for the child which will create a climate of confidence for his future learning efforts." Children of the poor, the memorandum reiterates, need "far more life experiences of success to supplant the frequent unsatisfying and unrewarding patterns of failure or the avoidance of failure." Programs should "maximize the opportunities for the child to *succeed* in what he is doing."

Again, the importance of including activities at which vulnerable children and their parents are likely to succeed may seem self-evident today. Yet, many programs designed for disadvantaged children still make the mistake of failing to begin with projects to which the children can bring some relevant prior knowledge or experience.

The Planning Committee memorandum also made frequent reference to the importance of parent involvement in the program. Three program objectives refer to the family, not just to the child, as the object of program intervention, and more than one page of the seven-page document is devoted to recommendations for parent participation. "Parents should be involved both for their own and their children's benefit. These parents need success experiences along with their children." Twenty-five years later, Head Start's parent involvement component is still the envy of many public school educators who have difficulty communicating with parents, much less getting them to volunteer in the classroom.

Given the widespread interest during the 1960s in improving children's intellectual capacity, I consider it a real victory that there is no mention in the Planning Committee's recommendations of raising IQs. One of the seven program objectives does specify "improving the child's mental processes and skills with particular attention to conceptual and verbal skills." But this language pales by comparison to the fervor of Hunt, Bloom, and other apostles of the environmental mystique.

Given the fact that most of the initial impetus for Head Start came from people who were interested in preventing mental retardation and in ameliorating its effects, it may seem strange that the Planning Committee document makes no provision for the inclusion of children with special needs. This absence requires a little explaining. Screening children for mental retardation was, I think, a casualty of an underlying racial tension, one that was no doubt aided and abetted by the predominantly white composition of the committee. One of the committee's few black members, Mamie Clark, shot down the suggestion to screen children for retardation because she felt IQ testing would discriminate against minority children. She showed keen foresight, because the heated controversy over the culture-fairness of IQ tests was just beginning to brew. Because of her concerns, the Planning Committee document indicates that screening for "special problems and special strengths" is a desirable part of an overall health evaluation of a child, but the decision about which screening elements to include is left up to the local community.

As another consequence of the same dispute, the committee abandoned any systematic effort to have Head Start serve children with special needs or disabilities. That came later, when a quota for handicapped children was established. Although we definitely thought that the program might head off some handicaps, originally there was no deliberate attempt to make a provision for children who already had disabilities.

A related battle developed over the whole issue of cultural deprivation. Once again, Clark led the opposition. I remember arguing with her that she couldn't have it both ways; if the children to be served by Head Start had not suffered any deprivation, there was no real rationale for the program. But at the same time I had to admit that the very term "cultural deprivation" was a misnomer. How could anyone be deprived of a culture? All one could be deprived of was the culture that someone else thought should be the norm.

To resolve the issue, the Planning Committee tried to play to the strengths of Head Start children and their families. Scattered throughout the Cooke memo is language emphasizing the diversity of the children to be served. "It should be recognized that children of the poor do not represent a homogeneous group," the document notes. "Rather, these children differ greatly in the diverse patterns of strengths and weaknesses which characterize their behavior."

A Texas-Style Beginning

Looking back on my involvement with the Head Start Planning Committee, perhaps the most remarkable aspect was that a group of experts, mostly academics, was taken seriously by the administration. Think of all the high-level commissions that have addressed various social or health problems since then, from the Joint Commission on the Mental Health of Children in the late 1960s to blue-ribbon panel reports on Head Start itself. Most of these recommendations are gathering cobwebs on the shelf.

There was one respect, however, in which both Shriver and Johnson ignored the consensus of the Planning Committee and other experts on early intervention programs. On the whole issue of the optimal program size for the initial phase of Head Start, we were dismissed as being naively out of touch with political reality.

Before the Planning Committee assembled, Shriver had asked the eminent Harvard psychologist Jerome Bruner how many children he thought the program could successfully serve the first summer. Bruner said it would be extraordinary if the program could serve as many as 2,500 children. "From a scientific point of view, that is probably what we should have done," recalls Shriver. "But faced with a national problem, to do only that would have been ridiculous."

No doubt aware of how we would respond, Shriver never asked the Planning Committee to address the fundamental issue of program size. Most of the committee members thought that Head Start ought to begin as a small pilot program and be tested. After all, most of us were academics, more familiar with conducting experiments than with launching government programs. How could a group of scientists say Head Start was going to be a good thing when it hadn't first been tested?

Despite that unofficial consensus, the committee, without ever voting on the issue, agreed to support—or at least not oppose—the Johnson administration's decision to proceed immediately with a nationwide Head Start program that would serve 100,000 children. The only reference to the issue in the Planning Committee document is a modest plea not to sacrifice quality for quantity: "During the early stages it would be preferable to encourage comprehensive programs for fewer children than to attempt to reach vast numbers of children with limited programs." Why did we all agree to stay silent on the basic issue of program size? The simplest answer is that we weren't really given a choice. As Bob Cooke put it, "Shriver didn't tell us as a committee that it had to be other than a pilot program, but he certainly let me as the committee chair know and convinced me that it was the way to go." Cooke remembers Shriver's telling him, "Look, you academicians are purists here. If the nation is ever going to have any program, it has to be done right away. If we study it, it will be studied to death and it never will come to fruition."

Cooke went along with Shriver because he respected his political judgment. After all, Cooke remembered the Peace Corps when it consisted of Shriver and a secretary. With Cooke on Shriver's side, the committee had little choice but to agree, even if only tacitly, that the program should begin on a large scale.

Recall, too, that the decision to go nationwide was made against the darkening clouds of the Vietnam War, and the mounting cost of what was already starting to look to many like a pointless conflict. Few of us on the Planning Committee really believed that an eight-week summer program could produce many lasting benefits in children's lives; we certainly didn't think that a couple of meals a day and some vaccinations could "cure" poverty. But the estimated $18 million price tag for the entire summer Head Start program was about the same as the cost of two fighter bombers at the time. If the nation could spend so much money on a war that was benefiting no one, why couldn't it spend a fraction of that amount on poor children in Head Start? The program certainly wouldn't do any harm; it might even do some good.

Beyond these rationalizations there was also the simple fact that we on the Planning Committee were like scholars in Camelot. Johnson and Shriver were accustomed to thinking big. They wanted Head Start writ large, Texas-style. Who were we to stand in their way?

President Johnson liked Shriver's vision of Head Start. Compared to the other theaters of the War on Poverty, such as CAP and the Job Corps, which dealt with unemployed inner-city adults, a program for poor preschool children looked like a winner with the public. Preschool children passed everyone's test for the "deserving" poor.

Lady Bird Johnson was also enthusiastic about Head Start. "The Head Start idea has such *hope* and challenge," she wrote in her diary after a meeting with Shriver in January 1965. "Maybe I could help focus public attention in a favorable way on some aspects of Lyndon's poverty program." She quickly accepted Shriver's invitation to serve as honorary chairperson of Project Head Start. Not all of us realized it at the time, but first ladies don't chair small pilot projects.

The Selling of Head Start

Once Lady Bird decided to hold a White House tea to kick off the program, the whole country began to join in the excitement. The initial idea was to hold a small reception to release the Planning

Committee recommendations and to recruit volunteers for Head Start. However, the reception soon became the social event of the season. Senators and congressional representatives started calling the White House to request invitations. "The real eye-opener was two governors' wives who phoned and said, 'I want to be invited,'" recalled Liz Carpenter, Mrs. Johnson's press secretary. One was Mrs. Orval Faubus of Arkansas; the other was Mrs. Hulett Smith of West Virginia. Apparently, Head Start was winning over even some politicians in the South, the region where Johnson was meeting the most resistance to his civil rights and War on Poverty initiatives.[26]

Ultimately, some 400 people crowded into the East Room of the White House for the ceremonies, followed by tea in the Red Room. The guests included politicians' wives, a Metropolitan Opera singer, and actress Gina Lollobrigida. Academics, particularly those of us specializing in research on mental retardation or early childhood education, were not used to this kind of attention. I remember one woman who kept asking me questions while the members of the Planning Committee mingled with the guests. I finally noticed her name tag; it identified her as Mrs. Robert McNamara.

Addressing the gathering, Mrs. Johnson asked for volunteers who would reach out to young children "lost in a gray world of poverty and neglect, and lead them into the human family." She went on to say that some children's cognitive systems had been so badly damaged by their low-income homes that they didn't know a hundred words. "Why," she added, "some of them don't even know their own names."

At this I cringed. Five-year-old children would have to be severely retarded indeed not to know their own names. Children who respond, "I don't know," when asked their names are exhibiting wariness of strangers, not lack of intelligence.

Yet, while some of the rhetoric that afternoon struck me as excessive, I have to admit it was also effective. As a result of Liz Carpenter's savvy, the national media covered the White House tea as a "society" rather than a "news" event. This was fortunate because it provided Head Start with the image of being a nice, respectable program. Society news coverage also contributed to the number of community groups who expressed an interest in submitting applications to sponsor a Head Start program. Some 200,000 people signed up to be Head Start volunteers, and groups started organizing Head Start programs in fraternal social halls, church basements, and wherever else they could find available space.

Three weeks after the inaugural tea, President Johnson announced he was almost tripling his original request for the summer program, from $18 to $50 million. The numbers kept going up until May 1965, when five times the original amount had been budgeted and over half a million children were to be enrolled. Indeed, three months before the first summer program opened, Johnson said that he had already "budgeted $150 million for fiscal 1966 to put Head Start on a year-round basis."[27]

This kind of wild escalation may be difficult to imagine today. But during the mid-sixties, President Johnson's economic advisers were actually projecting a $35 billion increase in revenues by 1970.[28] Sadly, Vietnam would soon consume all this and much more. But in 1965 the administration was not yet figuring the escalating cost of the war. Moreover, the Community Action Program still had an embarrassing budget surplus. Far from posing a financial problem for the administration, the creation of a nationwide Head Start program actually represented a solution—a worthwhile way to allocate the remainder of the unused CAP funds before the end of the federal fiscal year.

Without Johnson's early and enthusiastic support, Head Start never would have become what it is today. But his very interest in the program meant that it quickly took on a political life of its own. We on the committee had done our planning. Now the president and Lady Bird became involved in selling the program in terms ordinary people could understand. In the process they quickly fell into the IQ trap the Planning Committee had so carefully avoided.

The Cooke memorandum wisely set Head Start on a comprehensive course; we thought giving poor children shots and dental exams was as important as stimulating their verbal skills. However, our term "comprehensive child development program" was cumbersome and difficult to understand. The Johnsons and other promoters of Head Start found it simpler just to talk about IQ scores, and the media also picked up on the theme. Johnson even went so far as to later claim, "Project Head Start, which only began in 1965, has actually already raised the IQ of hundreds of thousands of children in this country."[29]

For those who had the job of selling Head Start, IQ-point gains apparently made the clearest and most convincing case. Jule Sugarman, who went on to serve as associate director of Head Start, recalls how during that first summer, Shriver said to him, "Now, I want to prove this program is valuable. In fact, I'd like to say how many IQ points are gained for every dollar invested."

"Sarge, that's only part of what Head Start is all about," Sugarman responded. But Shriver said firmly, "I want it done."[30]

Many of the academics involved added fuel to the IQ fire. When research on the first summer of Head Start came out showing an initial gain of 10 IQ points for the children who attended the program,[31] even the Planning Committee (by then called the Steering Committee) was impressed by the positive findings. About the same time, Shriver was asked to testify before Congress on the proposed Economic Opportunity Act Amendments of 1966. "What is the War on Poverty's greatest success which can be actually measured?" he was asked. "Project Head Start is OEO's greatest single measurable success," he responded. As his first example, Shriver said Head Start "has had great impact on children—in terms of raising IQs, as much as 8 to 10 IQ points in a six-week period."[32]

The selling of Head Start was also influenced by the nation's widespread faith in education as the key to eradicating poverty. So many immigrants had worked their way out of poverty through education. President Johnson shared this view and liked to think of himself as the original "education president." When I met him in the White House Rose Garden at the ceremony to announce Head Start's opening in May 1965, he quipped, "If it weren't for education, I'd still be looking at the southern end of a northbound mule."

Thinking back on Johnson's statements, I feel nostalgic that there was once a time that a national leader could be so optimistic about any domestic program. In that Rose Garden speech, the president said Head Start "reflects a realistic and a wholesome awakening in America. It shows that we are recognizing that poverty perpetuates itself. Five- and six-year-old children are inheritors of poverty's curse and not its creators. Unless we act these children will pass it on to the next generation, like a family birthmark."[33]

Still, politics and social science make uneasy bedfellows. At this first Rose Garden address on Head Start, President Johnson made a claim that no social program could fulfill. "This program this year means that 30 million man-years—the combined lifespan of these youngsters—will be spent productively and rewardingly, rather than wasted in tax-supported institutions or in welfare-supported lethargy."[34] Not only was the president implying that all poor children would eventually wind up in prison or on welfare, but that an eight-week summer program could prevent such a fate for every single child enrolled. Head Start was setting out to be an LBJ-sized program, and President Johnson's claims on its behalf were larger than life.

I confess that I had mixed emotions after Head Start was born. I felt proud to be part of a bold new experiment, one full of hope and promise. But I also feared for the future. Would Head Start children really grow up to become a strong generation, part of a new social order where poverty was not the major domestic problem? I began to worry that the overselling, particularly the emphasis on IQ gains, would come back to haunt the program, and that too much was being promised too soon. As it turned out, my fears were, if anything, too mild.

2

Miracle Workers

T HE DECISION TO LAUNCH HEAD START AS AN INSTANT NATIONWIDE program was risky, but it turned out to be right. Had the voices of caution prevailed, Head Start would have been too small to weather the storm just starting to break over the country. The rising cost of the Vietnam War would have destroyed the opportunity to mount a large-scale program. If Head Start had begun as a pilot project, it would have ended the same way.

Starting on such a grand scale, Head Start rapidly provided half a million poor children with services many of them had not experienced before: basic medical and dental care and two nutritious meals a day. Nationwide implementation not only made the program highly visible but also created the grass-roots support—and a potential vote from every congressional district—that would protect Head Start later on. Within a period of months, Head Start also provided a focal point for research and training in early childhood education. Arguably, these research and training opportunities stretched the program's impact far beyond the children it served directly. Ask one of today's leaders in child care or prekindergarten programs about his or her background, and chances are you will find someone who began as a teacher in Head Start.

But the rapid expansion of Head Start also had a price, namely the sacrifice of consistent quality. It is a price we are still paying, in the uneven nature of Head Start programs today. No administration, from Lyndon Johnson's to George Bush's, has adequately confronted the problem of program quality for Head Start. Ironically, the Johnson administration's decision to launch Head Start in such a precipitous fashion has left the program in the position of still needing to play catch-up more than a quarter of a century later.

Still, no one can deny that Head Start's early administrators pulled off a miracle. With an outpouring of public support, they managed to get the program off the ground in just 12 weeks from the time it was publicly announced. No other social program before or since has managed to accomplish so much in such a short time.

Project Rush-Rush

Even the initial decision about funding was made in a hurry. After showing the Head Start proposal to President Johnson, and getting the signal to go ahead, Sargent Shriver called Jule Sugarman, the OEO administrator who had served as executive secretary for the Head Start Planning Committee.

He put a basic, but hardly simple, question to Sugarman: "Now how much will the program cost, per child?" Of course, no one at OEO had had time to estimate the per-child expenditure, but Sugarman promised to look into the matter. "Fine," granted Shriver, "you have an hour!"[1]

"So another fellow and I sat down over a ham sandwich at the Madison Hotel and arrived at $180 per child for an eight-week program," Sugarman recalls. "We rushed that figure to Shriver. Sure enough, when the press releases came out, that was the figure used for the average cost per child."[2]

Sugarman notes with some amusement that a few weeks later, when the applications for Head Start funds started pouring in, every community, from New York City to the small towns of Kentucky, cited $180 as the estimated cost to serve each child. He remembers standing on the balcony of the old hotel that served as Head Start headquarters in those days, and yelling out, in mock anger, to the harried staff reviewing the stacks of applications below: "The next person who turns in an application with a $180 cost per child is fired!"

The hasty manner in which the cost was determined was representative of the way in which Head Start was implemented. Around Washington, it was a style that quickly won the program the nickname "Project Rush-Rush." Everything was rushed—from the initial selection of program sites to the design of the first summer's program evaluation. In order to open the program by summer, Head Start's administrators had only six weeks to collect applications and another six weeks to process them. The logistical problems were formidable. From scratch a system had to be developed for processing thousands of applications, awarding grants, and distributing funds to grantees.

Moreover, this rapid implementation was taking place in a nation that, at the time, had very little experience with early childhood programs. Kindergartens did not then even exist in 32 states, and prekindergarten programs for four-year-olds were unheard of. Very little federal funding was spent on child day care—about $46 million for the entire nation, according to Sugarman. Some child advocacy groups, such as the Child Welfare League, actually opposed any type of group care for young children on the grounds that it posed a threat to mother/child attachment. In addition, many public schools were still extremely segregated in the summer of 1965. These were the days when parent involvement in education usually meant no more than a PTA bake sale.[3]

To be sure, there were a number of small-scale early intervention programs targeted at disadvantaged children or those at risk of mental retardation, such as the Nashville project run by Susan Gray that the Shrivers had visited. In New York City, Martin and Cynthia Deutsch were collecting data on an excellent nursery school program for poor children. In Syracuse, Drs. Julius Richmond and Bettye Caldwell had started the Children's Center for infants in very low-income families. In my own city of New Haven, the Ford Foundation had funded a preschool program for 15 disadvantaged four-year-olds. It and other foundation projects were being observed as possible models for a national program to prepare poor children for school. However, most of these programs were being carried out independently, with little or no knowledge of each other until Head Start began to give them a focal point that linked them together.

The Right Staff

Head Start might never have materialized, much less survived, had it not had the right staff at the national level. Fortunately, Shriver chose wisely. As director, he selected a pediatrician, Dr. Julius Richmond, one of the few people in the country who had experience with the actual operation of a program serving disadvantaged young children. Shriver chose as associate director Jule Sugarman, who had already been extensively involved with the Planning Committee's recommendations for Head Start.

Richmond had started the program at Syracuse for disadvantaged infants as an outgrowth of some research he and Bettye Caldwell had begun in the 1950s. In an effort to trace the origins of psychosomatic disorders, they had, during the course of regular well-baby checkups, been using developmental scales and looking at parent/infant interactions. What they began to detect among these disadvantaged infants was a striking pattern of developmental decline toward the end of the first year, about the time when language functions would normally start to become evident.[4]

Richmond and Caldwell decided some kind of early intervention program was needed to prevent this decline. Because of the Child Welfare League guidelines against group care for infants, most of the Syracuse program was home-based. However, at Richmond's insistence, the program also included one full day per week in the Children's Center. This gave the staff an opportunity to observe the infants away from home and to determine whether the developmental decline was being averted.

When Richmond arrived at OEO to direct Head Start, he found his earlier experience at the Children's Center invaluable in giving him some clear ideas about what would and what wouldn't work. It was Richmond who decided that if Head Start was going to offer nutritious meals, at least one of them would have to be hot—not just sandwiches, or milk and cookies. His work in Syracuse also gave him the foresight to insist on a staff/child ratio that would ensure that Head Start children got individual attention. Sugarman had suggested a staffing pattern of one adult for every 20 to 30 children, a ratio typically found in kindergartens. But Richmond insisted on one adult for every class of 15 children, with two additional adults as teacher assistants. He didn't know if Head Start would succeed with this more generous ratio, but he was certain that it would fail with only one adult for every 20 preschoolers.[5]

Although Richmond was director of Head Start, he continued to serve as dean at the Upstate Medical Center at Syracuse. Thus, Sugarman had the major responsibility for the day-to-day administration of the program. Fortunately for Head Start, he had extensive management experience with a number of federal agencies, including a stint at the Bureau of the Budget. As Shriver puts it, "Jule was a career government servant, a bureaucrat with guts." Head Start needed a manager, someone familiar with the bureaucratic jungle, the traditions and procedures intrinsic to government at the national level. "If you are going up the Congo River, you better take someone with you who knows where the rapids are and where to spend the night."[6] It was Sugarman's unusual talent for being able to blend an understanding of the federal bureaucracy with the wisdom and will to circumvent it that made him invaluable to Head Start.

A Feast of Volunteers

Among Sugarman's many talents was an ability to make good use of volunteers, a talent that proved to be one of the master keys to launching Head Start in such a short time. It also fit in with Sargent Shriver's own enthusiasm for staffing social service programs, such as the Peace Corps, with volunteers.

Although most governmental grant programs, ironically enough, tend to favor the more affluent communities that already have the resources to submit a sophisticated proposal, Sugarman was determined that Head Start, a program for the poor, should reach out to the 300 poorest communities in the United States. To help solicit applications from these communities, Sugarman recruited a group composed primarily of congressional wives. Led by Lindy Boggs, wife of Louisiana congressman Hale Boggs, and Sherri Henry, wife of the Federal Communications commissioner, the group spent hours on the telephone trying to find people in those poor communities who would be willing to sponsor Head Start. These women contacted, among others, mayors, state legislators, and commissioners of welfare, often trying to get them to offer joint proposals so that the local leaders would understand they had to work together.[7]

The group also included Dorothy Goldberg, wife of Arthur Goldberg, then Associate Justice of the Supreme Court, and Sylvia Pechman, wife of Joseph Pechman, then director of the Brookings Institution. Recalling how they operated, Mrs. Pechman said, "Dorothy would call someone up and say, 'Sylvia, Lindy, and I have cleared our calendars to work with Head Start. Can you give us five days a week?'"[8] The women also persuaded national organizations—the Kiwanis and Lions clubs, local chambers of commerce, the National Farmers Union, the National Council of Negro Women, and the YMCA—to set up Head Start programs in communities and to contribute volunteers.[9]

Sugarman enlisted more than 100 federal government management interns—from some 40 government agencies, ranging from the Department of the Interior to the Internal Revenue Service[10]— to help poor communities develop grant proposals. Each intern was asked to donate four weekends, in order to travel to some of the poorest communities in the nation, and to help them to write acceptable grant applications.

The interns received the necessary training from Head Start staff during the evening hours, and then were teamed with an appropriate professional, such as a psychologist or early childhood educator from a university near the area where a Head Start center could be located. Sugarman's teams would literally sit down with the people in that community and help them write their grant application. By the end of that first summer, 240 of the nation's poorest counties, most of which were in the southeastern part of the United States, had developed Head Start proposals.[11]

Head Start was soon inundated with applications. Shriver remembers walking through the old, condemned Colonial Hotel in Washington, D.C., where Head Start was headquartered in the spring of 1965. The staff hadn't had time to buy file cabinets, and the hotel's bathtubs were filled with thousands of applications that had come in from all over the country. One tub held "A–B," another "C–D," and so on. Shriver recalls: "The hotel was a beehive of activity. There must have been a 150 people working there, of whom 140 were volunteers."[12]

The community and volunteer involvement in these early days of Head Start was simply unparalleled in a federally funded social program. Unfortunately, it is still missing in most publicly funded programs today, including those that are, from a fiscal standpoint, far more "accountable" than Head Start was at its outset. As Dr. Robert Cooke, chairman of the Head Start Planning Committee recalls, the program was handing out money to groups that could best be described as fly-by-night. Typically, a group of parents would get together with their pastor to set up a program in a church basement. They weren't asked to comply with the usual federal grant requirements, such as demonstrating the capacity to manage large sums of money responsibly. If the applicants had been asked to prove their financial accountability in advance, or to describe their previous experience in handling even as small a sum of money as $10,000, many of them would have been hard-pressed to do so. And yet, because there was such a high level of motivation at the grass-roots level, abuse and fraud in Head Start turned out to be minimal.[13]

Volunteer Medicine

Head Start was particularly successful in recruiting health professionals as volunteers. Richmond's contacts with the medical community were a key factor in this. First he secured the support of the

American Academy of Pediatrics; then he proposed that each state's pediatric association specify consultants to help with the Head Start children's checkups. Pediatricians lined up to help. Soon half a million children were receiving medical attention, many for the first time in their lives. They got fitted for eyeglasses, received treatment for ear infections that could have led to permanent hearing problems, and in general received a good deal of "remedial medicine," to use Shriver's term. Richmond also recruited one of his former students, John Frankel, from the Public Health Service to help secure dental services for the children.

Today, in many Head Start classrooms in Lee County, Alabama, the most striking feature is a four-foot model of a tube of toothpaste suspended from the ceiling. Class time is regularly set aside for children to brush their teeth after meals. This is a serious effort to give children a "head start" on reaching adulthood with a full set of teeth.

When a dentist visits the program at the beginning of each year, it is not uncommon to find children who already have eight or nine cavities. Many of the children have never seen a dentist before, and regular oral hygiene has simply not been a part of their life experience.

As a result of Head Start, not only the children directly participating, but also their younger siblings get on a program of dental care. "Bottle-mouth" babies, once a frequent occurrence in Alabama, are no longer prevalent.

At the beginning of the program, nearly a fifth of the children entering Lee County's Head Start suffer from iron-deficiency anemia. After a year of two good meals a day and, in some cases, iron therapy, virtually none of the children has this condition. In Lee County, therefore, a healthy start is clearly a vital part of a head start.

As impressive as these contributions of medical and dental help were, there were limits to how much free care health professionals were willing to donate. The American Medical Association and other health-care groups had long argued that nobody needed to lack medical care in the United States, and that income should be no factor in securing necessary treatment. Calling the AMA's bluff, Richmond decided against spending Head Start's limited funds on follow-up medical treatment and hospitalization, and chose to rely on private doctors or local government to finance the care instead.[14]

The Associate Commissioner of Health in California was furious with Richmond. "You're not paying for the health care?" he demanded.

"Well, you've always said that nobody needs to lack for medical care," Richmond responded. "Look, we didn't create the *need* for medical care among these Head Start children; all we did was spur the *demand*."[15]

Fortunately Medicaid was soon established, and it picked up much of the cost for the Head Start children's hospital care and other treatment. However, contributions of time on the part of health professionals, particularly in the area of mental health, remain an important part of Head Start.

To help promote voluntarism, Head Start developed an innovative approach. As a grant requirement, all Head Start projects had to contribute 20 percent of the total cost of the program. However, a large part of the local match could consist of nonmonetary contributions. A graded scale was developed to give communities credit for the value of the labor contributed, ranging from the hourly rate for a typist to that for a physician.[16] Thus volunteers, while not benefiting financially themselves, gained the satisfaction of knowing what percentage of the local match they had contributed.

The Spirit of Cooperation

While Head Start relied heavily on volunteers in those early days, there had to be a core group of paid teaching staff to run the local programs. Sugarman knew there were not enough teachers with experience in early childhood education to make the program work, so he sent out a telegram in late March 1965 to hundreds of universities. Please come talk to us about a training program, it said.[17] Ultimately, a six-day orientation program was offered by more than 200 colleges and universities. By the end of June, more than 44,000 prospective teachers had received their basic training through the university-sponsored sessions.

To visit the many fledgling Head Start centers, the program developed a technical assistance corps, which, at one time, exceeded 2,000 people. The Planning Committee itself became a resource for technical assistance, visiting some of the rapidly proliferating Head Start centers. Because the national Head Start office was so small, the members of the committee took on many staff functions. Fortunately, for a federally funded program, there was remarkably little red tape to contend with in Head Start's early days. For example, OEO simply gave us a book of airline tickets. It was like saying "open sesame" to the airlines; all we had to do was specify our destination and sign the ticket.

I remember visiting a Head Start program with Bob Cooke in the Watts section of Los Angeles during the summer of 1965. When we got there, we thought there was a holiday because everybody was out in the streets. Only later did we realize that the neighborhood was being burned down. We had wandered into the midst of the Watts riot! Interestingly, the Head Start workers were protected by the Head Start logo they wore on their sleeves—clearly a sign of the esteem Head Start enjoyed in that community. Today, unfortunately, Head Start programs are as likely to be targets of crime as any other establishment. But in 1965, if you wore the Head Start badge, you were safe.

The program's special status in Watts was not unique. As Head Start began during the summer of 1965, it seemed to bring people together all over the country, to promote a cooperative spirit. That spirit was reflected in a letter Julius Richmond received from a woman in Corpus Christi, Texas. "You'll be pleased to know," the woman wrote, "that Head Start here is under the sponsorship of the National Council of Jewish Women, located in a Lutheran Church, and serving children who are Mexican-American Catholics."[18]

Stephen Juan King, now in his late 20s, credits Head Start with ending his isolation as a black American, cut off from the experiences and opportunities of mainstream white America.

When King entered Head Start in Lee County, Alabama, nearly a quarter of a century ago, he and five brothers and sisters lived on the side of town where the pavement ends. As he told a Senate subcommittee in 1990, Head Start made it possible for him to attend movies for children at the local theater for the first time in his life. Being part of an organized activity made the "white-owned, white-operated, and normally white-patronized cinema less intimidating for a five-year-old black kid from Auburn, Alabama."

Perhaps the experience that made the most lasting impact on King's life was waking up to find his mother and the Head Start director, who was white, working together at his house. White people rarely ventured into black neighborhoods in those days, but since the Kings had no phone, this was the only way the two women could talk with each other on weekends or early mornings before work. Stephen King came to think of it as normal for people of different races to be colleagues and friends.

"The adults I met through Head Start—the teachers, nurses, administrators, volunteers, cooks, and others— were of African-American and European-American backgrounds," said King. "The center I attended was housed in a Quonset hut which was also a Sunday school area of an all-white Catholic church."

King went on to become the first black newspaper editor at his predominantly white high school, and later received a National Merit Scholarship. He is now about to complete doctoral work in Middle Eastern affairs at Princeton. Summing up what Head Start meant to him, King said,

*"I regard Head Start as the first step ... toward my full
participation as an insider in American institutional life."*

Finding space for Head Start programs was not always easy. In
Broward County, Florida, there were problems with the Ku Klux
Klan in one area, and with the John Birch Society in another, recalls Willette Hatcher, Broward's Head Start coordinator, and someone who has worked with the program for over 21 years.

"Many churches didn't want us," adds Cato Roach, one of the
county's black school principals who championed Head Start. "One
upper-middle-class church, which we called the pink elephant,
fired its minister when he told us to come on in." Members of the
congregation feared that neighborhood houses would go up for
sale, and that blacks would move in.

In other places there were happier endings. Marilyn ("Mickey")
Segal, now director of the Family Center at Nova University, and
her father, the late developer and philanthropist Abraham Mailman,
persuaded their synagogue to sponsor a Head Start program. To be
sure, it took a while before this program for poor children was fully
accepted. After all, nearly 150 Head Start kids were suddenly in the
midst of what had been a very white, sedate area. Among other ten-
sions that had to be overcome, the temple wouldn't allow Head
Start to use the kitchen because the food served was not kosher.
One day Segal was trying to cook a big pot of spaghetti on a hot
plate, when one of the synagogue sisterhood asked her what she
was doing.

"Cooking spaghetti," said Segal, as if to underscore the obvious.

A second query followed: "Why?"

"Because I can't use the kitchen," Segal responded.

"Well, tell you what," came the reply. "Why don't you put your
spaghetti next to my pot of chicken soup on the stove, and if they
don't fight, we'll continue."

The Temple Beth-el congregation gradually grew accustomed to
the presence of the Head Start children. The turning point came on
November 18, 1967. On that day, Sargent Shriver came to present
an award to the synagogue's Head Start program. All of a sudden,
recalls Mickey Segal, even those people who had put up with her

sponsorship of Head Start only because her father was a prominent member of the congregation were boasting about the program themselves.

Then the volunteer spirit became infectious. Segal's father asked a friend who manufactured sneakers to send some shoes for the kids aged two to six. Thousands of sneakers arrived in a matter of days, transforming Temple Beth-el into a virtual shoe store. The city of Hollywood, Florida, was about to junk an old airplane, but instead donated it for the Head Start children to play in. Then the synagogue got in on the action by providing an old bus. The children rapidly learned to climb in and sing, "The wheels on the bus go 'round, 'round, 'round." Foster grandparents began to volunteer their time to supplement the regular Head Start staff. Then Mickey Segal and her father started a "cots for tots" program, and got enough cots to equip every Head Start program in Broward County.

The Sacrifice of Quality

While Head Start did capture the hearts and minds of Americans in a way no other publicly funded social program has yet managed to do, the frenzied distribution of grants during that first summer contributed to a long-term problem that still plagues Head Start—wide disparities in program quality. While some Head Start programs are excellent, many are mediocre, and some are downright poor.

Haste was certainly an important factor, if not the only factor, in the uneven quality. I remember watching the screening process late one evening in the spring of 1965. Because a large, but temporary, labor pool was needed to process the applications, Sugarman hired substitute teachers to supplement the volunteers and help screen the grant requests at night. They had a virtual assembly line set up. The only sound was the repetitious thumping of rubber stamps as the reviewers scanned each application, checked five boxes, and sent them on for funding.

Impressed by the organization and the dedication, I nevertheless worried about the end product. I asked Sugarman if he was concerned about the quality of the applications. "Don't worry," he assured me. "Of course, we'll fund some bad programs. But after the program is implemented, we'll close down any programs that are bad and shift the funds to better programs."

Caught up in the spirit that night, I was prepared to believe Sugarman. But a few years later I found that it is not so easy for administrators to stop the flow of federal funds to a program once it has started. One of the first questions I asked after assuming the responsibility for overseeing Head Start in 1970 was how many of the original programs had been closed down. Dick Orton, another Head Start pioneer and someone who by that time was directing the Head Start bureau at the new Office of Child Development (OCD), paused and scratched his head. "Well, Ed, there *was* one program we *almost* closed down."

That program was in Boston. Apparently the Head Start bureau had learned that the staff there were using wooden sticks to discipline the children. But, Orton continued, it had not actually been possible to shut the program down. You see, Head Start is based on the principle of parent involvement, there were as yet no official policies prohibiting corporal punishment in the program, and the parents *wanted* the staff to hit their kids.

Thus, one of my first actions when I became responsible for administering Head Start was to send out a memo saying that no child would be subject to corporal punishment in the program; this seemed to me a minimum requirement for any program claiming to help preschool children.

For a program that was first and foremost promoted as a way to prepare poor children to do well in school, it is ironic that the disparities in Head Start's quality were especially noticeable in the area of early childhood education. Part of the problem was that early childhood educators were in the minority on the Planning Committee. In an effort to ensure that Head Start was a comprehensive program, particularly one that downplayed "cognitive" development, we may have paid too little attention to the educational component. We were unanimous in hoping that Head Start would be something more than a traditional nursery school; unfortunately, in some communities, it turned out to be considerably less.

Of the original Head Start Planning Committee members, only two were early childhood educators—James Hymes, once president of the National Association for the Education of Young Children, and John Niemeyer, who had for many years served as president of the Bank Street College of Education. They were highly respected leaders in their field, and they spoke out strongly on behalf of quality educational programs. However, they were simply outnumbered by committee members representing other disciplines.

As a result of the committee's relative de-emphasis of early childhood education, the seven-page Head Start planning document contained only general recommendations concerning the educational component. These recommendations were that Head Start should: (1) "provide a flexible schedule and program oriented to the needs of the individual child"; (2) "encourage exploration and manipulation of the environment"; (3) "develop such imaginative techniques as role playing, doll play, puppetry and dramatic activities"; and (4) "provide maximum variety of and opportunities for communication with special emphasis on conversation to strengthen verbal skills."[19] These were wise goals, but they were accompanied with no particulars about the training of the teachers who were to carry them out.

Head Start's founders and early administrators were also reluctant to be more specific about the educational component, in part because of political considerations. There was concern voiced by local school districts—and a lot of rumblings attributed to the John Birch Society—that Head Start represented an attempt to impose a national curriculum on school systems. For instance, according to Cooke, "the Los Angeles school system gave us a terrible time because they didn't want outsiders providing education."[20]

The relative inattention to Head Start's educational program also reflected a lack of consensus among early childhood educators themselves. As Richmond recalls, there was a lot of tension in the early childhood education community between the Dewey-oriented, free-play approach used in middle-class nursery schools and in Bettye Caldwell's curriculum, on the one hand, and the more structured approach used in Bereiter-Engelmann and Montessori, on the other. The proponents of the more structured approach argued that the free-play method was just going back to "show and tell."

To avoid getting into the fray, Richmond said he held back from releasing any single curriculum as a standard for Head Start. Instead he put out four or five "model curricula," including the Caldwell program, the Bereiter-Engelmann curriculum, and a learning-through-play model written by Jeannette Galambos Stone and Marjorie Graham Janis. The national Head Start stance was thus to be flexible on the type of educational technique to be employed, and to let communities choose their own approach.

The decision not to dictate the educational component was further reinforced by the philosophy of the Community Action Program staff charged with implementing Head Start. Their insistence that participation by the poor was more important than any particular curriculum instituted by professionals was based partly on a lack of evidence lending support to any one method over the others. More important, however, according to Head Start's first research director Edmund Gordon and his colleague Carol Lopate, the CAP staff's lack of interest in the particular education component was based "on the conviction that Head Start should and would become part of an increasingly strong movement among the poor of our country to take control of the course of their lives, including the education of their children."[21] This emphasis on parent involvement and empowerment was commendable; it would become one of Head Start's hallmarks. In the early days, however, the CAP staff displayed an almost disparaging attitude toward professionals in early childhood education, seeming to discount the views of even the most prominent educators. Like Ronald Reagan, who as president once suggested that anybody could take care of kids, the CAP staff seemed not to appreciate the distinction between the individual, informal care of one's own children and organized group care of other people's children.

Frances Degen Horowitz, then head of the department at the University of Kansas that ran the university's preschools, recalls the response she received when she submitted an application to establish a Head Start program in 1965. After assembling what she

43

thought was a proposal for a top-notch Head Start program, Horowitz received a call from Washington informing her that the budget was too high, and would have to be trimmed considerably. Horowitz protested, arguing that she had requested only what was absolutely necessary. She had a great deal of experience with preschool services at the University of Kansas and she knew what it would take to put together a quality program. The response, which Horowitz will never forget, was: "This is not supposed to be a quality preschool program; this is Head Start."[22]

Thinking back on the first two years of Head Start, which were mostly summer programs, often in makeshift facilities employing teachers who had minimal or no training in working with young children, Horowitz suggests it is little wonder that the first major national evaluation of Head Start was less than complimentary.

Short on Teachers

The principal problem with Head Start's educational component was the lack of trained teachers. James Hymes, who had argued during the Planning Committee meetings that Head Start needed teachers with bachelor degrees, continued to find the program lacking from an educational standpoint. The committee never did face up to the disadvantaged young child's need for skilled and trained teachers, according to Hymes, or the need for first-rate educational leadership in what was to be a massive educational program.[23]

Eveline Omwake, another premier early childhood educator and a good friend of mine, was so disappointed in the quality of Head Start as an educational program that she at first refused to write a chapter for the earlier volume on Head Start that I edited. She was afraid her chapter would be too negative.

After I explained that her perspective was vital to the book, Omwake finally wrote: "It is unlikely that even the harshest critic would want to see the overall project fail, but it must be said that for some children no Head Start would be better than what they are getting."[24] Like Hymes, Omwake was primarily concerned about the quality of the teaching in the program. She felt that OEO had placed too much emphasis on the goal of providing jobs for low-income parents at the expense of the quality of the children's program.

Even if OEO had told programs to hire trained early childhood teachers, however, there would simply not have been enough to staff more than a fraction of the Head Start programs in 1965. In many instances, there were not enough job applicants at any training level to fill all the necessary positions.[25]

At the local level, while a number of professional educators, namely public school teachers, were hired to work in Head Start, nearly half of that summer's staff had no previous experience with preschool or poor children.[26] Of those teachers who did have early childhood training, many left when school opened in the fall or when the national office began placing more emphasis on hiring low-income parents.

Finally, although Head Start benefited from the federal government's open purse during its first year of operation, the amount budgeted per child was still too little to allow for a quality educational program. Martin Deutsch, one of the first directors of a model preschool program for poor children, opposed the opening of a nationwide summer Head Start program precisely on the grounds that there was not sufficient time or funding to provide a quality program. He also felt that the summer budget of $180 per child was far too little; a good program, he thought, would cost at least $1,000 for each child enrolled.[27]

Rather than a minimal effort with a large number of children, Deutsch would have preferred a maximum effort with a smaller number. Deutsch also wanted to place the emphasis on hiring trained early childhood teachers, not on hiring staff from the community. Otherwise, he feared that the children might be blamed for the program's failure. Finally, he thought that two months was not enough time to mount a nationwide program.[28]

Deutsch's criticism created an uproar among the Head Start staff in Washington. It was fairly traumatic, because the program was still in its honeymoon period. The staff wanted reassurances from me and Urie Bronfenbrenner that the program was on the right track. Perhaps we didn't pay enough attention to Deutsch's concerns. There is a tendency in a bureaucracy, once a program is funded, for the people involved to circle it with their wagons and protect it, instead of taking the negative comments at face value and saying, Well, that person may have a point.

Nor did Head Start's quality as an educational program improve when it was converted to a 10-month program. While a full-year program had far more chance of making a meaningful difference in children's lives, Head Start did not have the resources for a longer program. Over 80 percent of the summer programs, according to Gordon and Lopate, had been sponsored by local school systems, which made sense because they had space that was not being utilized during the summer. However, when Head Start converted to a full-year program, many schools needed their classrooms back, and many of the teachers had to return to their regular jobs. As a result, Head Start had to scramble for staff and space. Equally serious, while a 10-month program was likely to cost at least five times as much per child as the summer program, the administration had budgeted only twice as much money.

During my own visits to Head Start centers, I found great variation. Play *is* the work of children, but it should not be random play. There has to be some structure. Some Head Start programs had the right ingredients—good teachers, some kind of curriculum to provide organization for the day, and a room divided into appropriate activity areas. In other programs the staff appeared to have given little thought to what they wanted to do; they were just filling up the day.

One center I visited in some ways epitomized what not to do in an early childhood program. Children were being instructed in the most authoritarian, "teach-for-the-test" manner. In almost a parody of Lady Bird's lament that poor children were so deprived that they did not know their own names, the staff had literally placed children with name cards in front of mirrors in an effort to drill them.

This exercise began to bother me so much that I tried what I called the "no name" experiment at a local Head Start center. Out of some 30 children, two or three did claim that they did not know their names. All but one, however, suddenly remembered in return for the reward of cookies and juice in another room. One little girl held out, continuing to insist that she didn't know her name. Finally, her older sister arrived to take her home.

"What's your little sister's name?" I asked her.

"Don't you tell him!" blurted out the younger child.

As one of the original Ford Foundation–sponsored preschools for disadvantaged children, the Head Start program in New Haven was initially everything that a Head Start program should be. It functioned so well that the national Head Start office distributed its curriculum nationally.

But by the late 1960s, under pressure to admit more children, but with no increase in funds, the quality began to decline. Class size increased, and each teacher had one classroom aide instead of two. Fewer and fewer lead teachers had bachelor's degrees in early childhood education or any significant training in how to work with young children.

Jeannette Galambos Stone was shocked when she returned to visit several centers in the city in the 1980s. The program had diverged far from her original vision of learning through play. The teachers seemed never to have heard of building on an activity that might actually interest preschool children. Rote memorization through intimidation would better characterize their pedagogical style.

In one center Stone observed, Miss Lynette (not her real name) drilled the children on the alphabet, telling them what to do and how to do it as if training soldiers for military duty. "No playing!" the teacher yelled.[29] When Miss Lynette had a song session, she yelled as she sang, and the children all yelled along with her. On another visit, Stone found the teacher instructing a child at the blackboard: "Don't draw ... don't do your own thing! ... Just draw on the dots!"

As lunch time approached, the staff yelled at the chil-
dren to sit at the table to wait for lunch. Tables were dirty,
and children raced around, fighting and screaming. There
were no blocks available, no paints or easel, and virtually
nothing constructive to do. By this time efforts to involve
parents had dissipated, and no one was keeping very good
records of the children's health services. What had begun
as a model program had degenerated into a nursery
school nightmare.

Hasty Research Measures

Like the other aspects of Head Start, the research and evaluation measures used to assess the program also suffered from the speed with which they were put together. For those early measures, I bear considerable responsibility.

There had been a tremendous fight on the Planning Committee concerning whether to have an evaluation component at all. The medical people felt that the purpose of Head Start was to feed children, get their teeth fixed, and offer them a pleasant experience. What was there to evaluate? It was clear Head Start would do no harm. There was also concern that the only existing measures of educational performance were based on what was expected of white, middle-class children. Their use would at best overlook and at worst disparage the abilities of the minority children enrolled in Head Start.

I was the member of the Planning Committee who fought the loudest for evaluation, but it was Dr. Julius Richmond who recommended that we go ahead. He had been hired to direct the program and was attending one of the last committee meetings before release of our recommendations. The Planning Committee document states only that "research and evaluation should be a key part of both local and national efforts," and that "the Office of Economic Opportunity should arrange for independent assessment of local programs for purposes of identifying successful techniques and programs."[30]

Richmond asked Edmund Gordon, then a researcher at Yeshiva University and now a professor at Yale, to direct the evaluation component. Gordon was an expert on compensatory education and a highly respected researcher. Gordon, who is black, hoped to overcome some of the resistance on the part of minorities to participating in research studies.

During the spring of 1965, Bronfenbrenner, Gordon, Richmond, and I met endlessly to debate which measures to use. Time was passing, and we still had not decided how to evaluate the summer Head Start program. Gordon and I convinced the group that it would be a mistake to use IQ as the measure of Head Start's success, but our problem was that there was no other standardized test available that was really appropriate for a preschool population.

"Look, we're sitting around the table doing what researchers always do," I remember saying. "We have to bite the bullet and get this done or we won't have any measures this summer."

Richmond said, "You're right—you do it, Ed."

We had a little over a week to decide on the measures before the first Head Start programs opened. We did secure one good measure, "The Preschool Inventory," from Bettye Caldwell, Richmond's colleague at Syracuse. It is an excellent instrument and is still in use. As for the rest of the measures, Gordon and I went back up to my research lab at Yale. I assembled a team of four or five of my graduate students. We looked through the panoply of possible measures, borrowed some, and adapted others. There was a parent interview form and a schedule for collection of demographic information, a form on health, and one on social competence or social maturity. The students were young and eager to help, and we worked around the clock, day and night, for about 10 days. It was a hectic time.

On the last day, Ed Gordon was desperate for the measures. He was late for the plane to Washington, and he couldn't wait any longer. He grabbed the last protocol off the mimeograph machine before the ink was dry, and he was off.

Once the measures arrived in Washington, there was no time left to validate those that had not been used previously. Worse yet, by the time the forms were printed and distributed, Head Start had already been underway for two weeks. The Head Start workers dutifully filled in the many forms and sent them in. But as the coup de grace for this initial research and evaluation effort, OEO had no way to process the score sheets. "We were inundated with data," said Gordon. "I had to get help from the Census Bureau just to manage it." The first batch of data that Gordon looked at covered 2,000 children. He never looked at the rest. Sugarman adds that somewhere in the archives there must be thousands of test sheets still sitting.[31]

As the chief person responsible for developing the first measures used to evaluate Head Start that summer, I have to say that they were a disaster. They were so badly done that the results could never be analyzed.

We won only one research and evaluation victory that summer, and that was to establish the principle that evaluation was important. Evaluation would at one point almost destroy Head Start, but it also gave the program credibility, and assured the public that it was not just another "do-gooder" program.

One of the basic problems with the initial evaluation effort was the sheer size of the project. Shriver was adamant that the assessment must include *all* the half-million children enrolled in the program. Richmond sensed this was a mistake. And today, if there were any one thing he would re-do about that first summer of Head Start, it would be to put more time into the design of a manageable national sample. That way we would have had data representative of the population served, but of a size that was possible to digest and understand.[32]

This first evaluation effort did produce the only comprehensive descriptive data on Head Start participants that summer—background of the teachers, the economic status of the families served, and how the children were recruited. But the unwieldiness of the data suggested to Gordon that the whole approach was a mistake, and convinced him that the evaluation effort needed to be much more decentralized and intensive.[33]

Based on the experience of the first summer, Gordon set up regional research and evaluation centers for Head Start. By providing funding to allow researchers to spend half of their time on Head Start, and the other half on their own independent projects, Gordon recruited some of the finest researchers in the field. Fourteen regional research centers were established, some of which eventually provided longitudinal findings demonstrating long-term positive effects of early childhood programs, such as the fact that the children who attended them were more apt to be in the right grade for the right age, and less apt to be in special education.

Problems with IQ Measure

The root problem with the research and evaluation in the early years of Head Start, however, was that we did not know what to measure. Public health researchers might have assessed the number of measles cases prevented, or the reduction in hearing or speech problems. Sociologists might have looked at the number of low-income parents who obtained jobs through Head Start. But the only people evaluating Head Start were psychologists, and, for a time, that greatly limited the focus of the research.

While Gordon and I were calling for the development of new research instruments that would measure changes in attitude, cooperation, and behavior brought about Head Start, many researchers continued to rely on standardized tests, most frequently IQ, to assess the program. Once Leon Eisenberg found a 10-point IQ gain resulting from Head Start, it became increasingly difficult to oppose the use of IQ as a measure. When Martin Deutsch obtained similar results, the *New York Times* reported that children gained an IQ point per month in his program. If so, many of us would have wanted to enroll our own children for 20 to 30 months at least.

Despite the initial IQ gains reported in these studies, I was increasingly uneasy about using IQ as a measure of Head Start's effectiveness. One day at Yale I was surprised to see the noted psychologist Herbert Birch coming out of the men's room near my office. He had come to Yale to review a research project.

"I used to think you were smart, Ed," he said to me abruptly. "But now I think you are the dumbest man I know."

"What do you mean, Herb?" I asked, trying not to seem too taken aback.

He retorted, "Anybody who would use change on the most stable measure ever discovered, namely IQ, to assess the effectiveness of a program must be stupid!"

I had never supported the use of IQ to assess Head Start, and had spoken out against it in the Planning Committee. However, the encounter with Birch made me want to challenge directly and publicly the studies showing IQ gains from programs like Head Start. I felt I had to expose the environmental bias behind this work.

My chance came a short time later at an international conference sponsored by the George Peabody Teachers College and the National Institute of Mental Health. It was, I think, my most difficult presentation ever. Heading up to the speakers' platform, I felt like I was entering a lion's den, the stronghold of the "IQ is plastic" proponents. Most of the speakers were decidedly in the environmentalist camp, and the session was chaired by Joe Hunt, my old debating partner and the most fervent supporter of the idea that early intervention programs could raise children's IQs. Even more intimidating, as I surveyed the room I realized that many of the presenters were influential in helping federal agencies and philanthropic institutes make decisions about where to direct their funds. This was not just a debate; it could well affect my future ability to obtain research grants.

In the opening of my presentation, I took a shot at Hunt and his student, Ina Uzgiris, the featured speaker at the symposium. I accused Dr. Uzgiris of showing a profound disrespect for the biological, constitutional, and/or genetic integrity of the human organism. My own view, which I developed at some length that day, is that all systems in the human organism are influenced by an interaction between genetics and environment.[34] Based on my own research, I was convinced that the environment had a much stronger influence on the motivational and emotional systems than on the cognitive system.

Not only did I think that it is important to take the biological integrity of the human organism seriously, but I was also concerned that an unbridled environmentalism would backfire. During the early twentieth century, there was a period in the treatment of retarded children when the notion of "mental orthopedics" was in ascendancy. Many workers felt that, given the right kind of experience and training, retarded children might become "normal." Soon state schools were set up to provide the training that would ultimately "cure" retardation. When the retarded children did not become normal, these schools simply gave up on any attempt at treatment. They became purely custodial institutions, and the treatment of retarded persons entered its darkest phase. My concern was that Head Start might suffer a similar fate, that overoptimism might lead to undue pessimism. Then the nation might be even less willing to help poor children than it had been before Head Start began.

I was the only voice at the Peabody-NIMH conference to caution against placing too much hope in the power to raise children's IQs. Despite the miraculous launch of Head Start, and its overwhelming popularity with the public, I feared the program was on a collision course, in danger of crashing into its own expectations. Head Start had been designed to de-emphasize cognitive development, yet it was being evaluated primarily on the most cognitive measure of all—IQ.

Rose Garden Promises

All these concerns about the rapid expansion of Head Start, and the fear that the wrong kind of promises were being made on the program's behalf, remained in the background as the first summer of Head Start drew to a close. And we might well have had the resources to address them without too much difficulty had the conflict in Vietnam not been escalating. As Johnson talked about Head Start that summer, he was in an expansive mood. When Julius Richmond visited him in the Oval Office during this period, the president said he wanted to give all children—all the children of the whole world—a head start.

On the afternoon of August 31, 1965, War on Poverty officials, members of the Head Start Steering Committee, and a number of Head Start children and their parents gathered in the White House Rose Garden. We were there for the president's announcement to expand Head Start to a full-year program. That gathering still strikes me as reflecting the real miracle of Head Start: a diverse people uniting through the political process to achieve a common goal. Here was an assortment of bureaucrats, experts, and academics brought face-to-face with the people who were usually defined as the problem it is their business to "solve."

We, the problem solvers, were standing somewhat awkwardly to one side; the Head Start children and their parents were gathered on the other side. We had all been involved in a common enterprise for weeks, but with the unfamiliar backdrop of the White House behind us, we felt a little unsure of ourselves, and of each other. A catalyst was needed to bring us together.

Suddenly, President and Mrs. Johnson strode into the garden. Adept politicians, they walked directly over to a little Head Start girl and picked her up. They hugged her, commented on what a pretty dress she was wearing, and said they were sorry it was such a hot day. They returned her to her parents, complimenting them on what a fine child they had. It was polished politics, and it worked. We all relaxed, felt good about what we had accomplished, and applauded as President Johnson made it official: Head Start was here to stay.

In his remarks that day, President Johnson noted that "This summer some hope entered the lives of more than 500,000 children, and those half million youngsters need that hope the most. Before this summer, they were on the road to despair. They were on the road to that wasteland of ignorance in which the children of the poor grow up and become the parents of the poor.

"But today, after the first trial of Project Head Start, these children are now ready to take their places beside their more fortunate classmates in regular school."[35]

Only one of the key Head Start officials, Ed Gordon, the man in charge of the massive evaluation of the first year's summer program, chose not to attend that ceremony. Still struggling to evaluate the first summer's data, he felt it was premature to announce that Head Start was a success.[36] But Gordon's reluctance went beyond questions of data. In the midst of the widespread killing of families thousands of miles away in Southeast Asia, he simply didn't think it appropriate to pay tribute to the administration's more compassionate policies at home.

3

On the Defensive

A S SOME OF US HAD FEARED, SOON AFTER THE FIRST SUMMER OF Head Start reports of "fade-out" in the program's effects on cognitive development began to trickle in. Three major studies—the Coleman Report, the Westinghouse/Ohio Evaluation, and a monograph by behaviorist Arthur Jensen—challenged the effectiveness of compensatory education for disadvantaged children. Head Start, the nation's favorite social program, was under attack, and those of us who had promoted evaluation were ourselves on the defensive.

First Signs of Fade-out

As early as 1966, a study of New York City children who had participated in Head Start in the summer of 1965 found that these children scored higher in "readiness to enter school" than did a similar group of disadvantaged children who had not attended Head Start.[1] However, after a few months in public school, the non–Head Start children had caught up in most areas. This study, led by Dr. Max Wolff, then senior research sociologist at the Center for Urban Education, found no significant differences in performance on an achievement test between the two groups of children six to eight months after Head Start.

Most educational researchers, including Wolff himself, interpreted these study findings to imply that the public schools were at fault. "Head Start cannot substitute for the long overdue improvement of education in the elementary schools which have failed the Negro and Puerto Rican children," said Wolff.[2] "Head Start children had a magnificent experience and had great expectations about kindergarten," he added. "When they were disappointed, they tended to give up."

In "Pre-School Education Today," published in 1966, Dr. Martin Deutsch, one of the original clinical experimenters to find a 10-point IQ gain among disadvantaged children attending preschool, pleaded against expecting miracles from Head Start. What was needed, he wrote, was an "early childhood concept" running from three years of age to the end of the third grade.[3] Picking up on the need for continuity to prevent fade-out, the Johnson administration devised a program called "Project Follow Through," which was designed to preserve the Head Start gains through the early years of elementary school.

Yet, it is one thing to say that one or two years of Head Start is not long enough to produce lasting cognitive improvements, and it is quite another to assert that, if the program were continued into elementary school, there would be long-lasting IQ effects. In reality, it was already clear that Head Start was not providing a huge pay-off in terms of cognitive development.

My own research suggested the reason for the apparent fade-out in the initial cognitive gains: the Head Start children didn't lose the increased cognitive ability when they entered school; they had never really had it in the first place. Reflecting on the 10-point increase in IQ that Leon Eisenberg had observed among children attending the first eight-week summer program of Head Start, I, along with Yale faculty colleague Earl C. Butterfield, questioned the assumption that the IQ test is a relatively pure measure of the formal aspects of the child's cognitive structure.[4] On the contrary, we argued, intelligence tests actually measure three distinct factors: (1) *formal cognitive processes*, all of the abilities with which Piaget and other workers were concerned; (2) *informational achieve-ments*, which reflect the content (that is, the things children know or know about) rather than the formal properties of cognition; and (3) *motivation and the emotional factors* in learning.

An economically disadvantaged child might have a perfectly ad-equate storage and retrieval system, a formal cognitive feature, to master quickly the correct answer to the Binet IQ test vocabulary item, "What is a gown?," but still might reply "I don't know" be-cause he has never heard the word "gown" and thus has had no chance to acquire this particular piece of knowledge. Or, the child may know what a gown is but respond "I don't know" in order to end the unpleasant business of dealing with a strange and demand-ing grown-up. This conceptualization suggested that performance on IQ tests can reflect factors having little to do with the formal thought processes that have been investigated by cognitive theo-rists.

In a now well-known study, Butterfield and I then concluded that the 10-point gain in IQ we observed among poor children at-tending a Head Start program had not resulted from an actual im-provement in cognitive processes, but rather from motivational fac-tors, such as a greater expectancy of success. Indeed, we found that we could produce the same 10-point "gain" by administering the IQ test under optimal conditions—for example, by having the tester rearrange the order of the questions, presenting the easier items first in order to assure some degree of initial success. The tester, at least initially, would also refuse to take "I don't know" as an answer, and continue to encourage the child to respond to the question.

The fact that the increase in IQ test scores resulted from the children's more positive attitude toward the test did not mean that the increase was unimportant. With respect to unambiguous im-provements in the child's basic cognitive functioning, we noted, the particular preschool program investigated in our study would have to be considered a failure. However, in terms of the child's compe-tence in performing tasks similar to those he or she would en-counter in everyday school experiences, the program must be con-sidered a success. In short, while the Head Start experience had not made the children more intelligent, it had helped them use the intelligence they had.

Our findings also helped explain why the IQ test score gains tended to disappear when Head Start children entered the public schools. After a year or so in the frequently less friendly environment of the school, the children's wariness of adults, and their expectancy of failure, probably returned.

Finally, as Butterfield and I noted, the study raised the intriguing question of exactly what standards should be employed to assess the value of programs like Head Start. We concluded that such programs should be assessed on the basis of how well they foster greater general competence among deprived children rather than on how much they succeed in developing particular cognitive abilities alone.[5]

The Coleman Report

About the same time the early childhood community was beginning to worry about the fade-out of Head Start's effects on cognitive development, a national study, *Equality of Educational Opportunity* (the "Coleman Report"), was released.[6] The study concluded that the quality of a school accounted for relatively little of the variability in pupils' achievement. On the contrary, the major factor affecting pupil performance in school, the study found, was the socioeconomic status of the home, and there was little that schools could do to reverse poverty-induced educational handicaps.

The Coleman Report findings suggesting that schools make little difference are no longer taken seriously. Michael Rutter in *15,000 Hours*, James Comer in *School Power*, and other researchers have since shown that variations in the quality of schools do indeed make a difference. Even James Coleman himself in a later study points out that some schools, namely parochial schools, do much better than public schools in forming a partnership with parents and the community to reduce school dropout rates.[7]

At the time of its release, however, the Coleman Report was

read by policymakers as yet another sign that compensatory education, even for preschool children, was unlikely to be effective. Calling the Coleman Report "a profoundly reserved statement" about the prospect that education could reverse the ill effects of poverty, Daniel Patrick Moynihan, who had served on the initial Johnson administration task force that designed the War on Poverty, said that in Washington "this was more widely grasped than might be thought."[8] The study began to push the pendulum from overoptimism concerning the effects of compensatory education to a nihilistic view that such programs were a waste of money.

Origins of the Westinghouse Report

With social scientists increasingly skeptical about the benefits of compensatory preschool programs, and even early childhood program developers far more cautious in their claims, time was running out for Head Start. Its very success in becoming almost overnight a nationwide program made it vulnerable. "The gamble of Head Start lay in its instant nationwide implementation," my colleague Sheldon White of Harvard pointed out. "By going into nationwide implementation, Head Start quickly went into annual costs of 350 million dollars, a considerable sum which might be used for other kinds of approaches and whose value calls for justification."[9]

A clash was brewing between Head Start and another federal creation of 1965—the Planning, Programming, Budgeting System (PPBS)—which reflected a growing commitment throughout government to increasing analysis and assessment of all government programs. In October 1965, the Bureau of the Budget issued a bulletin that required every federal agency to establish a central office for program analysis, planning, and budgeting. The idea was to make analysis a critical part of the decision-making process, as Secretary Robert McNamara had tried to do at the Department of Defense in the early 1960s.[10]

Although OEO was one of the first federal agencies to establish an Office of Research, Planning, Programs and Evaluation (RPP&E), it did not establish a separate evaluation division until autumn 1967.[11] Until that time, Head Start, like other divisions of OEO, had been given responsibility for its own evaluations. However, under the new organization, while the Head Start division would continue to have responsibility for program monitoring and research on discrete issues, such as which preschool curricula were most effective, the new agency-wide evaluation division would take charge of outcome evaluation, such as averaging over local variations in implementation, whether the overall program worked.[12] The agency-wide evaluation unit was, in effect, expected to be a sort of scientific auditing arm of OEO that asked the tough questions, such as, Given limited funds, what programs should be funded? and Which is more cost-effective—Head Start or job training programs?[13]

In March 1968, the new evaluation division at OEO developed a Request for Proposal (RFP) for an "overall" National Head Start Evaluation. The RFP spelled out a number of specific conditions for the evaluation: (1) Data were to be obtained on at least several thousand Head Start graduates of both summer and full-year programs for years 1965, 1966, and 1967; (2) the study was to use various measures to determine the cognitive and affective status of children; and (3) the study was to be conducted retrospectively, with a control group set up three years after the program began, rather than as a true experiment, in which children would be assigned at random to a Head Start or non–Head Start group. Finally, the entire study was to be completed by spring 1969, less than a year from the time the contract would be awarded.[14]

Before the contract was awarded, the Head Start research committee, consisting of Urie Bronfenbrenner, Edmund Gordon, and me, visited Bertram Harding, who had recently replaced Sargent Shriver as OEO director. Our goal was to persuade Harding to alter the study design.

The proposed study was terrible, we insisted. We argued that it would be a mistake in the first place to try to assess the "overall" impact of Head Start so soon after its establishment. Such an approach assumed that Head Start was a homogeneous set of programs, which was not the case. Furthermore, we explained that it was unwise to base an evaluation on the first summer of Head Start, which everyone knew had been a chaotic operation. In addition, the study design should not be limited to evaluating cognitive effects, but should also assess the program's impact on health, nutrition, and community involvement.

Most important, we pointed out that there was no way, after the fact, to get a control group equally matched to the children who had participated in Head Start three years earlier. What was really needed, we argued, was a longitudinal study, which would assess children before and after Head Start, and use a control group based on random assignment. In short, we anticipated many of the criticisms that would be made of the study eventually conducted by the Westinghouse/Ohio researchers, but our efforts to persuade OEO to revamp the evaluation design were to no avail.

The fact that OEO decided to proceed with the original study design over the opposition of the research committee still troubles me. But, in retrospect, I can understand the factors that led to OEO's decision.

Perhaps the most obvious reason OEO proceeded with the national impact study design was that they were unhappy with some of the early research that had been commissioned by the Head Start division. Robert Levine, director of the RPP&E office at OEO, and John Evans, head of the evaluation unit, "didn't like the nationwide evaluation we had done of Head Start during its first summer," according to Edmund Gordon, "and they liked even less the fact that I had backed away from that nationwide evaluation approach to a decentralized model."[15] Levine and Evans felt that the research on Head Start had so far been too limited to individual project evaluations, and that there was no good evidence as to overall Head Start effectiveness.[16] But somehow OEO's research and evaluation office missed the main point of that first summer's disastrous attempt: huge national evaluations are tremendously expensive, difficult to design, and frequently don't yield much usable information. That is precisely why Gordon had moved to a model of evaluating a series of individual programs.

Pressure to proceed with the national evaluation may also have been prompted by political concerns. Given the growing skepticism about Head Start among social scientists, there was a perception that some day soon the day of reckoning with the Bureau of the Budget or Congress would occur. As early as 1967, some Republicans, as part of a larger effort to dismantle the Community Action Program, were already proposing the transfer of Head Start to an educational agency or to the states. It was the perceived need to conduct the study and get the results rapidly that was used as the official OEO excuse for ruling out our suggestion for a longitudinal study design. The OEO research and evaluation team argued that "because the program was in its third year and there was, as yet, no useful assessment of its over-all effects, time was an important consideration in an ex post facto design."[17] Such a design would, in their estimation, "produce results relatively soon (less than a year), as compared with a methodologically more desirable longitudinal study, which would take considerably longer."

In summary, the chief reason our recommendations concerning the national impact evaluation of Head Start were overridden was that federal expectations of evaluation research were as overly ambitious and optimistic as they had once been of Head Start. Just as Head Start had been nicknamed "Project Rush-Rush" by Washington insiders in 1965, there was a hurried quality to the evaluation effort prompted by the same kind of idealism that, if you have the right idea, you should proceed with it on a grand scale and you can't go wrong. Referring to the RPP&E office in OEO, Jule Sugarman, who had administered Head Start since 1965, said, "These were not bad guys. They were scholars. But they perceived the state of evaluation to be much more advanced than it was."[18]

Although I think that OEO's research and evaluation office was guilty of nothing more than excessive enthusiasm for outcome evaluation research, I also suspect that an additional factor may have been operating in other divisions of OEO, which made it easier for the study to proceed unchanged. A split had developed in the Community Action Program between those who were education-oriented and those who wanted funds to go to noneducational programs. The original Community Action people were jealous of the popularity of Head Start and the way in which it was being favored by President Johnson. "The CAP bias was that Head Start was not as good as had been claimed," according to Edmund Gordon, who argued that the CAP division liked the Westinghouse study design precisely because they thought it would show Head Start in an unfavorable light. Wolff had already demonstrated fade-out in a small sample, and in Gordon's view, "the OEO people wanted to show it on a larger scale."[19]

I had also experienced the Community Action Program's jealousy of Head Start. I never went to a meeting at OEO where I was not reminded that Head Start was part of the Community Action Program. The CAP leaders clearly felt that Head Start was the tail wagging the dog. Their resentment focused primarily on the fantastic growth in Head Start's budget, which had enjoyed more than a three-fold expansion by 1967, while the CAP appropriation remained static.[20]

Regardless of OEO's motivations for proceeding with the ill-fated National Head Start Evaluation, the best Gordon and I could do was offer a token protest. When the contract came down for Gordon to review as an OEO consultant in June 1968, he refused to sign it. The contract was awarded to the Westinghouse Learning Corporation in conjunction with Ohio University, and the study was to be completed in less than a year, by April 1969.

The study sample was huge—composed of 1,980 Head Start and 1,983 control children, all of whom were in the first, second, or third grade. Instruments to measure cognitive effects were all well-known standardized tests: the Illinois Test of Psycholinguistic Abilities; the Metropolitan Readiness Test, a test used to assess children's readiness for first grade; and the Stanford Achievement Test. Westinghouse also developed three attitudinal measures for use in the study, but there was no time to test their validity, and, hence, the results on these measures tended to be dismissed.

In fairness to the Westinghouse/Ohio researchers, I think it's important to acknowledge that I know of no widely accepted attitudinal measure that was available at the time the study was conducted. There was Bettye Caldwell's Preschool Inventory, but, as the name suggests, it would not have been appropriate for school-age children. The best one could have done was to measure proxies for attitude, such as school attendance. Indeed it was the very absence of reliable measures of attitude and motivation that led so many researchers to focus on the well-established cognitive measures.

Politics of the Westinghouse/Ohio University Report

The Westinghouse/Ohio study was commissioned by the Johnson administration. By the time the report was nearing completion, however, a new president, Richard Nixon, was in the White House. Weeks before OEO had received even the first working draft of the Westinghouse/Ohio report, hints came out of its negative findings, and the Nixon administration started inquiring about the study.[21] Although there's no evidence that the White House influenced the findings, it certainly increased the pressure to release the report prematurely, and contributed to the publicity that the findings received.

Daniel Patrick Moynihan, a Democrat who had served as Assistant Secretary of Labor for Policy Planning and Research during the Kennedy administration and as a member of the White House task force that drafted the Economic Opportunity Act in 1964, was by 1969 assistant to the president for Urban Affairs. Nixon liked Moynihan. Indeed, Nixon's first Executive Order created a Council for Urban Affairs,[22] with the president serving as chair and Moynihan as executive secretary. John Ehrlichman's handwritten notes from the period contain the frequent reminder to place Pat Moynihan "near the President."[23] According to Moynihan, he was also "head of OEO on hold" while the administration searched for a new director for the agency, a post with an at best uncertain future.[24]

Moynihan called John Evans and Walter Williams from OEO's research division to the White House in mid-February to discuss the Westinghouse/Ohio study findings. Being called to the White House is far from an ordinary state of affairs. "It was exciting, and also a little intimidating," Evans recalls. "Moynihan was interested in the findings because President Nixon was preparing to make a major address on the War on Poverty program, including Head Start, and Moynihan wanted to include the findings in President Nixon's address," says Evans. "We alerted Moynihan to the preliminary negative results. Moynihan was disappointed; he did not relish the findings. But he had done some work at the Labor Department on compensatory programs, and he was not surprised."[25]

There are also other indications that the White House had been taking an active interest in OEO's research and evaluation unit. "We have been wrestling with the problem of what to do with OEO's research, planning and evaluation—how to maintain some Presidential control over these activities while shifting them out of the Executive Office," wrote Richard Blumenthal in a memorandum to Moynihan in March 1969.[26] Blumenthal proposed that a research unit, including a portion of OEO's RPP&E staff, be made a permanent subcommittee of the Urban Affairs Council and be charged with the responsibility for monitoring all federal experimentation and research in the antipoverty field.

Shortly after Moynihan was alerted to the preliminary negative findings in the Westinghouse/Ohio report, the press began to hear of the study. According to the *New York Times*, an unnamed "White House adviser spread the word that something important was in the offing and that the report would show that Head Start, and in fact compensatory education in general, simply does not work."[27] Moreover, President Nixon's message to Congress of February 19 on the Economic Opportunity Act, while reaffirming support for Head Start, predicted that a "major national evaluation" would soon confirm "what many have feared: the long-term effect of Head Start appears to be extremely weak."[28]

Moynihan was impressed by the Westinghouse/Ohio findings. As "had in effect been predicted by Coleman," Moynihan later wrote in *The Politics of a Guaranteed Income*, "Head Start wasn't working: The children were getting their teeth fixed, but little else that could be quantified."[29] But Moynihan maintains that he only alluded to these negative findings in the president's February 19, 1969 message in order to warn Head Start advocates that the report was coming. Furthermore, there is evidence that, regardless of

Moynihan's own views about Head Start's effectiveness, he was trying to perform damage control on the program's behalf within the
administration. As Moynihan points out, in the aftermath of the
Westinghouse report Nixon made several reassuring statements
about Head Start. For example, in the same February 19 message
that Moynihan prepared for the president, Nixon made a commitment that Head Start should continue, although with some new emphasis: "So crucial is the matter of early growth, that we must make
a national commitment providing all American children an opportunity for healthful and stimulating development during the first
five years of life."[30]

Moynihan also helped prepare a report released on February 19
that recommended the delegation of Head Start from OEO to the
Department of Health, Education and Welfare.[31] This delegation
would protect Head Start from any possible dismantling of OEO, as
well as allow the program to concentrate on improvements.
Referring to his role in drafting the "first five years" message and
the recommendation to delegate Head Start to HEW, Moynihan
says, "My thanks was to be generally accused of having commissioned and written the [Westinghouse/Ohio] report."[32]

Despite these signs that Moynihan was trying to protect Head
Start from being dismantled, it is also true that his principal interests were not in compensatory education or in any kind of social
service or education strategy. Although he had been one of the architects of the War on Poverty, he had been disappointed by its emphasis on community action, rather than on employment policy, or
what he called in his book *Maximum Feasible Misunderstanding*
"the vital task of reforming and restructuring the job market."[33]
While Moynihan did not really consider Head Start a bona fide part
of community action, neither did he see the early intervention program as an integral part of the jobs and guaranteed income strategy
he was already preparing for President Nixon. This strategy, the
Family Assistance Plan, would require child care in order to enable
welfare recipients to work, but it would not necessarily have to be
a comprehensive program like Head Start. And because Moynihan's
primary interests lay elsewhere, he may have been more inclined to
accept the news of the Westinghouse report's negative preliminary

findings at face value, rather than to examine closely the methods used to obtain them.

While Moynihan tried to buy some time for Head Start, the White House in general took pleasure in the Westinghouse report's negative conclusions. "The finding that Head Start was not an unmitigated success was seen as vindication of the Nixon administration view that the Great Society programs were ineffective," says Chester Finn, who worked for Moynihan then, and is now a professor at Vanderbilt University. It was not, as Finn explains, that Nixon or his major advisers opposed programs for young disadvantaged children; on the contrary, they proposed some of their own. It was that Head Start was a product of the War on Poverty, a symbol of the hated Johnson era.[34] President Nixon summed up his own sentiments in response to a decision memorandum on Head Start on March 19, 1969: "No increase in *any* antipoverty program until more research is in," the president wrote in bold ink across the top.[35]

Whatever the White House views on Head Start, once the president had announced that the long-term effects of Head Start were "extremely weak," there was enormous pressure to release the full study, and there was a flood of requests for a full disclosure of the study's findings. Evans now adds: "I remember being in a frantic state. There was pressure from Congress, who wanted to see the study; pressure from the press, who wanted a copy; and pressure from the Head Start community, who felt victimized."[36]

This political pressure to release the report prematurely certainly contributed to the controversy surrounding the report. Part of the problem with the Westinghouse report, according to Sheldon H. White, professor of educational psychology at Harvard and a consultant on the data, was that there was political pressure from both Congress and the White House to release it before it was ready. White and another consultant, William Madow, then a statistician at Stanford, had been campaigning for some basic changes in the analysis of the data as it had been originally planned. The first working draft in March did not address their recommendations, and a rather substantial revision was envisaged, with an extension of time until May 31, 1969.

By this time, however, Congress was in the midst of reviewing the authorization for the full antipoverty program. A conflict was brewing between congressional forces who sought continuation of the antipoverty program in its entirety and the new Nixon administration, which sought to make major changes in it. Clearly, a major national evaluation—particularly one that was negative—would be a key factor in such a conflict. As a result, according to White, OEO's request for an extension of time to May 31 was viewed as an attempt to submerge the impact of the study. There was talk of a congressional investigation, and so the working draft, with very few of the changes recommended by White and Madow, was released as a preliminary draft report on April 14, 1969.

Much Ado About Little

Considering all the controversy that followed the release of the Westinghouse report, I think it is important to separate the report's actual findings from its conclusions. In brief, 70 percent of the Head Start children studied in the Westinghouse/Ohio report had participated only in the summer program, and the report did not detect any positive effects of the summer initiative. In fact, there was a slight difference favoring the control children in all three grades. However, the study did find some positive effects of the full-year Head Start program among both the first- and second-grade children, with the number of children in the third-grade sample too small to make a determination. In the first grade in particular, the Head Start children did better than the control group on the Metropolitan Readiness Test, which might be considered the purest measure of the effect of Head Start, as yet uncompromised by the effect of further schooling. Furthermore, Head Start appeared to be more effective among certain subgroups, such as black children in large cities in the Southeast. And parents of Head Start enrollees were nearly unanimous in voicing strong support for the program.

Good researchers may disagree on the significance of these positive effects. Yet, given the fact that some positive findings did turn up on the full-year program, and that the strongest negative findings applied to the summer program, I question why the executive summary of the Westinghouse/Ohio report concluded so forthrightly that "Head Start as it is presently constituted has not provided widespread cognitive and affective gains," and that "its benefits cannot be described as satisfactory."[37]

The release of the National Impact Study of Head Start by the Westinghouse Learning Corporation and Ohio University was met with a barrage of criticism, and immediately led to a major controversy. Madow, the study's chief statistical consultant, resigned in protest and would not accept payment for his work because he considered the design flawed and the conclusions incorrect.

Many researchers voiced the same criticisms that Bronfenbrenner, Gordon, and I had earlier expressed of the proposed study design—that it erred by assuming that Head Start was a homogeneous set of programs, and that the control group had been selected three years after the program began.

Even the Nixon administration itself seemed divided about the reliability of the study. Despite the fact that the White House kept touting the Westinghouse report, Secretary of Health, Education and Welfare Robert Finch was quoted as noting that some of his staff felt the data were "sloppy." "The only thing we got out of the report was that summer programs are not as effective as full-year programs," Secretary Finch told the House Education and Labor Committee, "and we knew this from other studies."[38]

More precise criticisms followed. In a lengthy critique, Harvard researchers Marshall S. Smith and Joan S. Bissell re-analyzed the Westinghouse data.[39] Unlike Westinghouse, Smith and Bissell found that the Head Start group scored higher than the control group on the Metropolitan Readiness Test by a large enough margin to be considered "educationally significant." The reanalysis placed the Head Start children who participated in the full-year program in the 44th percentile, close to the national median, while the control group was in the 36th percentile. Differences were even more pronounced in the urban black full-year Head Start centers. There the Head Start children scored over 16 percentile points higher than the control children.

In what has become a classic statistical analysis, Donald Campbell and Albert Erlebacher, psychologists then at Northwestern, criticized the ex post facto, or after-the-fact, design used in the Westinghouse study. Because Head Start had already begun three years before the study was initiated, there could be no random assignment of children to treatment and control groups. The researchers tried to set up an after-the-fact control group that was equal to the Head Start group, but the control group they selected was from a higher socioeconomic status than the Head Start children, which, of course, tended to make Head Start look ineffective. Furthermore, the type of statistical analysis the Westinghouse/Ohio researchers used to try to compensate for the pretreatment differences between the Head Start children and the somewhat better off control children ironically created a further bias in favor of the control group.[40]

In response to this critique, Victor G. Cicirelli, the research director of the Westinghouse/Ohio project, admitted the "essential validity of Campbell and Erlebacher's argument," but argued that the effects of the bias "would be small in the Westinghouse study, too small to significantly alter its conclusions."[41]

Based on their analysis of the Westinghouse/Ohio study, Campbell and Erlebacher recommended "that no scientific evaluation be done at all in ex post facto situations. We recommend this not because we 'fail to understand that every program will be evaluated,' but rather because we judge it fundamentally misleading to lend the prestige of science to any report in a situation where no scientific evaluation is possible."[42]

Those of us who had been cautioning for years that the plasticity of intelligence had been exaggerated, and not to expect too much from Head Start too soon, were now in effect cautioning that there were limits to our own discipline, research, and evaluation, as well. It would be almost a decade before longitudinal findings would reveal some of the long-term effects of preschool for disadvantaged children, including being in the right grade for the right age, and not being in special education. Both of these outcomes would never have been detected in a retrospective study such as Westinghouse/Ohio because the control and treatment groups

71

matched children in part by grade level; children not in the right grade for the right age or in special education would have automatically been excluded from the sample. Yet despite the powerful methodological criticism of the Westinghouse/Ohio evaluation, it remained for a long time the definitive Head Start study. Moynihan later dismissed the methodological critiques of the Westinghouse Head Start evaluation as yet another indication of the liberal "unwillingness to face the finding of failure where it appeared, as recurrently it did."[43] This is all very surprising since Moynihan himself is a first-rate social scientist. Years later, the only reference in Princeton's Woodrow Wilson School of Public and International Affairs in the card catalog under "Head Start" was the Westinghouse/ Ohio report. Because the National Impact Evaluation of Head Start was the biggest study of Head Start available, it was long assumed to be the best.

While the Westinghouse report was being debated at the national level, it had an immediate impact on the people who ran Head Start programs locally. "When that report came out, it really was a slap in the face," said William Fillmore, president of the Head Start Association in Florida, and a Head Start director since 1967. "We had been working so hard to develop a positive image for Head Start. Suddenly, the people who had always felt that only school districts should run educational programs would point to the Westinghouse study and say, 'You see, Head Start is just another baby-sitting service. You don't really do all the things you say.'"

What the Westinghouse study did not measure, however, was Head Start's effect on children's curiosity and leadership potential. In the early 1970s, Fillmore conducted his own follow-up study on the children who had been in his Head Start centers in St. Petersburg, Florida. He distributed a questionnaire to elementary school teachers. "How do you see the children who have been in Head Start?" he asked them. The answers he got back were sur-

prising: "The teachers said the children who came from Head Start asked too many questions, which is exactly what we taught them to do," said Fillmore. "The teachers were in effect saying that these children made them work too hard. They couldn't just sit behind their desks with the children in front of them in a neat row." [44]

The Jensen Report

Matters hardly improved for Head Start when, very soon after President Nixon alluded to the negative findings in the Westinghouse report, University of California educational psychologist Arthur Jensen published his monograph emphasizing the genetic influence on IQ scores.[45] Most of the 124-page article was a sophisticated discussion of the nature of intelligence, the distribution of intelligence, and the inheritability of intelligence. All but 10 pages on black-white differences in intelligence were on nature versus nurture, with Jensen leaning heavily toward nature. But the first paragraph almost gratuitously proclaimed, "Compensatory education has been tried and it apparently has failed." Compensatory education programs designed to raise the intelligence of disadvantaged children were misdirected, he argued, because hereditary factors were so important. While acknowledging that environment played a role in "at least some of the variance between racial groups in standard intelligence," Jensen said, "the possible importance of genetic factors in racial behavioral differences has been greatly ignored, almost to the point of being a tabooed subject, just as were the topics of venereal disease and birth control a generation ago."[46] Citing evidence that he said showed that blacks scored some 15 points lower on IQ tests than whites, Jensen then argued that programs like Head Start fail because they do not focus on skills that require a low degree of abstract intelligence.

It is doubtful that many policymakers followed the Jensen argument closely on the vagaries of the heritability of intelligence, and the article's findings were largely drowned in accusations of racism and a furor over whether the article should have been published at all. Yet, coming on the heels of the Coleman and Westinghouse reports, Jensen's article signaled the end of an era of naive environmentalism. It was once again acceptable to question whether any compensatory program could overcome poor children's genetic limitations. The "chill" in the intellectual climate toward Head Start would soon threaten to cool the political enthusiasm for the program as well.

Nixon Administration Quandary: What to Do with Head Start?

Given the series of negative scientific blows to compensatory education in 1969, the Nixon administration had the ammunition to try to end Head Start then. However, whether because of the support of Moynihan and Finch for the program, or the president's own inclinations, it did not. Instead, on April 9, 1969, Nixon announced the establishment of the Office of Child Development, which would, among other functions, house Head Start.[47] In this statement the president renewed his pledge to a "national commitment to providing all American children an opportunity for healthful and stimulating development during the first five years of life." The Office of Child Development would report directly to the HEW Secretary. On the subject of Head Start, Nixon said only that "Preliminary evaluations of this program indicate that Head Start must begin earlier in life, and last longer, to achieve lasting benefits." Toward this end, Nixon endorsed the expansion of the Parent and Child Centers, a program serving children from birth to age three, and Follow Through, designed to further the progress Head Start made once children entered elementary school. The only concrete negative consequence of the Westinghouse findings that day was the announcement that summer Head Start programs would be reduced, a move that many Head Start advocates would endorse themselves.

Nevertheless, even after OCD's creation, Head Start's future remained precarious, primarily because of its association with the War on Poverty. According to White House assistant John Ehrlichman's notes from a meeting with President Nixon on May 22, 1969, the administration was definitely considering massive changes, if not the elimination, of several key antipoverty programs. "President wants Shultz to get *rid of Job Corps*," Ehrlichman wrote by hand. On the subject of Head Start, Ehrlichman's notes from the meeting indicate that it "may be too late to abolish" it, with a notation that House Education and Labor Committee Chairman Carl Perkins was too powerful a supporter of the program with whom to reckon. But as the president had indicated earlier, "*no increases*" should be considered for Head Start in its present form.[48]

And at a time when Head Start was already suffering from the effects of previous reductions, this was bad news for the program indeed. The Nixon administration was clearly on record wanting to do something to help young children, but its support for Head Start was lukewarm indeed.

4

My First Crisis

JUST AS THE NATION'S LOVE AFFAIR WITH HEAD START WAS COOLING, the Nixon administration asked me to run the program. There are two puzzling questions here: Why would the administration pick me for the job, and why would I accept it? The answer to both questions is the same: the early years of the Nixon administration were far different from the latter.

Typically, appointments for positions such as director of the Office of Child Development and chief of the Children's Bureau, for which I was being considered, are reserved for party loyalists as a reward for their work during a presidential campaign. Yet, in the six to eight interviews I had with HEW officials, the question of my politics never arose. Apparently no one was concerned that I had opposed a major evaluation of Head Start that the president seemed to like, or that I was apolitical. As Elliot Richardson noted in his book *The Creative Balance*, President Nixon initially imposed fewer restrictions upon political appointments than did many of his successors—fewer, according to Richardson, than President Carter, and far fewer than President Reagan.[1] Indeed, the only partisan question prospective political appointees had to answer during the screening process was, "Did you campaign for the president's opponent?"

Not only was the screening process relatively open, but many of the people conducting it for HEW were at least as liberal as I. "This was the northeastern wing of the Republican party," recalls Robert Patricelli, who conducted one of my interviews for the position in Washington, "and we chose all kinds of people with nontraditional Republican backgrounds."[2]

Credit for the openness in the appointment process during the early years of the Nixon administration must also go to the president himself, who after all selected Moynihan as an adviser. No less a liberal columnist than Meg Greenfield has noted that the early years of the Nixon administration were the most progressive of the second half of the twentieth century in terms of domestic policy. Commitments to improve "the first five years of life" fit right in with Nixon's proposals for a negative income tax and national health insurance.

"It is perhaps the ultimate irony," notes Moynihan, "that the Nixon proposal for a negative income tax was drafted by Democratic advocates who not months earlier had the same proposal rejected by the Johnson administration."[3]

Hence, it is no surprise that I accepted the offer. While I had some doubts about leaving my research at Yale to become an administrator, I was attracted by the administration's expressed interest in early childhood. There was also the possibility that I would be able to help shape the child care component under the Family Assistance Plan, the president's proposal to free families from dependence on welfare. The opportunity to start something new, to be the *first* director of the Office of Child Development, was also appealing.

As for the Westinghouse report, the prospect of having to defend Head Start against that study if anything made the job more appealing to me. I had always been concerned about the quality of Head Start, and I knew that it had not yet become the program I would like to evaluate. But I never believed in the integrity of the Westinghouse/Ohio data. Having grown up in a tough, poor neighborhood myself, I've always been committed to the idea that young children deserve a childhood, one that is relatively carefree and protected. For many children, Head Start was their only chance at that kind of childhood. I was determined that no statistically flawed research study take that opportunity away from them.

Warning Signs

Nineteen seventy was hardly the best time to assume the leadership of Head Start. During that spring and summer, there were numerous developments that did not bode well for the program. First, President Nixon continued to tout the negative findings of the Westinghouse report in his references to Head Start. In a special message to Congress on educational reform on March 3, 1970, Nixon included Head Start in a general dismissal of compensatory education: "The best available evidence indicates that most of the compensatory education programs have not measurably helped poor children catch up ...," he said. For the third time in a year he alluded to the Westinghouse report, which concluded that Head Start had no lasting impact on children's IQ scores or other indices of cognitive capacity. "In our Headstart program where so much hope is invested," he said, "we find that youngsters enrolled only for the summer achieve almost no gains, and the gains of those in the program for a full year are soon matched by their non–Headstart classmates from similarly poor backgrounds."[4]

There were also structural changes taking place in the administration that threatened to lessen the influence of those most sympathetic to Head Start. Moynihan had been "promoted" to Counsellor to the President in November 1969, and on March 12, 1970, the Urban Affairs Council, which Moynihan had run, was replaced by the Domestic Council.[5] John Ehrlichman was named the head of the new council and the president's Chief Domestic Assistant. At the same time, the Bureau of the Budget was renamed the Office of Management and Budget, and Secretary of Labor George Shultz was tapped as its new director. When passage of the Family Assistance Plan ran into trouble in the Senate Finance Committee in April 1970, suffering another setback in November of that year, it was generally considered a defeat for the administration's liberals. The invasion of Cambodia that year placed all of the administration's more constructive domestic proposals in jeopardy with a testy Congress.

Finally, the negative findings on the effects of compensatory education had taken their toll on Head Start's budget. Congressional appropriations for Head Start had slipped from $349 million in FY 1967 to $325 million in FY 1970. Some Head Start funds had been diverted from direct services to research and development. The House of Representatives was proposing a further reduction in the program's appropriation. While the Nixon administration was planning to request a small increase for Head Start to $339 million for FY 1971, it was actually $30 million less than the administration had requested the previous year.[6] Furthermore, given the previous reductions in service and the level of inflation, the budget request was not sufficient even to restore the 1967 level of services.

Head Start parents, the people who knew the program best, sensed that the program was in danger. Soon after the official word of my nomination in April 1970 for the post of Chief of the Children's Bureau and director of OCD, I was invited to give a lunch address before the New England Association of Young Children (NEAYC) at the Park Plaza Hotel in New Haven. Walking across the New Haven Green from my office at Yale to give the speech to this predominantly white, middle-class group of nursery school teachers, I did not expect a hero's welcome, but I hardly anticipated a picket line.

I arrived at the hotel to be greeted by about 30 placard-carrying Head Start mothers, most black, who had rented a bus to come down from Rhode Island and voice their grievances. They were demanding entrance to the luncheon address, but they could not pay the $6 luncheon fee. My academic credentials and role on the original planning team for Head Start meant nothing to this group. They had only one concern: Was I going to help save Head Start?

I was willing to sit down and talk with the Head Start parents. After all, they were my new constituency, and Head Start was their program. But this was a highly confrontational period, and the NEAYC conference organizers didn't know how to handle it. They were offended by what they saw as the Head Start group's unruly behavior, especially their "refusal" to pay for the lunch. In spite of the fact that the 30 mothers posed no real threat to the some 400 NEAYC members, the conference organizers were also afraid. So, instead of offering to buy their lunch, or at least find them some chairs in the back of the room, NEAYC actually locked the mothers out and called the police.

Finally, after my address, the hotel management let me meet with the Head Start mothers in a room upstairs, though only on the awkward condition that there be a police officer stationed at the door. Maybe the Head Start parents thought that if I had been nominated by the Nixon administration, I couldn't be any good. Perhaps they had information I didn't. In any case, one mother stood up and asked a very legitimate question.

"Are you going to cut the budget?" she asked.

"I've just been nominated," I said, "and I don't yet have any say on the budget."

"Well, we just want you to know what a good program it is," another woman said, "and to let you know we can't stand any more cuts."

The dialogue continued, and I'm sure I didn't really satisfy their concerns. But somehow at least I had the sense to listen, and as our meeting progressed, the tone became friendlier. Always before my connection to Head Start had been as a planner or researcher; this was my first real encounter as an official directly responsible to the families Head Start was intended to serve. So the confrontation turned into an opportunity for me to learn what Head Start was all about—a partnership between the federal government and parents.

Lessons from the Office of Management and Budget

Not long after I had moved to Washington to assume the OCD responsibilities, I went to what I thought was to be a routine meeting at the Office of Economic Opportunity. A representative from the Office of Management and Budget (OMB) went up to the blackboard and put up this plan, to begin in FY 1972: "Phase out one-third of Head Start the first year, one-third the second year, and eliminate the entire program the third." Suddenly, it appeared that I had not been hired to direct Head Start, but rather to dismantle it.

In retrospect, I'm not sure how serious this phase-out plan was, or from how high up in OMB it emanated. The plan may have been only a trial balloon floated to see how much resistance it would encounter. What is clear, however, is that during the summer of 1970 the president's interests were shifting toward his New Federalism proposal, including plans for revenue-sharing and decentralization. These plans would push federal policy in the opposite direction from Head Start, which depended on federal categorical grants that went directly to communities, bypassing governors and mayors.

In July 1970, Donald Rumsfeld, the former Illinois congressman who had been tapped to lead the Office of Economic Opportunity, submitted a memorandum to Ehrlichman and Shultz summarizing the problems with federal grant programs. According to the memorandum, federal grant administration was overly complicated; processing time for applications was too long; and grant programs were poorly coordinated and not systematically evaluated or eliminated if proven ineffective.[7] However, it was difficult to address any of these problems because of the considerable impact of special-interest groups, including professionals and service recipients. In short, in attempting to redirect federal grants, the administration would be up against the so-called iron triangle, whereby interest groups ally with executive agency specialists and congressional subcommittees to protect pet programs.

Given this situation, the Rumsfeld memorandum, with the support of a work group including OMB assistant director Richard Nathan, recommended that OMB take the lead in promoting the principles of decentralization by interjecting them into the FY 1972 budget process. "There are a thousand decisions which present several options for the use of money," the memorandum noted. And Head Start, a program that epitomized the iron triangle by totally bypassing state and local government, was unlikely to be high on the list for continued funding in such a climate.

I certainly could not afford to take any budget cut proposal associated with OMB lightly. In pre–David Stockman days, the OMB may not have been the best-known advisory arm of the White House, but it was certainly one of the most powerful. In fact, OMB had more clout than the Cabinet, because the agency determined the budget requests for every other executive agency in Washington. How well any agency head's budget fared depended in large part on what some anonymous OMB analyst felt about the agency and its programs. The OMB not only helped shape the president's budget decisions; its staff also wrote the testimony delivered by executive agency officials before Congress, and sent someone to listen to how the officials responded to questions. I recall during a "little Cabinet" meeting conducted in HEW by George Shultz, a federal health official who innocently dared to challenge this OMB role. Wouldn't it be better, this kindly older physician ventured, if the administration just gave agency officials guidance on policy, and allowed the officials to deliver testimony to Congress in their own words?

"You will read the OMB testimony word-for-word," Shultz replied sharply. "And anytime you can't, don't let the door hit you in the butt on your way out."

With this introduction to the mighty power of OMB, along with the common knowledge that the Nixon administration was looking for War on Poverty programs to eliminate, the Head Start phase-out proposal seemed to me a real threat. It would be hard to overestimate the sense of betrayal I felt. Sitting on a park bench, I asked myself how I could have had all those visits with the administration recruiters, and nobody had ever mentioned there was a plan to eliminate the program. Now the questions I'd been asked at the Park Plaza Hotel by the Head Start mothers a few months earlier took on a new dimension. Perhaps I had been duped into accepting this position; after all, if you want to dismantle a still-popular program, what better way to defuse criticism than to get one of the program's original planners to do it?

Richardson to the Rescue

Soon after my encounter with OMB, I went to talk with Elliot Richardson, who had just replaced Robert Finch as Secretary of the Department of Health, Education and Welfare. Referring to the phase-out plan for Head Start, I said, "I can't do this, and I won't."

Fortunately, Richardson gave me his full support. He was not impressed by the Westinghouse report. Trained in philosophy at Harvard as well as a graduate of Harvard Law School, Richardson was a quick study in psychology. He noted that the last place one would expect a program like Head Start to make significant changes was in cognitive development, the area most subject to innate capacity.[8]

Richardson also proposed a strategy for how to fight the phase-out proposal: publicize Head Start's strengths, so that OMB and the president's other advisers would know what would be lost if the program were eliminated. Using Richardson's strategy, I mounted a virtual campaign on behalf of Head Start and the Office of Child Development. During the first summer and fall after becoming OCD director, I made a whistle-stop tour of the nation while visiting all the regional offices of OCD, seizing every press opportunity, including the *National Enquirer*. When asked about the Westinghouse report, I argued that the measures used in the report were much too narrow. Don't crucify the child on the cross of IQ, I said. Always I would repeat the theme that what we should be evaluating was not Head Start's impact on cognitive ability, but rather its influence on the motivational factors that lead children to make the most of the cognitive abilities they have. Head Start should be evaluated on much broader criteria, such as not only school performance but also health, nutrition, and attitudes toward self and society.

And I pointed out that on some of these nonacademic dimensions, Head Start had already been a successful effort. In terms of health care, for example, more than one-third of Head Start children had been found to have identifiable physical defects, and, of these, over 75 percent had been treated. Head Start had become the nation's largest deliverer of health services to poor children. In dollar cost, if Head Start did nothing else but get medical attention to these children, it would be a valuable long-term investment. But, I said, it has also improved the quality of life for countless children and families.

Most important, I had to undo five years of overselling of Head Start, while still putting across the message that it was a good investment. The purpose of Head Start was not to turn all ghetto children into geniuses, I explained, but to help them get out of the ghetto. Head Start's purpose should be to increase the social competence of disadvantaged children, and their overall social competence—their ability to do well in school, stay out of trouble with the law, and relate well to adults and other children—is as much a product of goals and attitudes as it is of IQ scores.

In fact, the evidence on behalf of Head Start then was weak. At the time, there were not many well-executed evaluations to draw on to make the case for Head Start. It would be almost a decade before longitudinal findings appeared, showing that disadvantaged children enrolled in quality preschool programs were more likely to be in the right grade for the right age, and much less likely to be in special education. On the day I was sworn in as OCD director, however, I was able to release the Kirschner report, which found that Head Start had been an effective instrument for community change, acting as a catalyst for making health and educational institutions pay more attention to the poor. Those communities that had a Head Start program experienced far more improvements in the responsiveness of these institutions to poor families than those that did not have a program. This may have constituted only indirect evidence of Head Start's value, but we had to make the most of it, because it was the best we had.

In defending Head Start, I got away with surprising candor. I don't want to sound like I'm arguing with the president, I told a *Washington Post* reporter the first month after my nomination, but the Westinghouse report is deeply flawed. "New Head Start Chief Hits Report Nixon Used," the *Washington Evening Star* reported on the day I was sworn in.[9] Asked about my political affiliation during that first press conference, I said only that my politics were children. A story the next day noted: "Provocative statements flowed from him faster than reporters could take them down."[10] This might be a fine tribute for a professor, but it was hardly a welcome accolade for a bureaucrat.

Did the provocative statements provoke? Once I did get a call to come to the White House to discuss some remarks I made. With regard to low infant mortality rates, I had stated at a news conference in Dallas, this nation is not even in the top ten nations of the civilized world. "But how," Ed Morgan, who later was jailed for his Watergate involvement, asked me, "can anything be so wrong with the nation's children when Richard Nixon is president?"

White House Lessons

My real problem was not White House opposition, however, but White House disinterest. Part of my reason for accepting the position at OCD was the president's speech on "The First Five Years," in which he suggested that the only thing wrong with Head Start was that it didn't start early enough. I referred to the speech constantly whenever the press challenged the sincerity of the Nixon administration's commitment to early childhood programs. Despite my inclination toward professorial independence, I was trying to be a good player on the president's team. Thus, I was disappointed by the outcome when I tried to discuss the speech with him during a meeting in the Oval Office.

"That was a wonderful speech," I said.

"Oh, yes." He quickly dismissed the topic, saying, "You should talk with Pat Moynihan—he wrote that." By that time, the Family Assistance Plan was in trouble, and Moynihan's days in the Nixon administration were numbered.

During my meeting with the president, his every gesture and response was directed at terminating contact; he simply refused to engage. I'm not sure if his primary discomfort was with me, or with the policies I was promoting, but he was the most uncomfortable man I have ever met. There was no spontaneity to him, and he wouldn't make eye contact. In any case, far from giving me any direction on what the Office of Child Development he had created should do, Nixon just quickly reached into his desk drawer and grabbed several sets of presidential cufflinks and golf balls.

"But you already gave me a set the first time we met," I protested.

"Oh, no, take them, take them," the president said. "You never know when you might need them."

I had been invited to the White House as a member of the administration; I left feeling more like a member of a visiting delegation.

Indeed, I know of only two occasions when the Nixon White House directly sought the aid of the Office of Child Development. The first occurred early on when I was asked my opinion about a recommendation by a New York physician that all six-year-old children be tested for criminal tendencies. "Idiotic" was my response. The second request was for advice on how to get a picture of the president with some adolescents. In this era of campus protests against the Vietnam War, no one could figure out how to get a picture of the president with some young people without something bad happening. A dozen senior HEW officials flown out to a conference on adolescence in Santa Cruz were asked to try to come up with a plan for how to get the photo. I said there was no way the president could be placed in the middle of a thousand students on a campus without a demonstration. But as a psychologist I knew that how people behave depends a lot on the setting and the situation. Why not take five or six adolescents to the summer White House in San Clemente, I suggested. After all, how likely were they to act up in the president's study? Five students were flown by helicopter to San Clemente, and President Nixon got his photo opportunity without incident.

Finding a Mentor

I would never have been able to protect Head Start from the budget axe without HEW Secretary Richardson's support. The key to my getting to know Richardson was OCD's placement in the Office of the Secretary, a situation where I reported directly to him. The fact that I had the same access to the secretary as did the commissioner of education and the commissioner of social and rehabilitative services made it possible for this small new agency with a $1.5 million budget (excluding Head Start) to have a much greater influence than it would otherwise have had.

At one point when there were concerns that too many offices were reporting to the secretary directly, there was a reorganization plan to place OCD under an assistant secretary.

"What's your point of view?" Richardson asked me.

"Sometimes there are criteria more important than the neatness of an organizational chart," I said, adding that he might consider hearing directly from the offices that deal with the most vulnerable citizens—children and the elderly. Richardson walked over to the chart and drew a straight line from the Office on Aging and the Office of Child Development to his own office.

Not only did I have regular access to the secretary, but we developed an intellectual exchange. No two individuals could have come from more different backgrounds. I'm the son of an Eastern European Jewish immigrant; his roots go back to the Mayflower. While Richardson was at age eight the president of the Herbert Hoover Club at Boston's Park Street School, I was watching my mother count how many extra guests were accompanying my father home from synagogue, so she could figure out how much water to add to the soup. While Richardson was at Harvard Law School, I was attending a vocational high school in Kansas City. I got my own "head start"—or at least my ticket to college—in high school debates on whether 18-year-olds should have the vote, and in oratorical contests sponsored by the Women's Christian Temperance Union.

Richardson's Boston Brahmin manner at first intimidated me. But I soon found that this seemingly austere man had many other dimensions. My first indication of Richardson's playful nature came during HEW meetings, when he would carry on a very high level of debate—and all the while be drawing elaborate doodles. Nor were Richardson's drawings limited to doodles: on my wall today I still have a New England scene that he painted.

Perhaps even more unexpected than his humor and

creativity was the concern he showed for the people who
worked for him. Here, after all, was a man in charge of a
budget as large as those of most countries. Yet, when my
father died unexpectedly, one of the first people to call was
Elliot Richardson saying how sorry he was.

Yet Richardson at this time was not just a privileged prince of the eastern wing of the Republican party. He was also a man who had come from a family of physicians, and who, upon the death of his mother while he was still a toddler, was raised by a much-loved nanny who had been a social worker. Richardson was interested in the substance of child and family issues, and he used to amaze me with his understanding of psychology. He was, for example, very concerned about the effects of labeling children with disabilities. I responded with a proposal for a major study on the effects of labeling, which Richardson quickly approved. The study, which we contracted with the late Nicholas Hobbs of Vanderbilt, turned out to be a landmark, *The Futures of Children;* it concluded that children should be labeled only when the value of the potential services to be gained from the label is greater than its negative consequences.

Richardson and I used to have weekly meetings called "one-on-ones," and after a time word got out about these exchanges. For a period he and I had regular Friday noon discussions, and other HEW staff would bring brown bag lunches in order to watch the debate. Once the topic was what kind of programs for children are most cost-effective. Everyone expected me to say Head Start, but, since we did not yet have the evidence, my response was maternal and child health programs. Sometimes the discussions, such as one on child safety, led to concrete policies, such as support for child safety caps on bottles.

Another time the issue was what to do about lead paint. Richardson, who was interested in voluntarism, wondered if there were some way to have volunteers go into the slums to take down the lead paint that was harming so many children. I was enthusiastic, and he was enthusiastic. Unfortunately, a later analysis by the Assistant Secretary for Planning estimated the cost of removing the paint, even with the use of volunteers, at $10 billion, and the unexpectedly high estimate squashed that.

Issues such as labeling and lead paint may seem only indirectly related to Head Start, but I think the trust that developed between Richardson and me was an important factor in protecting the program during this period.

Shoring Up OCD and Head Start

Another part of protecting Head Start was to build up its host agency—the Office of Child Development. OCD at least had the merit, from a political standpoint, of being the new administration's creation, rather than a leftover from LBJ. I saw three main responsibilities for the agency. The first was to administer social action programs for children, such as Head Start and child care, and, in particular, to improve the quality of Head Start. The second was to begin coordinating children's programs across agency lines, eliminating duplication, a goal that was popular with OMB. And the third was to serve as an advocate for children in the Capital, and to develop the kind of children's lobby that had not really existed since the early days of the Children's Bureau, when groups of mothers systematically visited communities to determine the causes of infant mortality. In retrospect, this last goal for OCD may have been naive, but I still consider it important.

The real problem facing Head Start, of more long-term significance than the initial negative research findings, was the disparity in quality across Head Start centers. Despite my public pronouncements on behalf of Head Start and my criticism of the Westinghouse report, I knew from my own visits to centers that the quality of Head Start programs varied enormously.

To address the issue of quality, I quickly announced a major quality-surveillance plan of 150 Head Start programs. The idea was to find the 50 best programs, and then to use these as a guide for developing performance standards to monitor all the programs.

Having the right instincts about program administration, however, is a lot different from being able to implement them. Running a university research lab with a handful of staff was hardly adequate preparation for dealing with the bureaucracy associated with a nationwide program that by that time had a budget of over $325 million. Jule Sugarman, the masterful administrator whom I had hoped would stay on as a deputy director, left OCD soon after my nomination in order to take charge of New York City's Human Resources Administration. I had hired two excellent young people as assistants: Dr. Donald Cohen, who had then just completed his medical studies and is now the director of the renowned Yale Child Study Center, and Carolyn Harmon, a political scientist who had done her doctoral work at Yale. But none of us had any experience with the federal bureaucracy. The truth is that, as a result of my administrative inexperience, my first few months at OCD were in many ways a disaster. I would hold staff meetings, and ask people to do things. They would agree and indicate that they would get right on it, and a few weeks later when I checked nothing had been done.

Aware that I was flailing my arms in the wind, I called in a management consultant, Chris Argyris, an old friend of mine who had been at Yale but by then was at Harvard. I didn't learn much from Argyris directly, but just the fact that I was able to get a consultant of his national reputation won me some points with the HEW hierarchy, whose highest respect is reserved for good managers. Argyris was more forthright with Larry Lewin, a young consultant I finally hired to do an organizational study. "If you're not willing to tell Ed he's the problem," Argyris told Lewin, "you aren't worth anything as a consultant."

Later Lewin pointed out to me what was already obvious, that I had serious management problems compounded by the difficulty of trying to merge two different organizations—the old Children's Bureau with the militant Community Action types who had led Head Start at OEO. "You are exactly what this organization needs," as Lewin put it, "but you are not all that it needs."

Clearly, I needed a deputy who understood the federal bureaucracy. I assigned Lewin the task of finding such a person. The secret of whatever administrative success I enjoyed thereafter thus
had a name: it was Saul Rosoff. Saul had done some hard jobs in
other agencies, including pulling off the difficult feat of moving a
large section of the Public Health Service from Washington to
Baltimore. While I tended to overwhelm my staff with too many
ideas, Saul was a master at bringing out the best in staff; he would
call in everyone in his office to work together on a problem, and be
willing to talk as long—and provide as many doughnuts—as necessary to complete the project. He would hold meetings before important meetings, so staff had a chance to work out the wrinkles in
their presentations before they were given publicly. Saul was not
only good at converting a staff into a team; he was also a good
strategizer who never called attention to himself. I became the
front man with the ideas; Saul would turn the idea into a program.
Saul in effect served as a professor of public administration for me,
while I taught him child psychology.

Another challenge was to garner the respect of regional HEW
directors and to address the split between CAP leaders and Head
Start parents and staff at the local level. From that perspective, the
turning point for me was a visit to Marin City, California, in October
1970. I was there to visit a Head Start center with a few of my staff,
including regional liaison Clennie Murphy and Head Start educational curriculum coordinator Jenni Klein. During the course of the
visit, the regional people asked me, "Would you be willing to meet
with a few Head Start parents?"

The regional people took us into a huge shed, where there
must have been 800 angry-looking people. I was totally taken by
surprise. There were microphones set up, and seats on the stage,
as if the whole event had been carefully planned. Soon after we
went up on the stage, a group of protesters slammed the doors and
said, "You can't leave until we say." It was hot, and the atmosphere
was so charged that I had the feeling that at any moment the
demonstrators might storm the stage. Jenni Klein, who had fled
Hitler in 1939, became extremely frightened. "This is just like Nazi

91

Germany," she said to me. I stood up and said that I would stay there as long as the group wanted, but that one of my staff members was ill. If the protesters would allow her to leave, I'd try to answer their questions.

After Klein was allowed to leave I found that the demonstrators' prime concern was to protest a potential budget cut. Actually, it was the House of Representatives, not the Nixon administration, that was proposing another $5 million reduction in Head Start's budget that year. Whatever the Nixon administration's long-term plans for the program, the president had actually requested a $14 million increase for fiscal year 1971. This would not have been enough to restore the damage done over the previous three years, or to compensate for inflation, but it was technically not a "cut." Nevertheless, so far as the demonstrators were concerned, all the blame belonged with Nixon. They were angry and did not want to hear any explanations to the contrary.

After several hours of harangue, much of which seemed to have been directed from a script, one of the ringleaders demanded, "How much is the Nixon administration spending on the Vietnam War?"

"I haven't the slightest idea," I said, "because my job is to administer Head Start."

"Well," the woman exploded, "you ain't nothing but a boy. You don't know nothin'. Why didn't they send a man to talk with us?"

Then the Kansas City Ed Zigler came forward. I'm short, but as a youth I had developed a reputation as one who never held back from a fight. I told the audience I didn't like it when black men were called boys, and I didn't appreciate the adage any more when it was directed at me. If anybody doubted my manhood, I suggested he step outside and we'd settle it.

This exchange altered the mood of the audience. An elderly black woman rose to speak. She revealed perhaps more clearly than anyone ever has before or since to me just how Head Start has managed to survive so many years. "Dr. Zigler, I know about Head Start," she began. "My daughter died in an automobile accident, and I have had to raise her two children. One child had Head Start, and the other didn't, and I see the difference. If you will see to it that Head Start is not cut, then you can cut part of my Social Security check to pay for it."

The Art of "Coordinating"

My second major goal for the Office of Child Development was to coordinate the multitude of federal programs for children that had grown up over the years. If Head Start could be seen by the White House and OMB as part of an effective agency, I thought the preschool program might benefit from the association.

As critics had long pointed out, there were hundreds of programs for children spread out across at least a dozen agencies, including Maternal and Child Health, the National Institute for Mental Health, the Office of Education, to name just a few then within HEW. Since the public response to my coordination proposal had been favorable, and OMB liked it, I couldn't understand why my initial overtures met with so little enthusiasm from the various agency heads. Finally, I asked Elliot Richardson. He leaned back in his chair and laughed. "Coordination may sound like a great idea to you," he said, "but to a bureaucrat, it means you want to take over his program and put it in OCD."

Realizing that as long as I headed up the effort it would get nowhere, I asked Brewster Smith, a respected scholar outside government and a past president of the American Psychological Association, to lead an Interagency Panel on Children. Since neither I nor anybody else from OCD was claiming to be in charge of the panel, it was no longer a threat to other agencies. With the skillful staff work of Edith Grotberg, who had already been meeting informally with other agency officials about research issues held in common on children, the panel flourished, and, as of this writing, still exists.

OMB was flabbergasted. The panel made a "map" of the existing programs in all federal agencies designed to serve children in the first five years of life, and identified some gaps as well as dupli-

cations in services. In fact, I think the success of this panel probably did more than anything else to enhance OCD's credibility with
OMB. Always frustrated by the waste and inefficiency caused by
duplication and lack of coordination of social programs, OMB itself
had tried in the past to bring some order to children's programs.
With some tangible evidence that OCD could perform a useful function, I hoped to convert the architect(s) of the Head Start phase-out
plan into a kinder and gentler OMB.

The "Loyal" Advocate

My most difficult function, to some extent self-imposed, at OCD
was that of advocacy. I took seriously the 1911 law creating the
Children's Bureau and assigning it responsibility for continually
taking readings and reporting on the status of the nation's children.
For many years, the position of director of the Children's Bureau
was essentially nonpolitical. When I said that the U.S. infant mortality rate compared unfavorably with that of other developed nations, or that many of our child care centers were poor in quality, I
thought I was just fulfilling the requirements of that 1911 law. To
stop sharing these facts would not only have been unethical; it
would have been illegal.

But I now acknowledge that, increasingly, there is an inherent
conflict of interest between being a presidential appointee and
being an objective, nonpartisan advocate for children. I tried to be
as outspoken as the Children's Bureau chiefs of old, when presidents would come and go, while the Children's Bureau chiefs
stayed on for a decade. More and more, what used to be nonpartisan advocacy positions in government are politicized. Thus, since
1972, there have been at least a dozen directors of the Office of
Child Development and Children's Bureau. Positions such as director of the National Institute of Health have been held vacant for a
couple of years because the administration couldn't find a person
with the "right views."

While trying to remain a loyal member of the administration, I certainly used the well-known technique of citing the president's record to try to get him to do what I wanted, giving him credit for things I wished he or Congress would do. Hence, since the president was on record endorsing a $386 million child care component to be part of his welfare-reform proposal, the Family Assistance Plan, I touted this constantly, adding that I was appalled that it had not received more grass-roots support.

Working with Congress

Another strategy in protecting Head Start was to develop a rapport with the key House and Senate leaders charged with overseeing the program. On this score, I had a rough start. Early on when I was testifying before the House Education and Labor Committee, the subject of the Westinghouse report came up. For the most part, I said, I didn't put much stock in that report. But there was one conclusion with which I agreed totally. The report's finding that the summer program did not accomplish very much was right on target, and I recommended that Congress consider phasing out the summer program entirely, and channeling all of those funds into the year-long program.

"You shut down a single summer Head Start program," the committee chairman, Carl Perkins of Kentucky, shouted down at me from the committee platform, "and I'll have you down here the next day, if I have to subpoena you."

Perkins's outburst was a total enigma to me. Why wouldn't the committee chairman want to save money on a wasteful program, and redirect it to a more worthwhile activity? I asked my staff, other colleagues, and Secretary Richardson. Nobody could give me a plausible explanation. Finally, I asked John Brademas, who was then chairman of a subcommittee under Perkins. Reluctant to violate the congressional rule of loyalty, this Rhodes Scholar would only say, "Well, Ed, he's the committee chairman; he can do what he wants." Finally, seeing that I still didn't have a clue about the chairman's behavior, Brademas took pity on me. Using the Socratic method, he asked me: "Ed, who teaches in the summer Head Start program in Kentucky?"

"School teachers who are moonlighting during summer vacation," I replied.

"Ed," he continued, "whom does the chairman of the House Education and Labor Committee depend upon to man the phones during an election and get out the vote for him?"

Oh, I guessed, school teachers, and the mystery was solved. It should be noted that the summer program was not entirely eliminated until 1982, at which point Representative Perkins was gone.

Fortunately, I had more success with the congressional appropriations committees. In fact, preparing to testify before the Senate Appropriations Committee was like preparing to take doctoral orals. Not knowing what questions would be asked, I read voluminously and tried to be prepared with the cost per child of every service someone conceivably might want to pursue. I asked my staff to try to guess the questions, and we even staged mock rehearsals. After the testimony, one was graded by one's own agency staff, depending on how much of the president's request for the program the committee ultimately appropriated.

As I became more at ease with Congress, I stepped into a professorial mode. After one such occasion, Secretary Richardson showed me an OMB report on my testimony: "Dr. Zigler gave his usual tutorial." At the same time, most of the points I won came by managing not to sound academic. One time after concluding my testimony, a representative interrupted me to say, "You don't sound a bit like a professor. You're spiffy, and full of pep, and you sound like you know exactly what you're talking about."

Dealing with the Enemy

All my worries about Head Start's budget prospects came to an unexpected conclusion in November 1970. Secretary Richardson was holding an HEW retreat at Camp David. Soon after our arrival, a call came that some 500 parents of Head Start children from as far away as Mississippi had assembled in the HEW auditorium back in Washington. They were demanding to talk to the secretary about possible cuts in the Head Start budget, and they were announcing the establishment of a National Head Start Committee to advise the federal government on the program.

While OMB's phase-out plan of the previous summer still lingered in the back of my mind, Richardson's strategy of emphasizing Head Start's strengths appeared to have worked, and there had been no more public promotion of this drastic proposal. Nevertheless, because the administration's budget request was not sufficient to cover inflation, we were preparing for possible further reductions in Head Start services. Meanwhile the House was proposing a $5 million reduction in the program budget, while the Senate was asking for a $73 million increase, and the whole issue was stuck in conference committee.

As the federal official responsible for Head Start, I left the retreat to go back to Washington to try to handle the demonstration. Once I got there, it was clear the demonstrators were not about to leave the auditorium. "Zigler must go! Zigler must go!" they kept shouting. I was in no position to tout my own efforts on Head Start's behalf over the past months, and, in any case, they were in no mood to listen to them.

Finally, after about six hours, Secretary Richardson and OEO director Donald Rumsfeld returned from the retreat. Richardson promised to urge the conference committee between the House and the Senate to "come out with enough money to carry forward the program ... without any cuts this year."[11] Although this promise did not go much beyond what the administration had already requested, it sounded like a major concession; it may have even contributed to the final congressional appropriation of a $35 million increase over the previous year and the first real increase in the program's budget since 1967. The future of Head Start was still far from secure, and the program's budget did little better than keep pace with inflation over the next few years, but at least we had bought some time.

Relations between the Head Start parents and the administration were further improved by James Farmer, HEW assistant secretary for administration and former head of the Congress on Racial Equality. Observing that many of the parents had traveled a long way to get to Washington, Farmer said that they must be very tired after spending all day in the HEW auditorium. And he arranged for them to have dinner in the cafeteria of a local school.

As I worked my way out a back door of the auditorium, I bumped into Daniel Schorr, who was covering the demonstration for CBS News. "Not much like academia, is it, Dr. Zigler?" he remarked ruefully.

5

Maximum Feasible Parent Participation

O NCE THE ISSUE OF HEAD START'S IMMEDIATE SURVIVAL HAD BEEN resolved, my major challenge was to develop the program's parent involvement policy. The Head Start Planning Committee and the program's early administrators had launched the trend toward parent involvement in education and social services, and Head Start parents had emerged as the program's most effective defenders. Nevertheless, when I became director of the Office of Child Development in 1970, there was still considerable controversy concerning what form parent involvement in Head Start should take: Were parents to run the program or merely be participants in its parent education services?

Origins of the Controversy

The roots of the controversy concerning the role of parents in Head Start really date back to the program's formation in 1965. The Planning Committee's recommendation for parent involvement represented a revolutionary step at the time. Previous architects of programs for children tended either to place parents and children in separate groups or to ignore the parents entirely. By contrast, the Planning Committee took the stance that children would benefit from their parents' direct involvement in the program, and that the best way for parents to learn about child development was through actual participation *with* their children in the daily activities of the program. The planning document recommended that Head Start offer parent education activities to "help parents deal with general and specific problems of child-rearing and home-making." Parents were also to "fill many of the non-professional, sub-professional, and semi-professional roles" in the program as maintenance staff, cooks, and teacher aides.

But the Planning Committee stopped considerably short of recommending parent control of Head Start. Rather than advocating a directive role for parents, the committee recommended that parents only "assist in planning the program of the center, its hours, location, program, etc."[1] The majority of the Planning Committee thus viewed parent involvement as a kind of "hands on" approach to parent education.

Some members of the Planning Committee were uneasy even with this limited conception of parent involvement.[2] James Hymes, Jr., a committee member who was then a professor of early childhood education at the University of Maryland, wanted a much more professional early childhood program, taught exclusively by staff with degrees in early childhood education. At the other extreme, Mamie Clark, one of the black scholars on the committee, initially opposed the whole idea of parent education in Head Start because she feared it might disparage black culture or attenuate its strength. Clark was reacting against the "deficit model," which was popular in the sixties and which equated poverty with "cultural deprivation."

The tension about the deficit approach added up to the following dilemma: On one side, if Head Start parents, whether black or white, had no educational or parenting skill deficits, and no problems but lack of money, why were we doing the program? Why not just issue each family a check? On the other, there would be no meaningful parent participation in any program that did not demonstrate full respect for parents.

It was Urie Bronfenbrenner who offered an approach to parent involvement that was not tied to overcoming some alleged cultural deficit. Bronfenbrenner was already beginning to formulate his ecological approach to child development—the idea that you can't help the child without helping the family and building a social policy hospitable to families. This ecological approach applied to all programs designed to help young children, whether their families were rich or poor. The basic insight was this: No one- or two-year program is likely to make lasting improvements in any child's development *unless* the program helps parents become the agents of change, reinforcing positive changes in the child long after the formal program's conclusion. Nevertheless, Bronfenbrenner's view of parent involvement was focused primarily on improving the relationship between parents and their children. His main goal was to empower parents to be better parents, rather than to organize them for social action.

"My original conception of parent involvement in Head Start was quite different from what it turned out to be," Bronfenbrenner recently explained.[3] To him parent involvement did not necessarily mean participation on committees or organizing for political action but rather having parents become "captivated" by their own children, supportive of their education, and irrationally committed to the idea that their children mattered.

Bronfenbrenner recalled paying a visit in 1965 to a Head Start center in western Appalachia that came close to this ideal. There was no way to reach the program by public transportation, and no street address. When he finally found the program, he asked the director, a minister in his late eighties, about the level of parent involvement in the center. "See for yourself," the director advised.

As he entered the center, there were 200 children, sitting in straight rows on old benches, drawing pictures with crayons. "Pacing about the room," according to Bronfenbrenner, "were three women and a man, each

> *armed with a flyswatter, and all actively involved in swat-*
> *ting any flies that dared to alight on any strikeable sur-*
> *face, including the more level facets of children's*
> *anatomy."* [4] *The parents were determined that nothing*
> *should interfere with their children's opportunity for edu-*
> *cation.*

Leaders of the Community Action Program (CAP) that served as the "host" agency for Head Start placed a different emphasis on parent involvement. The primary goal of CAP, of course, was to overcome poverty. The CAP philosophy tended to see the root cause of poverty as disenfranchisement from established social structures, and factors such as racism and classism, not a deficit in education or parenting skills.[5] Therefore, CAP leaders viewed parent involvement primarily as a way for parents to develop an alternative power structure to challenge the established institutions, such as schools, that had so far excluded them from any position of authority.

Polly Greenberg, a former OEO staff person who helped introduce Head Start in seven southeastern states, illustrates this view of parent involvement eloquently in her history of the Head Start program run by the Child Development Group of Mississippi: the CDGM goal for Head Start, according to Greenberg, was to "build the iron egos needed by children growing up to be future leaders of social change in a semifeudal state." [6] The Head Start centers would serve as the nucleus of an "experimental" private school system for black children that would be run by their parents and volunteers. Only if the children saw their parents in positions of authority in Head Start, as teachers rather than "teacher aides" who were little more than glorified maids, would they respect their parents. In short, in Greenberg's view, the only meaningful parent involvement in Head Start would be parent control and ownership of the program. And she adds that the CAP leaders were "nervous" about Head Start's "service delivery" orientation, which they feared might limit the power of poor parents to "plan, decide, and advocate (agitate) for the children before the powers that be—the mayors, et al.—[would] declare that Head Start people were, quote, 'too political.'"[7]

The first major clash, and in Greenberg's view the decisive conflict, on the role of parents in Head Start erupted when OEO temporarily cut off the funding for CDGM after its first year of operation and gave the grant to another group that was perceived as less threatening to whites in Mississippi. The superficial reason was CDGM's bookkeeping; however, the real issue was that Mississippi Senator John Stennis had the power to stop the whole War on Poverty if he could prove that any local program had misused money. Sargent Shriver was convinced that Stennis planned to use the CDGM case to do exactly that.

The dispute over CDGM is the subject of Greenberg's 825-page book, and it is far too complicated to discuss in detail here. But given the controversy concerning parent involvement during the early days of Head Start, it is little wonder that no clear policy on the role of parents developed at the federal level during the first year of the program's implementation.

Bessie Draper's Vision

Much of the practical wisdom of the federal policy that eventually developed on parent involvement in Head Start can be traced to Bessie Draper, who joined the national Head Start staff in 1966 as its first parent-program specialist. Draper had what might be considered an unorthodox background for developing parent involvement policy. Her training was not in child and family development or social work, but rather in labor and industrial relations. She had worked for the Urban League and then became Equal Employment Opportunity officer for the Missouri State Employment Service. It was precisely Draper's training and experience in helping adults that allowed her to come up with a workable approach to parent involvement, a synthesis of the various strategies of educating parents, enfranchising them, and helping them secure employment.

At the time Draper joined the Head Start national staff, parent involvement had not really been defined in federal rule or policy. She recalls a conversation with Jule Sugarman shortly after she joined the staff, when she asked him for direction:

"If we knew what parent involvement should be," Sugarman told her, "we wouldn't need you."[8]

Draper turned for direction to the law that provided the auspices for Head Start. "I looked back at the Economic Opportunity Act and found a phrase to hang my hat on—'maximum feasible participation of the poor,'" she said. Draper interpreted that phrase to mean that parents should be full partners in the design and delivery of services.

Draper had three children of her own, and in the 1950s and early 1960s, the attitude of educators was "Bring us your children and you go away while we educate them." Particularly as a black parent, Draper had problems dealing with the educational establishment. With two university degrees, she certainly considered herself better equipped to deal with the schools than black parents who were themselves undereducated. "Yet," she said, "I still found it a challenge."

Draper decided that she wanted parent involvement to mean that parents would be "equal partners" with the professional staff. The biggest obstacle to this vision was that parent participation and parent involvement were not initially seen as a separate component of Head Start, but rather as a division of social services. For example, Draper said she was initially expected to work under the supervision of the social services staff. Ironically, one of the problems she had with social workers was that they did not stress involving parents in the lives of their children. "The philosophy I found in social workers working with a low-income population," she said, "was almost patronizing, not one of encouraging self-determination."

Aware that she was charting new territory, Draper hired a group of consultants from a broad array of disciplines—sociologists, psychologists, social workers, educators, and persons from all ethnic backgrounds, including an Apache chief—to help give some shape to the parent involvement component. These consultants had to agree to commit two days a month of their time. Unlike many consultants, they did not just "meet." Rather, they spent most of their time visiting

Head Start programs and evaluating the extent to which parents were participating in the program, and determining what factors seemed to promote or discourage that involvement.

When Harold Hines's first child was enrolled in Head Start in Miami in 1966, he never went to the center or even met his son's teacher.

Then one day when his younger son was in Head Start, the boy came home wearing different clothes than he had put on that morning. "I asked him why, and he told me he'd messed his pants, and that the teacher had bathed him and changed his clothes," said Hines. "At the time I knew that I would have beaten the hell out of my son for such behavior."

Hines waited to hear what punishment the teacher had applied, but the boy said that didn't happen. "I thought about somebody showing that kind of love to my child, and the next morning I went to the school to meet the teacher," said Hines. "She handed me my son's clothes from the previous day, all washed and ready to wear the next day."

Moved by the kindness, and frankly determined not to let the teacher's love for his child outshine his own, Hines attended the Head Start center meeting that evening. It was not only his first Head Start meeting, but also his first meeting of any kind as an adult. The center was having an election of officers. "They thought a male image would be good for the program," said Hines, "and I happened to be the only father there, so I became president."

At the time, there was no structure for parent involvement, no real council. Hines started organizing parents and eventually began attending regional meetings on Head Start. A short time later he was offered the position of parent involvement coordinator for the entire Head Start program serving Dade County.

Draper developed a parent involvement section of the Head Start policy manual in 1967, which spelled out four basic functions for parents: (1) participating in the decision-making process about the nature and operation of the programs; (2) participating in the classroom as paid employees, volunteers, and observers; (3) receiving home visits from Head Start staff; and (4) participating in educational activities. This policy manual gave parents on the Policy Advisory Group the right to participate in the selection of the Head Start program director and to help establish the criteria for the selection of other staff. But it did not give them the power to approve or disapprove those selections. The manual also mandated that "parents are one of the categories of persons who must receive preference for employment as non-professionals" in Head Start.[9]

The next important landmark in the development of parent involvement policy in Head Start was the publication of a manual in early 1969 entitled *Parent Involvement 10A—A Workbook of Training Tips for Head Start Staff*.[10] This was developed by Draper and the consultants with the help of Helen Alexander, a volunteer in the national office who gave an entire year of her time to the project.

As a series of "training tips," the 10A workbook did not carry the force of a policy mandate, but it did help explain the various structures intended to facilitate parent involvement. These structures included the Parent Advisory Committee at the center level, the Policy Advisory Committee at the delegate agency level, and the Policy Advisory Council at the grantee level. Fifty percent of the members of each of these groups were to be parents of Head Start children, with the other 50 percent being community representatives from various public and private neighborhood, professional, civic, and social organizations that had a concern for children. The workbook also suggested duties for each of these advisory committees, including participation in the development of procedures for recruiting, screening, hiring, and terminating Head Start employees and approving the appointment of the center director.

While the 10A workbook suggested structures for parent involvement, it placed equal emphasis on giving practical suggestions for how parents could be involved. One section suggested possible jobs for Head Start parents in the program, such as teacher aides, shopping aides, and group leaders in activities for Head Start parents. Another section suggested topics for parent meetings—how to buy a used car, dos and don'ts of buying on credit, workshops to make inexpensive toys, and how to evaluate a prospective Head Start employee.

"Most of the parents had always been on the other side of the job interviewing table," said Draper.[11] When confronted with a job applicant, therefore, she thought their tendency was to base the decision to hire simply on the fact that the applicant needed a job. Thus, the 10A workbook was designed to teach parents that they had the right to evaluate an applicant based on one key question: "Will this be a good person to work with my child?" While many Head Start parents tended to be too accepting in hiring Head Start staff, according to Draper, other parents got swept up in the power trip of hiring and firing. "They would say 'hire and fire' as if it were all one word," she said. "I would say, but wait a minute, there is something that goes on in between."

Draper also fought many bruising battles to persuade Head Start officials to hire specific staff to facilitate parent involvement. Various members of the national staff would decide that parent involvement stretched through the whole Head Start program, and that, therefore, no specific staff for parent involvement were necessary. But Draper felt that if parent involvement were everybody's job, it would be nobody's job. Thus, she considered it a great victory when the 10A workbook spelled out the suggested staff positions for parent involvement: one Parent Program Assistant for every 60 children to develop plans with parents and staff for parent activities; one Parent Program Developer to supervise every 10 Parent Program Assistants; and one Parent Program Coordinator per grantee. All of these positions were independent of and equal to the social service staff at their level. Finally, she won the battle to have a parent involvement specialist in each regional office.

In addition to defining parent involvement and giving it a structure in federal policy, Draper, guided by the Parent Program Planning Consultants, developed some insights that are central to Head Start. While some people wanted to make it a requirement that parents participate a certain number of hours in Head Start, Draper said, "You can't require; you have to entice."

She also fought hard for Head Start to set aside funds for recreational or social activities for parents, and for parents to have the power to decide how these funds would be spent. Fifty cents per child of the program budget was set aside for parent activities. However, when a group of Head Start parents in New York decided they wanted to go to Patricia Murphy's Restaurant for a candlelight dinner, a local staff member said, "They can't do that." But Draper approved it. "I really thought I was going to lose my job over that," she said, adding that the parents probably learned more from raising part of the money for the dinner and arranging for the bus to transport them there than they did from most of the Head Start staff-initiated parent education activities.

Under Draper's guidance, the policy of parent involvement in Head Start was evolving toward a self-help approach. In part, the policy was designed to assist parents in gaining the organizational skills necessary to be full partners with professional staff in running the program. The policy was also designed to allow parents to decide what kind of parent education they did want. Many of the original Head Start parent education activities consisted of lectures on child development. Parents did want some information about children, but they redirected educational efforts to matters of more immediate interest. Parents began to share their own skills in everything from meal preparation to hair cutting. In short, Bessie Draper helped put a practical face on the concept of "maximum feasible parent participation." "Maximum feasible" was defined as a full partnership role for parents with paid professionals, but a role that stopped short of exclusive control by parents.

New Policy on Parent Participation

Despite the progress in defining and building the parent involvement component of Head Start, when I became director of the Office of Child Development in 1970 there was still considerable confusion about the role of parents, particularly in the areas of program direction and community activism. There were struggles for control among Head Start parents, staff, and administrators, and, in turn, between all segments of the Head Start program and the Community Action Program.

In the area of program direction, we received complaints from some Head Start programs that CAP was forcing Head Start to hire unqualified staff. In New Orleans, for example, Head Start complained that they were having to turn away qualified applicants in order to hire the people designated by the CAP agency.

There was a lot of misunderstanding according to Bessie Draper. "Parents were supposed to start out as aides in the Head Start program. But in order to progress to higher positions, they were supposed to go on to get a credential. I wouldn't want a Head Start parent to be a Head Start director just because he or she was a Head Start parent."[12]

Furthermore, not all the Head Start "parents" on the various advisory committees and boards really had children in the program. According to Draper, some were activists just using the program as a platform. For example, she recalled one man who presented himself as a poor parent but was a college graduate. "He wasn't poor," she said. "He was just broke." And Draper later found out that the child he was supposed to be representing "wasn't his child at all."

Part of the problem stemmed from the tendency of white people to think all black people were poor. White Head Start staff used to ask Draper if she had been a Head Start parent. At the time, her husband, who had been a professor of law and later a judge, was deputy director of the Equal Employment Opportunity Commission.

By the time I arrived in Washington, D.C., social activism in Head Start was becoming a two-edged sword: it was helping to keep the program alive, but it was also alienating some key members of Congress. Making courtesy calls to key senators shortly after my arrival on the job, I learned that my scheduled appointment with Senator Russell Long, chairman of the Senate Finance Committee, had been shifted to the Senate Steam Room. While I stood dripping in a suit, Senator Long, wrapped only in a towel, lectured me that he didn't want any more Head Start funds going for Community Action activities.

"Why should I pay poor people to stir up trouble," Senator Long asked, "when I can't find anyone to iron my shirts?"

Nor was the congressional criticism of activism in Head Start confined to white southerners. The late 1960s and early 1970s was a period of politics by confrontation; marches and sit-ins were common forms of persuasion in attempts to increase society's responsiveness to the poor. It is hardly surprising that when the status quo was attacked, established members of society retaliated. Mayors and governors lost little time informing Congress that Community Action funds, including Head Start's, were financing militants. This reactionary wave reached its peak about the time I arrived at OCD in 1970—the same year I learned of the three-year plan to phase out Head Start.

Coming on the heels of the recent release of the Westinghouse/Ohio report raising skepticism about Head Start's effectiveness, any notion in Congress that Head Start money was being spent on inappropriate forms of activism was simply a perception the program could not afford. As OCD director, I felt I was having to defend Head Start from all sides. I could have handled either the Westinghouse report or the concerns about publicly financed activism, but it was difficult to tackle both at once.

The whole issue of *parent* as opposed to other forms of *social* activism came to a head for me in a meeting in my office in 1970. A number of local Community Action Program leaders had come to present me with some "non-negotiable demands." "We're going to tape everything you say," they said, a tactic not particularly conducive to an open, honest discussion. We were sitting around the table in my office. I had decided that Head Start was to have a single goal—improving the social competence of children and their families. In short, I wanted to concentrate on the development of high-quality programs. I was aware that if you change society, you can also make life better for children, but I didn't think we should attempt broad-scale social change with Head Start's $400 million budget. These CAP leaders didn't like the fact that I had decided to cut off use of parent activity and training funds for some forms of activism, such as protests and sit-ins.

Finally, one man got frustrated. Standing up at one end of the table for emphasis, he said, "Dr. Zigler, you don't understand. We are interested in systemic change. We are willing to give up a whole generation of our children in order to get it." I stood up at the other end of the table, and said that he might be willing to give up a generation of children, but that I was not, and that was not my mission in OCD. His children had a right to be all they could be, I said, and that was what Head Start was about.

It was at this point that I made a critical decision: while rejecting use of Head Start funds for some forms of community activism, I decided that federal policy should give parents clear authority to determine the nature of local programs. And I asked Bessie Draper to develop a policy that would allow us to enforce the decision-making role of parents in Head Start. Up until this point, the guidelines on the parents' right to participate in the hiring and firing of Head Start employees had been just that—guidelines. But in 1970 we issued a new section on parents for the Head Start policy manual. This policy, known as 70.2, for the first time spelled out the specific responsibilities of the Head Start policy committees at the center, delegate agency, and grantee agency level. To eliminate any possible confusion about the division of responsibilities, a chart in the new section outlined the respective roles of the delegate and grantee agency boards, policy committees, and Head Start directors. The chart indicated areas where parents had to be consulted, where they had operating responsibility, and where they had the power to approve or disapprove. At the same time, the name of the policy-setting groups, half of whose members were required to be parents of Head Start children, was officially changed from Policy Advisory Council to Policy Council. The Policy Council was specifically given the power to approve or disapprove the hiring and/or firing of the Head Start director at the delegate agency and the grantee agency level, and to approve or disapprove the program budget.

Strengthening the power of parents in Head Start decision making, particularly in the area of personnel administration, was not universally welcomed. No sooner had the policy been announced than I got a call from some school superintendents representing grantee agencies who complained that schools *never* share power with other groups on the hiring and firing of school employees. We had to de-fund Head Start programs in Kansas City and Omaha because they refused to comply with the new policy on parent involvement, and we threatened to de-fund several others.[13]

Even some of my own OCD staff disapproved of the policy giving parents clear decision-making power. I remember one meeting where a Head Start parent literally came to blows with one of my OCD staff members. "There was blood on the floor," Bessie Draper recalls. In retaliation, my staff member wanted me to punish all Head Start parents by removing their power to make decisions in the program.

Given the political climate and the internal opposition, why did OCD stick by the new parent participation policy? I expected parents to make mistakes and learn from them, just as we at the national office were doing. As a member of the original Head Start Planning Committee, I also believed that parents are their children's best advocates and that parental participation in decision making would most effectively guarantee Head Start's quality.

Beyond these basic principles, I was convinced by Bessie Draper. Her common-sense approach to the policy impressed me. While committed to the goal of making parents equal partners with Head Start staff, she did not romanticize their poverty. "The law [the Economic Opportunity Act] didn't say that poor people were supposed to run the program by themselves," said Draper. "If they already had that kind of skill, they probably wouldn't be poor. The word in the law is participation, not control."[14] Draper was not blaming the victim. Coming from a background as an employment counselor, Draper's approach was to empower people by encouraging them to develop necessary skills.

In addition to the section on the parental role in decision making, the new parent involvement policy also spelled out the Head Start policy on home visits: Head Start staff were to visit parents of enrolled children at least three times a year, if the parents consented. This was the forerunner of all of the home-visitation projects today, such as Parents as Teachers, and David Olds's home-visitation project in Elmira, New York. Finally, the new policy clarified Head Start's stance on community activism. Parent activity funds could be used to work on community problems and "common concerns, such as health, education, welfare, and housing." However, in order to prevent use of such funds for sit-ins and other clearly disruptive tactics, Head Start program proposals henceforth had to contain a specific request for parent activity funds, and a general explanation of the types of activities for which the funds would be used.

In summary, the 70.2 policy for the first time spelled out the duties and powers of parents in Head Start in such a fashion that the policy could be enforced. The policy struck a balance between parent involvement as a vehicle to empower parents as decision makers, and as a tool to educate and counsel them. Perhaps the best tribute to this policy is that, as of this writing, it remains unchanged as part of the Head Start Performance Standards.

Effects of Parent Involvement

Given the central place of parent involvement in Head Start policy, there has been surprisingly little research on its impact on children, parents, or communities. There are strong suggestions, however, that parent involvement—in a variety of forms—improves the long-term outcome for the children. The MIDCO report noted a direct relationship between the children's progress and the degree to which their parents participated as decision makers and learners in Head Start, although it was not clear whether parent participation caused the children's progress or merely correlated with it. Edmund Gordon, Head Start's first research director, has suggested that the development of leadership potential among the poor might be an important factor in optimizing the growth of children. Gordon pointed out a finding in the Coleman Report that had gone relatively unnoticed—namely, that with the exception of family background, the variable most related to school performance was the child's sense of control of the world he or she inhabits. How does a child's sense of control develop? Based on modeling theory, children will believe that they can influence their own destinies if they have the opportunity to interact with adults who themselves have that world view.

The importance of parent involvement, in the sense of home visits to parents, has also been suggested by High/Scope Foundation's research. In a follow-up study of disadvantaged children participating in the Perry Preschool Program, children who received biweekly home visits *plus* preschool fared better as young adults than did those who had only had the benefit of the preschool program.

Even the highly critical Westinghouse/Ohio report was positive on one score: parents liked the Head Start program; more than 80 percent of parents covered in the Westinghouse study thought their children had improved as a result of Head Start. Positive parental attitudes toward Head Start's effect on children take on more significance when one considers the tendency for poor parents, especially poor urban parents, to lose hope for their children. Thus, any program that can raise parental aspirations will help to shape children's accomplishments.[15]

"What difference has Head Start made to your family?" I remember asking a Head Start mother who approached me some years ago after a speech.

"Well, it's simple," she said. "When my daughter used to give me pictures she had drawn, I'd think to myself, that's the ugliest picture I've ever seen, and wad it up and toss it in the wastebasket. After she was in Head Start, I'd take the picture, ask her to tell me about it, and post it proudly on the bulletin board."

As my Yale colleague Victoria Seitz and others have suggested, there may well be a snowball effect operating here. The parent's more positive attitude toward the child increases the child's self-esteem, which furthers the child's accomplishments, which in turn enhances the parent's satisfaction with the child.

There is considerable anecdotal evidence about the impact of Head Start on the lives of parents themselves: in *Head Start*

Success Stories, 79 parents relate the impact Head Start has had on their lives.[16] One story after another reports the experiences of parents who started out without even a high school diploma, became involved as parent volunteers in Head Start, then took on leadership roles on the Policy Committee, and ended up getting college degrees. Ernestine Carrasco, for example, started out as a parent volunteer in the Carlsbad, New Mexico, Head Start in 1966. The program helped her obtain her Graduate Equivalency Diploma (GED), and go on to get a bachelor's degree and finally a master's degree in education. Carrasco became a public school teacher, created the district's first bilingual kindergarten, and in 1979 was promoted to elementary school principal.

"When I talk with some of these women who are Head Start's success stories," said Rossie Drummond Kelley, Head Start's public information director, "they often tell me how 'those Head Start ladies' stayed on their backs until they got involved. What happened to their kids happened because the parents changed."[17]

Frankie Brundage King cried when her mother told her she was going to have another baby. According to custom in their rural Alabama county, this meant that King, the oldest daughter, would have to drop out of school to care for the infant. Married herself at the age of 16, King had six children by the time she was 26. She got a job as a maid and thought that was the end of her education and her opportunities.

But then King started attending meetings of the Alabama Council on Human Relations, the organization that sponsored Head Start in Lee County, Alabama. They encouraged her to go back to school and gave her the confidence that she could learn. King also began working for Head Start. "She started out as a secretary who could not type," said Nancy Spears, Lee County Head Start director. Due to a speech impediment, King was at first even afraid to answer the phone.

With the support of Spears and Head Start parents in

*similar circumstances, however, King acquired secretar-
ial skills and obtained a Graduate Equivalency Diploma.
"I went to school half a day, and worked eight hours in the
afternoon and at night for Head Start as a clerk-typist,"
said King. "It was the first job I ever had that did not include pushing a mop or dusting a table."[18]*

*Empowered by a new sense of pride, and the sense that
she could make a better life for herself and children, King
enrolled in college part-time. By the age of 37, the same
year her oldest son graduated from college, King obtained
her bachelor's degree. All six of her children completed college as well, and King is now the human services coordinator for the Alabama Council.*

Despite numerous success stories, studies are just beginning to attempt to quantify the impact of Head Start parent involvement on families. One such study examined the effects of parent involvement on Head Start parents' psychological well-being. Mothers who participated reported fewer psychological symptoms, greater feelings of mastery, and greater life satisfaction at the end of the program.[19] Another study, the Head Start Family Impact Project, found that parent involvement in a Minnesota Head Start program increased the sense of family cohesion and adaptability, and the researchers speculate this will eventually improve the children's performance in school.[20]

But what is needed is research on how participation in Head Start affects the whole fabric of parents' lives—their employment, housing, and overall socioeconomic status. At the same time, we need a realistic yardstick by which to measure the effectiveness of Head Start's parent involvement policy. Even if only 1 percent of the over 10 million parents associated with Head Start over the last 25 years represent "success stories," a hundred thousand families in this nation are as a result now leading much better lives.

More data are also needed on the extent of parent involvement in Head Start. Although Head Start Statistical Fact Sheets maintain that over 443,000 parents volunteered in the program in 1989, or nearly one parent for every child enrolled that year, there is little indication of the extent of their involvement. That is, did the parents attend one parent meeting a year, or did they volunteer several hours a week in the classroom? The Family Impact Study found that Head Start parent involvement ranged from 0 to 154 hours over a six-month period, averaging to less than one hour per week.[21] And Head Start directors report informally that parent involvement has declined over the years.

Another missing piece of information concerns the effects on the children enrolled of Head Start's policy of encouraging parent employment in the program. We know that, nationwide, over one-third of Head Start staff are parents of children who are past or present participants in the program. But do children fare better in those Head Start programs that employ large numbers of Head Start parents as teachers, even when that means that few of the teachers have college degrees in early childhood education? Or do children do better in those programs that place a higher premium on employing early childhood professionals, at the expense of not hiring as many Head Start parents? In short, while few would now challenge the importance of involving parents as employees and volunteers in Head Start, what balance between paraprofessionals and professionals works best for the children?

Head Start's parent involvement has clearly had a positive effect in terms of encouraging parents to obtain training in child development. Under the Head Start Supplementary Training Program, by 1973 more than 12,000 Head Start staff, many of them parents of children enrolled, had received college training for credit and 1,000 had received either A.A. or B.A. degrees.[22] Through the Child Development Associate (CDA) program, which was initiated under my direction in 1972, over 30,000 Head Start teachers and home visitors have obtained this competency-based credential.[23]

At first, Ophelia Brown's employment with Head Start did not seem to represent much progress. Despite the fact that she already had 30 college credit hours, more training than many of the white teachers in Head Start in Miami at that time, Brown was hired at the lowest level of teacher assistant. She was treated like the center's domestic; she alone swept the floor, took the children to the bathroom, and gave them baths.

Far from being discouraged by this experience, however, Brown was all the more determined to get enough training so she could not be held back. Through Head Start Supplementary Training, she got her associate's and then her bachelor's and master's degrees in early childhood education at the University of Miami. During this time, Brown was raising a family and working full-time for Head Start during the day, while attending school evenings and weekends.

"I started as a teacher aide 1, moved up to teacher aide 2, then teacher, then center director, then field operations supervisor, then region director, then Head Start director, and now director of a new combined Head Start, Youth, and Family Development division of the Community Action Agency," said Brown.

Over the years, the Dade County Head Start program had gone through many nationwide searches for directors. "They would hire Ph.D.'s from New York to Oregon," said Brown, "and then have me fill in when they left." Finally, Head Start parents petitioned Brown to take the position, and she was hired as the Head Start program's 19th director.

Head Start has thus provided leadership training and career development opportunities for thousands of Head Start parents. To date, however, Head Start's employment and training efforts have probably been overly focused on careers in early childhood. The goal was not to have Head Start parents become permanent Head Start employees, according to Bessie Draper, but to "move them up and out" of both Head Start and poverty. Washington and Oyemade fault Head Start's parent involvement policy for not placing more emphasis on economic self-sufficiency. "In the final analysis," they write, "the solution to poverty is jobs and a decent income."[24] And they argue that Head Start should place greater emphasis on programs to help parents improve their employability.

Recent welfare reform legislation, the Family Support Act (FSA) of 1988, requires parents on AFDC with children over age three to be employed or in a training program. Given the fact that nearly 50 percent of Head Start parents are on AFDC when their children enter the program, this legislation seems to demand that Head Start improve its linkages with employment and training programs beyond those geared simply to providing training in early childhood education.

Nevertheless, at its best, I think Head Start already comes closer to embodying the kind of two-generational approach that seems most likely to help families overcome poverty.[25] And Head Start's economic empowerment strategy may depend on preserving its voluntary nature. It would be interesting to compare the effectiveness of Head Start's parent employment and training activities with those of the Jobs Opportunities and Basic Skills (JOBS) program mandated through FSA. While it is likely that a higher percentage of JOBS participants secure training and employment, it may well be that the people who secure jobs through Head Start find more lasting employment.

Bessie Draper tells the story of a New York City Head Start program that was having difficulty getting the fathers involved. So they set up a social night for the men on Tuesday evenings.

The leader of the group was a janitor, employed at Queens College. The men got some lumber and built themselves a Ping-Pong table. Then they repaired some of the furniture for the program. Then they started talking about jobs. In New York, there's an examination you have to take to become an "engineer," or the equivalent of a janitor, in a large building or institution. So the men decided to have

*a study group to prepare for the entry-level position for
this occupation. As a result, several men secured jobs and
moved their families to a better place.*

*"The key to this success was that it was self-motivated,"
Draper says. "If we had mandated that the men take
courses one night a week, it would have been a total flop."
But when the motivation comes from within, people are
more apt to develop a commitment to the jobs they secure.*

It is Head Start's two-generational strategy that separates it
from so many other job-training and early intervention programs.
Too often job-training programs have focused on the parents, while
placing the children in poor-quality child care arrangements that do
little more than prepare them to be the next generation of welfare
recipients. At the same time, many early intervention programs,
particularly those based in the public schools, have focused on the
children, with little interaction with their parents. Newer programs,
such as Even Start, established by the Department of Education in
1988 and operating in 119 sites across the nation, offer adult basic
education, early childhood education, and parent-child activities.
But it is Head Start that set the trend.

New Outlet for Parent Activism

Head Start's parent involvement component has had an interesting
side effect: the emergence of the National Head Start Association.
In 1973 Head Start directors formed a national association, and the
following year parents and staff were admitted to the organization.
By 1976 the National Head Start Association (NHSA) was com-
posed of four groups—parents, directors, staff, and "friends" of
Head Start, with parents representing the largest component.
Arvern Moore, a former Head Start parent from Holy Springs,
Mississippi, is the current president of the organization.

The National Head Start Association has played a central role in many of the program's battles with Congress over the years. Relying on telephone networks and mailgrams, and, at least in the early years, less than an $8,000 national budget provided by private donations and dues, the NHSA has helped win numerous appropriation increases for Head Start as well as a major congressional victory to keep the program out of the Department of Education.

Earlier sit-ins and marches by Head Start parents and staff, where the goal was broad social change and the target was the "establishment," understandably alienated some members of Congress. Even the HEW sit-in during my first year as OCD director, while it helped achieve the short-term specific goal of protecting that year's budget, could not have survived very long as an effective lobbying tactic.

The organization of the National Head Start Association, however, lifted parent participation into a whole new realm of political education. Developing increasingly sophisticated lobbying techniques, such as an elaborate state-by-state contact list, which could reach all the congressional committees charged with supervision of Head Start, made the NHSA a force with which Congress—and presidents—must reckon.

The National Head Start Association embodies both the parent education and parent empowerment components of "maximum feasible parent participation," and it does so in a manner that is even palatable to conservatives. By serving as spokespeople for Head Start's family-centered approach, Head Start parents won over New Right leaders of the 1980s, such as Senator Orrin Hatch of Utah and Senator Jeremiah Denton of Alabama.

"The best part of Head Start volunteerism is that the majority are parents of children who are now, or who have been, enrolled in Head Start," wrote the erudite Senator Hatch in support of Head Start's reauthorization bill in 1984.[26] "This involvement appropriately highlights the role of parents as the prime educators of preschool children."

"What I like is Head Start's family-centered nature," Senator Denton told Nancy Spears, a fellow Alabaman and chair of NHSA's Education Information Committee that year. Responding to the self-help message in Head Start parent Frankie King's testimony before his committee, Senator Denton told Spears that he "never could have made it if he had to face as many obstacles as she had."[27]

With new friends like Hatch and Denton, Head Start's parent involvement policy came full circle. Once the most controversial aspect of Head Start, parent involvement became the policy that made the program most politically viable.

6

Head Start Meets Child Care

T HE HIGH POINT OF MY TERM AS DIRECTOR OF THE OFFICE OF CHILD Development was the passage of the Comprehensive Child Development Act of 1971—a bill that embodied my greatest hopes, but also led to my greatest disappointment.

In this legislation, Head Start almost became the foundation for a nationwide network of child care centers that would still be the envy of most child advocates. The Child Development Act had federal standards to protect the quality of care, federal money to train child caregivers, and allowed the use of federal funds to purchase child care facilities. The Act authorized $2 billion for child care—more than twice the amount found in the next major child care legislation enacted two decades later, the Child Care and Development Block Grant of 1990. Perhaps most revolutionary, the 1971 bill even stated that its purpose was to lay the groundwork for universally available child care services.

Like most legislation that portends real change, the Child Development Act of 1971 resulted from a temporary convergence of otherwise disparate interests. Some supporters were primarily interested in protecting Head Start and its Community Action Program base, while others wanted to consolidate Head Start with child care so that parents on welfare could go to work. Still others wanted to ensure that federally funded child care programs were of good quality and to open up these programs to all children of working parents, not just those who were poor.

Timing is everything in legislation, and, as a result of this convergence of interests, there was a brief moment when comprehensive child care legislation was possible. "It may sound mystical," notes Jack Duncan, a Washington lobbyist who at the time was staff director of the House Education and Labor Committee that sponsored the legislation, "but everything was in place for action."[1]

The Comprehensive Child Development Act managed to weave its way through Congress with strong bipartisan support. But the Republican support ultimately unraveled, providing an opportunity for a devastating presidential veto that would rule out any significant child care legislation in the United States for at least 20 years. As the OCD director who almost had the opportunity to set child care in this nation on a quality course, that veto remains the greatest disappointment of my professional life.

Shoring Up Head Start versus Broader Goals

The drive for the 1971 bill really began in 1969 in the aftermath of the Westinghouse report and concerns about the future of Head Start. In May 1969, Senator Walter Mondale, a Democrat from Minnesota and chair of the Subcommittee on Children and Youth of the Senate Committee on Labor and Public Welfare, introduced the Headstart Child Development Act. This bill proposed a massive expansion of Head Start from a $325 million to a $5 billion program over a five-year period. At the same time, it would have extended the program to nonpoor families on a sliding scale fee basis. Services would be comprehensive, including prenatal care for pregnant women. Head Start funds would be used to ensure the quality of child day care programs, and a common set of standards was to be developed.

Although the bill would have expanded both eligibility and services, it seemed primarily designed to shore up Head Start as a Community Action Program (CAP). Preference for grant applications would have been given to CAP agencies, Head Start would have remained within the Office of Economic Opportunity, and emphasis would have been placed on hiring indigenous low-income persons as Head Start personnel. These provisions were prompted by fears that the Nixon administration's plan to move Head Start to HEW was only the first step in abolishing the Community Action Program, and transferring Head Start to the states. Nevertheless, I opposed the provisions giving preference to CAP, regardless of the quality of the application. Such a policy seemed to subordinate the needs of children to another—albeit worthy—goal of organizing communities to fight poverty.

Meanwhile, Democratic Representative John Brademas of Indiana, chair of the Select Subcommittee on Education of the House Committee on Education and Labor, was working on legislation to coordinate and improve the quality of all federally funded child care programs. The starting point, according to Jack Duncan, who helped draft the bill, was the concept of Community Coordinated Child Care. Jule Sugarman was proposing the establishment of nonprofit "4C" agencies where families would be able to select from a variety of publicly funded child care programs.[2]

About the same time, other prominent voices were also calling for child care coordination. A special Head Start Advisory Committee, chaired by Charles Schultze, former director of the Bureau of the Budget under President Johnson, reported early in 1969 that "the objectives of day care and Head Start are in many ways similar, though not identical."[3] Schultze added that much of the knowledge gained in the Head Start program might profitably be applied to child day care, and that the two programs should be jointly administered. Nixon's new HEW Secretary Robert Finch adopted the same line, announcing that the Office of Child Development would provide "a single focal point within HEW" for child care and preschool programs.[4]

Brademas introduced the bill, the Comprehensive Preschool Education and Child Day Care Act, on August 13, 1969. The key objective of the 1969 bill was to bring together child day care, Head

Start, and preschool programs. At the federal level, instead of scattering the responsibility for child care across seven federal agencies, all early childhood programs would be located in OCD.

"One of my concerns was standards," says Brademas, a Rhodes Scholar with a doctorate who later served as president of New York University.[5] The 1969 legislation called upon HEW to establish for all child development programs, insofar as possible, a common set of basic requirements. By making OCD the lead federal agency for child development programs, Brademas also hoped to undercut the tendency to subordinate children's needs for quality care to other goals, such as getting their parents off welfare or using child care as a vehicle to employ low-income people. As his first witness on the Comprehensive Preschool Education and Child Day Care Act, Brademas called Milton Akers, executive director of the National Association for the Education of Young Children. Asked what were the principal lessons learned from Head Start, Akers said, "For a while we wanted to give jobs to everybody—that was the important thing. But now parents are beginning to see their kids are being sold short without competence."[6]

Another motivation behind the attempt to coordinate child care programs in Brademas's bill was the concern that existing federal policy was promoting socioeconomic segregation; it clustered poor children in one set of early childhood programs, such as Head Start, while children of wealthier parents attended other types of child care. "I was impressed by the findings of Jim Coleman," Brademas says, "that poor children do better developmentally when they are mixed with middle-class children."[7]

Initially, the Head Start program at Temple Beth-el in Hollywood, Florida, did have a social and economic mix of children. Marilyn Segal, a leader in early childhood education and daughter of a wealthy philanthropist, initiated the first Head Start class at the temple. She made sure that half the children came from full fee-paying families, including her own four-year-old handicapped daughter, Debbie.

*But soon the federal government ruled out having
equal numbers of children from economically disadvantaged and more affluent families. Head Start began to require that the parents of children financed by Head Start
hold meetings separately from the children of full fee-paying parents.*

*This may have made sense from the standpoint of pro-
moting Head Start as a self-help group for impoverished
parents, but it was too bad in many ways for the children.
"You can only break down stereotypes if you work and
play together," said Segal. "When we had the socioeconomic mix, all of the parents, including the upper-income
parents, would visit the program and get close to the children." Segal often wonders how the first group of Head
Start children who experienced the mixed setting have
fared compared to later participants in the program.*

From the opening hearing on the Brademas bill in November
1969 through the last one in March 1970, over a thousand pages of
testimony were collected. Many issues that Congress has yet to resolve in child care—staff-child ratios, the universe of eligibility,
whether schools should be involved—were being discussed in
enormous depth over 20 years ago, notes Brademas, adding that
much the same rhetoric is still used today.

The key battle that would seal the fate of the Comprehensive
Child Development Act two years later was already taking shape in
1969. The primary difference between the Mondale and Brademas
bills that year concerned whether federal funds should flow directly to Community Action Programs, or be channeled through
state commissions. Whereas Mondale was mainly attempting to
expand and build upon Head Start programs under the auspices of
antipoverty agencies, Brademas was trying to design a new child
care system extending equal status to all publicly funded early
childhood programs—state-financed preschools, federally funded
child care, and Head Start. And, in so doing, Brademas was willing
gradually to turn over to the states the decision-making power over

distribution of federal funds for child development programs. In his 1969 bill, state commissions composed of representatives from local education agencies, CAP agencies, and public and private child welfare groups would prioritize grant applications for approval by the HEW secretary. After two years, these state commissions themselves would have the power to approve grants and distribute federal funds.

Brademas was careful to retain some protection for existing Head Start programs. First, CAP agencies would have representation on the state commissions. Second, the bill, by grandfather clause, mandated that the state commissions give priority to refunding Head Start programs in existence prior to July 1969. But many Head Start and CAP advocates thought any state role in Head Start would undermine leadership by poor—and especially by minority—parents in the program.

Neither the Mondale nor Brademas child care bills introduced in the House and Senate in 1969 made it out of committee. However, in highlighting the issue of whether federal funds for child care programs should flow through state commissions or directly to CAP agencies, these 1969 bills set the stage for the 1971 debate.

White House on Quality Care: Rhetoric or Reality?

The White House was primarily interested in child care as a tool for welfare reform. Nixon's Family Assistance Plan, or FAP, was designed to reduce welfare rolls by placing recipients in employment and training programs. The architect of the plan was Daniel Patrick Moynihan, assistant to the president for Urban Affairs in 1969 (and later a principal author of the welfare reform measure, the Family Support Act of 1988).

The major obstacle in getting welfare mothers to work was the lack of affordable child care. Yet the administration's first version of the Family Assistance Plan paid little attention to child care, and was virtually silent on issues of quality. Of the 100-page bill that passed the House in April 1970 just as I was preparing to assume the leadership of OCD, only three pages concerned child care. HEW was to receive "such sums as may be necessary" to make grants or contracts for child care, to any public or nonprofit private agency that demonstrated a capacity to work effectively with the local manpower agency. With regard to the nature of child care to be provided, the bill said only: "Such projects shall provide for various types of child care needed in the light of the different circumstances and needs of the children involved."[8] The Family Assistance Plan, in proposing a guaranteed income for families—whether single-parent or intact—was one of the most radical pieces of legislation ever offered by any administration. By contrast, FAP's child care section was pallid indeed.

Yet I was convinced that FAP offered a major opportunity to expand and improve the quality of child care in our nation. First, there was the sheer magnitude of new child care arrangements that would be needed. In the first year of operation alone, service would be required for over 450,000 children. This represented a program as large as Head Start itself. Second, there were the president's statements about child care. "The child care I propose is more than custodial," the president said. "The day care that would be part of this plan would be [of] a quality that will help in the development of the child and provide for its health and safety, and would break the poverty cycle for the new generation."[9] Finally, the very fact that President Nixon created OCD seemed to me a sign that the administration was serious about quality programs for children. References to child care in the FAP bill might be vacuous, but I saw them as a vacuum waiting to be filled.

So, from the day I started at OCD, I tried to put the administration in a position of leadership on the issue of child care quality. Various officials had been talking quality, but nobody was leading the charge. As one of my first initiatives, I had OCD convene a conference on child day care. Over a thousand people attended the 1970 conference at Airlie House, Virginia. My main goal for the conference was to produce some manuals, in effect "cookbooks," on the principles of quality care and the key components of infant, preschool, and school-age child care. The conference underscored some differences among child care advocates about what consti-tutes quality care. Some proponents thought all child care should be comprehensive, including medical and social services, while others felt that a developmental level of care was sufficient for all but the most disadvantaged children. "Developmental" meant that the care was age-appropriate, with sufficient numbers of staff trained to work with the particular age child. Participants were unanimous, however, that child care should be something more than custodial care, or "just baby-sitting."

These debates helped precipitate my decision that it was neces-sary to revise the 1968 Federal Interagency Day Care Requirements (FIDCR). While the FIDCR enjoyed a near sacred status among child care advocates, the standards were written in such ambigu-ous terms that they were virtually unenforceable. In fact, soon after their promulgation in 1968, the Social and Rehabilitation Service sent informal assurances to the states through HEW's regional of-fices that the standards would not be enforced. Thus, in 1970, with the support of HEW Secretary Elliot Richardson, I set about revis-ing them. My intent was to produce a set of standards that could be used for child care under the Family Assistance Plan, Head Start, or any of the various child care proposals making their way through Congress.

While the 1972 standards developed at OCD would have slightly reduced some of the staff-child ratios established in 1968, in other respects they were more stringent. Volunteers and support staff, such as cooks and custodians, could no longer be counted in the staff-child ratio. Furthermore, unlike the FIDCR, which specified a one-to-five staff-child ratio for a wide span of age groups, the 1972 revision attempted to recognize the developmental needs of chil-dren at different ages. More protective ratios were recommended for infants and toddlers, whereas the standards for school-age chil-dren required less staff supervision.

I also spoke out in favor of a socioeconomic mix in Head Start and all child care programs. Middle-class and lower-class children would both grow from interaction, I told the *Washington Post*. As an ex–lower-class child, I rather resented the implication that they would not.[10] We couldn't continue sending poor kids to one place and more affluent kids to another, I added. Federal policy should promote integration by socioeconomic class, not just race.

Studies had indicated that task persistence, verbal skills, and self-concept of disadvantaged children improved more in Head Start classrooms that included children from more affluent homes.[11] There were also studies indicating that children from middle-class homes had something to learn from poor children; for example, the less advantaged children tended to be more spontaneous and emotionally expressive, qualities that enabled them to take pleasure in creative activities.[12] Allowing a mix of children in Head Start would also open up the program to children just above the federal poverty level. I thought many of these children needed Head Start just as much as those whose family income met some arbitrary limit set in Washington.

At 7:30 in the morning, at least 30 Haitian families are already waiting to enroll their children in a new Head Start program scheduled to open the following week in Fort Lauderdale, Florida.

Anticipation is high: the children are dressed in their Sunday clothes, with girls in bright-colored ruffled dresses, and boys in shirts and ties. One boy even sports a back pack that says, "School Fun." Several fathers and one grandfather are among the adults seated on child-sized blue plastic chairs in the Head Start classroom. Each family has been given a number, indicating who should receive priority for the limited spaces in the program.

"Number one," calls out the social worker who holds the combined position of social services and parent-involvement specialist for Head Start in Broward County, Florida. She speaks quietly with parents to protect their privacy, but her frustration is obvious in her deepening frown. Most of the children have no documentation of immunizations or a recent physical examination, and many have never been to a doctor. Even though all of the families

live in a very low-income area of Fort Lauderdale, the majority are above Head Start's income ceiling.

"I'm sorry, but you earn too much money," explains a Head Start community worker, after reviewing one family's check stubs. The mother and father together had managed to earn just over $20,000, not a lot to support three children in Fort Lauderdale, but still well above the federal poverty level for a family of five.

"Is there nothing I can do?" asked the father, as he looked down at his little girl in the red-ruffled dress. "What if my wife does not work?"

"I wish that we could admit every child who comes through the door," says Willette Hatcher, Broward's Head Start coordinator, "because many are just above the limit and fall through the cracks." But only half of the 4,000 children estimated to meet the poverty-level guidelines in the county are enrolled in any early childhood program. As a result, Broward does not even exercise the federal option to allow 10 percent of the children in Head Start to be above the poverty level.

My recommendation for socioeconomic integration did not sit well with some Head Start advocates. When I first called for a mix of children in Head Start in August 1970, I was denounced as a reverse Robin Hood. "Trying to give everybody a head start is a contradiction in terms," a *New York Times* editorial said.[13] Even if middle-income families paid for their children to be in the program, some Head Start leaders worried that their very presence would overpower poor families and make them less likely to participate fully.

Less than a year later, the *New York Times* reversed its position, praising the Family Assistance Plan in a July 1971 editorial for not limiting services to the most deprived, and for including child care on a sliding fee scale. But the early dispute on the issue of socioeconomic mix was yet another sign of the differing philosophies among child care and Head Start advocates. Were we primarily trying to develop self-help programs for the poor, where it would make sense to cluster poor children and their parents together? Or was the primary goal to foster the optimum development of children, who appeared to benefit more from a heterogeneous group?

Coalition of Advocates

The advocates who supported legislative initiatives leading up to the 1971 child care bill had a wide variety of goals, ranging from the protection of Head Start as an antipoverty program to the development of more federal support for child care for children of working parents.

Many of the child care advocates of the late 1960s and early 1970s had come of age during the civil rights movement and the early days of the War on Poverty. They were determined to protect the gains that had been made. No child advocate more embodied this spirit than Marian Wright Edelman, then director of the Washington Research Project and now head of the Children's Defense Fund, the nation's premier advocacy organization for children and families, particularly those who are poor. She had experienced discrimination as a black child growing up in South Carolina, but she had also been taught that it was possible to address wrongs through a strong family, education, and community service.[14]

After graduating from Spellman College and Yale Law School, Edelman opened a legal office in Jackson, Mississippi, in 1964 to support civil rights efforts. When the state of Mississippi declined to apply for Head Start funds in 1965, a group of private, public, and church organizations formed the Child Development Group of Mississippi (CDGM) to submit the application. Edelman became an influential CDGM board member. Later, when the white leadership in Mississippi struck back by accusing CDGM of mismanaging funds, she helped save the program by finding a new director, and persuading the local leaders to attempt to work within the system to regain federal funds.

But the experience of having the Office of Economic Opportunity turn its back on CDGM also taught her a lesson. "I learned that even good friends would do you in," Edelman said recently. "We needed an early alert system to anticipate political attacks on Head Start."[15] The battle to re-fund Head Start in Mississippi thus prompted her decision to move to Washington in 1968 and ultimately to form the Children's Defense Fund. "Head Start was the impetus for CDF's beginnings," she said, "and for identifying the big gap between federal legislation and implementation."

With the Mississippi experience behind her, Marian Wright Edelman became a strong foe of channeling federal funds for education through the states. One of her first initiatives in Washington was a study of the implementation of the Elementary and Secondary Education Act of 1965. The study showed that while a lot of money was going to state education agencies across the country, very little of it was reaching poor children. Thus, Edelman immediately saw efforts to transfer Head Start to state educational agencies as a threat to the program's very essence. To help protect Head Start, she brought together a coalition of groups with a direct interest in child care. This Ad Hoc Coalition on Child Development included several labor unions, the National Organization of Women, the National Welfare Rights Organization, and the Day Care and Child Development Council of America.

Out of that coalition came the comprehensive child care bill. "My goal was to protect Head Start, but to couch it in terms of child care," said Edelman. "There was a separate section near the end of the bill that protected Head Start, which was my primary agenda."

While Marian Wright Edelman was working to save Head Start for poor children, middle-class working mothers were also beginning to develop an interest in child care. Between 1965 and 1970, the number of working women with children under 14 jumped 45 percent—from 3.5 million to 5 million, and there was no indication that the trend would stop.[16] The emergence of this middle-class interest in child care prompted John Brademas's optimism that the time was right for child care legislation. "I am confident there will be strong support for early childhood legislation," he said on the day he opened hearings on the Comprehensive Preschool Education and Child Day Care Act of 1969. A June 1969 Gallup poll indicated that two out of three Americans favored providing federal funds for child day care.[17]

The Day Care and Child Development Council of America was the leading advocacy group on behalf of child day care for working parents. Led by Baltimore socialite Theresa Lansburgh, board members included business executives, politicians of both parties, early childhood educators, and researchers. I joined the board in 1969. For a time, Mrs. Richard Nixon served as honorary chairman.

One of the high points for this growing coalition for child care was the White House Conference on Children in December 1970, with over 4,000 participants. Out of a long list of recommendations, this conference gave top priority to expansion of comprehensive child development programs, including health services, day care, and early childhood education. Both Mondale and Brademas referred to this recommendation frequently in support of their child care bills introduced a few months later.

At the same time, the White House Conference on Children was in some ways a harbinger of problems to come. In preparation for the conference, I spent several hours with Stephen Hess, conference director, persuading him to include a single sentence mentioning the Office of Child Development in President Nixon's speech. OCD had been established by Executive Order, not legislation, and I knew that we needed something more binding to secure its future as the focal point for early childhood programs. "Help me legislate OCD," I said to my friends and fellow advocates at the conference. "Oh, we are, Ed," they said. "In fact, we're doing something better than that—we're trying to get a Cabinet level office for children."

It was my first brush with a tendency that seems endemic among child care advocates, whereby their vision of the perfect frequently becomes the enemy of the good.

Far-sighted Proposal

Brademas and Mondale worked closely on the development of their respective versions of the Comprehensive Child Development

135

Act introduced in spring 1971. The bills were nearly identical on many points. Taken together, they amounted to the most far-reaching child care legislation Congress has ever proposed, even more than two decades later.

First, Mondale and Brademas were in agreement on the issue of child care quality. Both bills called for federal standards for child development programs. Funds were earmarked for pre-service and in-service training of both professional and paraprofessional child care staff. The federal government would also help finance the renovation or purchase of child care facilities. The Office of Child Development would be legislated as the principal agency for the administration of the Act and for the coordination of programs relating to child development.

Second, Mondale and Brademas agreed on the importance of comprehensive services. Both bills provided for physical and mental health services, the identification of special needs, and the inclusion of services for children with disabilities.

Finally, Mondale and Brademas agreed upon a goal that few politicians would even dare utter out loud today—the goal of universal access to child care services. The preambles of both bills contain the following phrase: "it is the purpose of this Act ... to establish the legislative framework for the future expansion of such programs to provide universally available child development services."

Republicans joined in the support for the Comprehensive Child Development Act. In the Senate, Jacob Javits of New York and Richard Schweiker of Pennsylvania joined Mondale and other Democrats as initial cosponsors of the bill. In the House, four Republicans were among the nine original sponsors of the legislation. Ultimately, the House bill was cosponsored by 120 members, over one-third of whom were Republicans.[18] Orval Hansen, Republican from Idaho, spoke out particularly strongly on behalf of the Child Development Act: "This legislation before us today is truly landmark legislation in terms of its potential effect on the future of the country. The good it can do can have a more far-reaching impact than any of the major education bills enacted during the past 20 years."[19]

Stumbling over Delivery System and Eligibility

Despite the unprecedented bipartisan support for child care legislation, there were two major stumbling blocks to the bill's passage—disagreements over the delivery system and the income ceiling for eligibility. Underlying the resistance to compromise on these issues were differences in the House and Senate positions on the Family Assistance Plan itself.

The most intractable problem was the disagreement over the delivery system. As had been clear in their proposed child care legislation in 1969, Mondale and Brademas disagreed on the role the states should play. Mondale favored an expansion of the Head Start model, whereby all federal child care funds would flow directly to community agencies on a grant application basis. Brademas preferred that the funds go through a state commission.

Brademas thought some state supervision was needed to monitor the program. "Administrative workability was very important in my mind," he said. "The idea that the federal government would have to be in direct touch with thousands of community agencies all over the nation would have been an administrative nightmare."[20] Brademas was also a political realist. "Because of the scope of what we were trying to do," said his subcommittee staff director Jack Duncan, "we knew we would never prevail without strong bipartisan support."[21] And Republican support depended on granting some role to the states.

Initially, Brademas's 1971 bill would have limited prime sponsorship of child development programs to states and cities with populations of over 500,000. Communities were to submit applications to the prime sponsor through a local council, much like the Head Start Policy Council. The prime sponsor would then submit the application to the federal government, with the HEW secretary having the right to override the prime sponsor's recommendation and directly fund a local program.

During the course of subcommittee debate, however, the bill was revised to allow cities with populations as small as 100,000 to serve as prime sponsors, probably because this was the number the administration had selected for its proposed manpower development programs. At the time, I remember thinking it was a reasonable compromise.

Unfortunately, the Senate version placed no limit on the size of the community that could submit an application for funding to the federal government. Mondale made a strong argument against allowing states to be prime sponsors, without really explaining why there should be no restriction at all on the number of such sponsors. "I think it is time we learned that money sent out from the Federal Government by way of the States, through the State bureaucracy, to the localities gets to be pretty thin by the time it reaches the end of the pipeline," he said. "It is terribly important that we make money available directly to community groups and local governments."[22]

In testimony on the Senate bill, Marian Wright Edelman was adamant on the issue of the federal-to-local administration. "The heart of this bill is the delivery system," she said. "Those of us who have worked with the poor, the uneducated, the hungry, the disenfranchised have had long and bitter experience in how legislative intent is thwarted in the process of implementation; the way money is spent often is more significant that the fact that it is spent." And she warned that those concerned with equal opportunity and civil rights would oppose extending any control of the child care funds to the states.[23]

The dispute over size of the prime sponsors reached a peak when the bill came before the full House Education and Labor Committee. Committee chairman Carl Perkins, Democrat from Kentucky, speaking on behalf of the many small counties in rural America, wanted to eliminate or reduce the 100,000 requirement. Knowing that any further reduction in the population requirement for prime sponsors would jeopardize Republican support, Brademas risked Perkins's ire and held for the higher limit.

Another major area of controversy on the Child Development Act of 1971 was that of eligibility for free child care. Both the House and the Senate agreed that there should be a socioeconomic mix in child care, but they disagreed about the income level above which families should have to pay a fee.

The final House bill provided for free services to families with incomes up to $4,320 for a family of four, the proposed cutoff for family assistance at that time, and payments on a sliding fee scale for families above that level. The Senate bill provided for free services up to the so-called lower living standard established by the Bureau of Labor Statistics at $6,960 for a family of four.

Behind the scenes, Head Start advocates, as I had learned earlier, were not so sure they wanted a mix. "Marian's concern was for poor children," said Brademas. "I argued that poor children would be better off in a socioeconomic mix. If you can build a broader base politically, you can both have a substantially better program and build the support to get the funding to serve all children."[24]

Within the administration, there was also disagreement. HEW was willing to consider some federal assistance for child care for the families just above the family assistance cutoff. However, the Office of Management and Budget was concerned about the $13 billion, four-year price tag on the bill. They wanted to restrict federal funds for child care to persons eligible for the Family Assistance Plan; families above that level would have to pay the full cost of care.

Trouble over FAP

Differences in the House and Senate stance toward child care in some ways mirrored differences over the Family Assistance Plan itself. The House passed the Family Assistance Plan by a two-to-one margin in April 1970 and a slightly revised version again in May 1971. Given the House Democratic leadership's support of welfare reform, Brademas from the beginning saw FAP as an opportunity to win the Nixon administration's support for his child care measure. He was therefore inclined to make some compromises necessary to accommodate the administration's interest in child care.

By contrast, the Family Assistance Plan quickly got mired in the Senate. Ironically, Senate conservatives thought the welfare reform measure would exacerbate the work disincentives in the existing welfare system. Meanwhile, Senate liberals thought that FAP's guaranteed income ceiling was too low, not realizing that once the principle of a guaranteed income was in place, there would be opportunities to raise it.

Mondale frequently expressed deep reservations about FAP. "The President's Family Assistance Plan, pending in Congress right now," he said, "would force mothers of school age children to work even during hours when the children are not in school."[25] As for preschool children, Mondale wondered whether they were not better off in programs lasting several hours a day like Head Start, rather than in all-day programs designed to accommodate working mothers. He was also concerned that the administration would try to convert Head Start into a full-day program without increasing the expenditure per child, a policy that would surely undermine Head Start's quality.

Thus, while Mondale was totally committed to providing comprehensive early childhood programs, he was less than enthusiastic about any policy that seemed to encourage welfare mothers to place their children in all-day care. Furthermore, Marian Wright Edelman's Ad Hoc Coalition on Child Development included some prominent foes of FAP—the National Welfare Rights Organization, which argued that FAP's workfare provisions represented an attack on minorities and motherhood, and several labor unions, which feared that the guaranteed income might undermine union membership. Perhaps Mondale and Edelman were less willing than Brademas to compromise with Republicans on the child care bill in part because they would have preferred not to tie child development programs to welfare reform at all.

Administration Deadlock

The Nixon administration continued to be divided on child care legislation. In fact, Secretary Richardson had to cancel his scheduled testimony on the Child Development Act three times. According to Kevin Phillips, then a *Washington Post* columnist, the major obstacle to administration support was Richard Nathan, assistant director of the Office of Management and Budget (OMB). Nathan had served as chairman of the task force that came up with a blueprint for the Family Assistance Plan, and he was trying to safeguard its day care component from what he saw as the detrimental competition of the larger child care bill.[26]

In an effort to break the administration's deadlock on the bill, Richardson had been running back and forth between the White House and the Hill. Brademas was on Nixon's enemy list. So even in these pre-Watergate days, Richardson had to be careful about where they met. I also participated in numerous meetings with Brademas and Mondale, usually in hotels away from their offices. Both Richardson and I knew we had to make the Comprehensive Child Development Act as consistent as possible with the Family Assistance Plan in order to secure White House support.

An Unexpected Breakthrough

Much to everyone's surprise, in June of 1971 Richardson won out over the forces opposed to the bill within the Nixon administration. In a letter to Mondale, the secretary, with White House approval, stated his general support for comprehensive child development legislation that would: (1) "consolidate and coordinate" federal day care and child development programs; and (2) assist in the development of a delivery system for day care and child development services. Richardson also supported two principal service targets—the provision of child care for children of low-income working families, and the provision of child development services for children, regardless of the work status of their parents, to the extent permitted by budgetary resources and with priority to economically disadvantaged children.[27] Finally, Richardson reiterated his support for the Revised Federal Interagency Day Care Requirements, and noted that these standards would govern child care under the 1971 version of the Family Assistance Plan.

Richardson's statement was the breakthrough we had been waiting for. Stephen Kurzman, assistant secretary for legislation in

HEW, and I were then sent to deliver friendly testimony on the bill before the Senate Subcommittees on Employment, Manpower and Poverty and on Children and Youth. We told the subcommittees that the administration endorsed the principle of a delivery system for day care and child development services that would serve families of all income levels. We went along with the lower income limit of the House bill, providing free services to those with incomes under $4,320 for a family of four, while above that level families would pay on a sliding fee scale basis. On the issue of prime sponsorship, Kurzman said the administration preferred to deal with states or with cities with populations exceeding 500,000. Based on the experience in Head Start, where the federal government had difficulty monitoring the quality of programs administered by over 1,000 grantees, the administration thought it unwise to deal with more than 100 prime sponsors. "We are talking about such an enormous expansion of facilities and units within the next few years that when you compare it to the scale that is now in operation," Kurzman said, "it would require a much, much larger Federal bureaucracy and a great inability, in our judgment, to manage and monitor effectively the quality of the services provided."[28]

Finally, on the issue of quality of care, I testified that OCD had analyzed the costs of custodial and developmental care, and found a way to provide a developmental quality of care within the administration's budgetary guidelines. We actually broke down the costs of staffing, transportation, equipment, and so on, projecting a cost of $1,594 per child per year for developmental care meeting our proposed standards. Since we estimated that two-thirds of the children would be school-age and thus need only part–day care, the average cost per child would be $700. Thus, the $700 million the administration budgeted for child care—including the $386 million in new monies, plus the existing expenditures for child care—could serve a million children. We may have fudged on the proportion of school-age children a bit, but at least the estimated expenditures were based on the cost of implementing quality care.

Richardson's letter and Kurzman's and my testimony seemed to provide a "green light" for child development legislation. Even though the administration's preference for a 500,000 population limit for prime sponsors remained a problem, there were indications that the White House might not balk at the House-proposed figure of 100,000.

Last Chance

Unfortunately, instead of embracing the administration's offer on comprehensive child care legislation, child care advocates held out for more. One evening that fall there was a secret meeting in Baltimore at the home of Terry Lansburgh, the president of the Day Care and Child Development Council of America. I was trying to get the group to go along with the administration's position. Please accept this, I told them. If the limitation on prime sponsorship size really does prove unfair to community-based programs, we could always amend the legislation the following year.

By this time, the right wing had risen up against the bill, picketing Mondale, Brademas, and me, and flooding the White House with letters opposed to any child development legislation, on the grounds that it would destroy the American family. There was no corresponding stack of mail from advocates. Most disappointing was the absence of strong support from the women's movement, which had much to gain from national child care legislation. I have never understood why the movement did not make child care legislation more of a priority. If affordable, quality child care were available to all, both men and women would finally be able to work without harming their children.

With this new opposition in mind, I warned the group of child care advocates assembled at Terry Lansburgh's home that I was beginning to hear threats of a presidential veto. If the advocates kept insisting on allowing every community, no matter how small, to serve as a prime sponsor, I feared the bill might go down. I begged them to support the administration's proposal, and added that it might be their last chance. "Oh, Ed, you don't understand politics," they said. "Nixon will never veto this bill in an election year." I may not be much of a politician, I responded, but there is nothing wrong with my hearing.

For me, that meeting was a turning point in the child care battle. Had I won the argument on prime sponsors with the advocates, the history of federal support for child care might have been different. On my way back to Washington that night, my car broke down. I felt as if it were an omen of the legislative breakdown to come.

The first evidence of real trouble appeared when the House took up the bill on September 30, 1971. Brademas had succeeded in sustaining the 100,000 population requirement for prime sponsors in committee over the objections of chairman Perkins. But when the bill reached the floor, Perkins struck back. He rose to propose an amendment slashing the population requirement to 10,000.

"You have to understand that Carl Perkins represented a district in Kentucky where 10,000 was a big number," said Brademas.[29] As Perkins said, his own Pike County, the largest county east of the Mississippi in geographic area, had a population of only 60,000 and would not qualify as a prime sponsor under Brademas's rules.

Brademas, taking pains to state that he disliked having to disagree with his distinguished committee chairman, tried to explain that the population limit did not mean that smaller areas would lose out on child care services. Local policy councils from such areas would still submit applications for funding child care; it was just that the federal government would deal directly only with larger units of government.

Republicans tried to support Brademas. Orval Hansen even warned that a further reduction in the population requirement would jeopardize Republican backing. "I have continued to support this legislation, even though I have had to concede certain points upon which I was not in full agreement," he said. "I hope that this debate does not bring us closer to the point where too many concessions have been made and continued support of the bill is brought into serious question."[30]

But Perkins prevailed in the floor vote, reducing the population requirement to 10,000. Perkins also took revenge on Brademas for having challenged him. Because there were still differences in the

House and Senate Economic Opportunity Act amendments to which the child care legislation was attached, the bills had to go to a joint House and Senate conference committee. "Perkins knocked me off the conference committee," said Brademas. "It was the only fight we ever had."[31]

It was unprecedented for the author of a major piece of legislation to be excluded from a conference committee, and Brademas's absence proved costly. Without Brademas to restrain them, the conference committee went wild. Not only did they reduce the population requirement for prime sponsors even further, to 5,000, but they also added a provision that was a slap in the face to the administration: the final language in the Conference Report mandated that programs follow the 1968 Federal Interagency Day Care Requirements, rather than allowing the revised standards we at OCD had worked so hard to develop.

During the conference deliberations, Elliot Richardson knew that the bill was headed for trouble with the White House. On November 15, 1971, Richardson met with the president and John Ehrlichman, Nixon's chief domestic adviser. When they told him that right-wing opponents of day care were pressuring the president to veto the bill, Richardson said a veto opposing any federal role in child care would be inconsistent with the administration's involvement in the process. "I would be placed in an exceedingly embarrassing position," said Richardson. Reminding the president of his own positive statements on the importance of quality child care for welfare mothers, Richardson added that he had given friendly testimony on the child development bill, and that the testimony had been cleared by the White House each time. The meeting ended when Ehrlichman told Richardson to keep the president in touch, without making any final commitment on the bill.[32]

The final Conference Report was filed on November 29, 1971. The provision allowing communities as small as 5,000 to be prime sponsors infuriated House Republicans because they felt that the conference committee had ignored their views. Soon the bipartisan support for the bill began to unravel. Although the Conference Report passed 63–17 in the Senate in December, the margin of victory was much narrower in the House. Of the 186 House members who voted against the bill, 134 were Republicans. On December 7, three Republicans who had been among the strongest supporters of child care legislation—John Dellenback of Oregon, Albert Quie of Minnesota, and Orval Hansen of Idaho—voted against the final bill.

The next day President Nixon met with OMB director George Shultz and Ehrlichman. The first item on the agenda was the Comprehensive Child Development legislation, which had just reached the president's desk. Patrick Buchanan, the speechwriter Nixon called in when he wanted to draw blood, was assigned to work on the veto message. According to Ehrlichman's notes, Buchanan was told to "put in what the right wing wants to hear."[33]

Opportunity Lost

I was at a meeting in San Francisco when the call came from Elliot Richardson: the president had vetoed the legislation, and Richardson didn't want me to learn this first from the morning newspaper. It would be difficult to overestimate how discouraged I felt. I had been working on the bill for two years, and all of a sudden it was gone.

Had President Nixon restricted the veto message to criticism of the prime sponsorship mechanism, or the cost of the child care legislation, we could have attempted another bill. But instead he offered a sweeping indictment of the whole concept. "For the Federal Government to plunge headlong financially into supporting child development," the veto message said, "would commit the vast moral authority of the National Government to the side of communal approaches to child rearing over against the family-centered approach." The rhetoric had the same ring as an earlier column by James Kilpatrick, who had written that the bill would make sense in "the context of a Sovietized society," but "that if Richard Nixon signs it, he will have forfeited his last frail claim on Middle America's support."[34]

No one close to the Child Development Act of 1971, however,

thinks that the right-wing attack was the major factor behind the president's veto. More important reasons no doubt included the declining fortunes of the Family Assistance Plan. Moynihan had left the White House, and while the administration was still pushing FAP, its passage seemed less likely. Without FAP, the administration would have no use for an expensive new child care program.

Another important factor behind the veto, according to Elliot Richardson, was the cost and the unworkability of the child care legislation. Had Nixon really thought the federal government should not be involved in child care, he would not have continued to support child care as a provision of welfare reform. Since Nixon had decided to veto the bill anyway, however, he merely used the occasion to throw a bone to the right wing.

Jack Duncan, who had worked so hard with Brademas to maintain bipartisan support for the bill, does not even think cost was the major reason for the veto. While acknowledging that the administration did have concerns about the bill's price tag, Duncan is convinced that the president would never have risked such a stinging veto, or perhaps a veto at all, had the strong Republican support for the bill in Congress not collapsed. But in light of the conference committee changes in the bill, the Republicans felt a sense of betrayal. Republican supporters, such as Albert Quie, were disgusted with the way a process they had taken so seriously had fallen victim to politics-as-usual. According to Duncan, they were so angry with what Perkins, the advocates, and the labor unions had done that they thought it might be better to let the measure die, and wait for another day. "They didn't realize that there would never be a chance again."[35]

Mondale and Brademas did introduce similar legislation in the next session of Congress, but they did not really expect it to be enacted. By that time, Brademas was aiming for a position as House Speaker, and Mondale for an eventual run for the White House. Child care had begun as a bipartisan issue; after the veto, it became too hot for any leader with higher political ambitions.

When Mondale and Brademas tried to reintroduce some aspects of the child care bill in the Child and Family

*Services Act of 1975, right-wing attacks on the legislation
rose to the level of a well-orchestrated hate campaign, re-
plete with elaborate falsehoods.*

*Returning for a visit to his home in South Bend,
Indiana, Brademas was shocked to turn on the television
and hear the local anchorman denouncing him in an editorial for sponsoring "anti-family" legislation. Brademas
must not have been raised right, the anchorman continued, or he could never support a bill that would take children away from their parents and give them to the
Department of Health, Education and Welfare.*

*Brademas immediately drove down to the station, and
demanded to see the anchorman. "Jack, you didn't even
read my bill, did you?" Brademas asked him.*

"No, John, I didn't," the anchorman conceded.[36]

*The anchorman retracted his statement, but the ven-
omous mail campaign against child care legislation effectively blocked it for years.*

Retrospect

Twenty years later, my emotions about the defeat of the Comprehensive Child Development Act of 1971 have cooled a bit. I can
concede that those advocates who opposed any state role in child
development legislation or restriction on the size of prime sponsors
had a point. Head Start as we know it might not exist today, at least
in places like Mississippi, had the legislation allowed states to
serve as prime sponsors. Head Start's federal-to-local delivery system has provided the political support necessary time and again to
defend the program from the threat of budget reductions and other
destructive policy changes. Furthermore, even had Brademas and I
won on the prime sponsorship issue, no one can be certain that
Richard Nixon would have signed the bill.

But I remain troubled by the opportunity we lost. Child care remains a massive problem in this nation. More than two decades later, we still have three separate systems for child care—Head Start for children from poverty-level families; federally funded care with no federal standards for children from other very low-income working families; and a hodgepodge of frequently unreliable arrangements of mixed quality for everyone else. Had the defenders of children—advocates, congressional supporters, and, most especially, the President of the United States—been a little more willing to compromise in 1971, millions of Americans would be better off today. We had the opportunity to develop a quality child care system, but we let it slip by.

7

Keeping the
Experiment Alive

WHILE WORKING TO COORDINATE CHILD CARE WITH HEAD START, I was also trying to promote it as the nation's laboratory for quality programs for children. Some efforts would work, others would fail, but my job was first and foremost to keep the experiment going.

Partly, this was a deliberate strategy: in the first years after the Westinghouse report, there was no hope of a significant Head Start expansion. We were at best in a holding pattern. I took to heart the advice of HEW Secretary Elliot Richardson, a sailor, that if you don't keep moving, you eventually sink. So I tried to dazzle people with all types of new demonstration projects, some directly connected to Head Start and others designed to benefit all children. I wanted Congress and the public to associate both Head Start and OCD with such a blur of useful activity that the administration would not dare close them down.

The notion of Head Start as a national laboratory also fit my philosophy. I have always thought of Head Start not as a static program, but as an evolving concept. Head Start should be a model of the very best and most innovative in child and family services. Far from being restricted to one center-based "treatment," Head Start should offer a range of options, from home-based to full-day programs, or whatever can best meet a particular family's needs. Head Start should embody the experimental approach to social reform outlined by Donald Campbell, former president of the American Psychological Association. Campbell envisioned a society that is not afraid to try out new and different ways to solve social problems. Once we learn which programs appear to work and which do not, we can "retain, imitate, modify, or discard" them as we progress toward better solutions.[1]

Head Start began in the spirit of experimental social reform, and I was determined to keep that spirit alive. One way was to press for program improvement. Members of the Head Start Planning Committee knew that the program was far from perfect, so now was the time to refine it. This effort led to the development of the Head Start Program Performance Standards, which were and remain the principal vehicle for monitoring Head Start's quality. Experimentation also involves innovation, so during my tenure we tried out new ways to serve children and families, such as Home Start, Health Start, and the Child and Family Resource Program. The Child Development Associate Program, an effort to train and credential child care workers, and Education for Parenthood, a school course for teenagers, also originated at this time.

While we worked to find new and better ways to serve children and families, we also had to keep track of how the original Head Start program was faring. A program that is meant to help preschool children be better prepared for school should seemingly be judged on how they do when they enter school. Yet, the first major study I commissioned during this period produced another "fade-out hypothesis," that the boost children received from Head Start was short-lived. This study in some ways was an even greater threat to Head Start than the Westinghouse report. However, this report in turn inspired the Consortium studies that uncovered the so-called sleeper effects, such as that quality early intervention programs reduce grade retentions and special education placements. It took a daring experimental attitude—and a lot of patience—to uncover such benefits, and we are still discovering more today.

Climate of Resistance

The initial climate at OCD was hardly conducive to either improvement or innovation. It was bad enough in the minds of Head Start staff left over from the Johnson era that the agency had been created by the Nixon administration; to underscore their resentment of this fact, shortly before the first visit of a high administration official staff members placed pictures of the president in the OCD toilets. Worse yet, OCD was the product of a forced marriage between the most unlikely partners—the Children's Bureau staff, a seasoned group that had changed very little since the bureau's formation in 1912, and Community Action Program activists who had been in charge of Head Start at the Office of Economic Opportunity. Many of the CAP people were convinced that the creation of OCD was only the first step in dismantling Head Start, and that I was eager to begin the dissolution.

The old guard at the Children's Bureau saw no reason to engage in any flighty new research and demonstration projects; they were used to dispensing research funds through the usual channels without benefit of peer review. Some Children's Bureau officials even resisted racial integration, repeatedly turning down minority applicants who were well qualified for research positions. Finally, I placed a highly respected black pediatrician, Dr. Rick Greene, in charge of the whole operation as associate director of the Children's Bureau.

As for the Head Start staff, they, too, wondered why we had to bother with new programs like child care and Education for Parenthood. Why couldn't we just work on Head Start? And understandably, those staff members who had come from the Community Action Program really missed the era of high hopes, when Head Start could do no wrong. The whole idea that we needed to improve Head Start in order to save it was foreign to them; any suggestion that the program needed tighter management seemed to violate the very spirit of spontaneity and community control that had made the program unique. Head Start, they feared, would become just another government program immobilized by its own regulations.

I guess you might say that many people at OCD were less than thrilled by my appointment as their director. I might never have been able to bring these disparate groups together had it not been for the hiring of Saul Rosoff as my deputy. Saul weeded out the few people who were truly intransigent, brought out the best in the many who remained, and attracted new talent to the agency as well. Together we built a team comprised of some of the brightest, most dedicated individuals with whom I have ever had the opportunity to work.

Improving Head Start

Basically, OCD was confronted with a two-fold and to some extent contradictory challenge. We needed to tighten up Head Start's management to improve program quality, but we also needed to free up local programs to offer more than one standard center-based option. And we didn't have much time to accomplish these objectives. So we proceeded down both tracks, developing program standards and self-assessment and monitoring procedures, and at the same time developing and disseminating alternatives to the basic Head Start classroom model.[2] Eventually these dual efforts became known as the Improvement and Innovation Plan. This formal document amounted to a blueprint for Head Start for many years to come.

The "improvement" part of the plan had to come first both in name and degree of effort, because Head Start's future was not very secure in the early 1970s. Even though we averted a budget cut during my first year as OCD director, the program remained, as my insightful administrative assistants Carolyn Harmon and Edward Hanley put it, "highly vulnerable to attack on administrative grounds."[3]

The problem was that there was no real system of accountability. Not only had the War on Poverty deliberately avoided the classical model of making federally funded programs accountable to state or local general-purpose governments, but no alternate system of management had been substituted. That is, while the federal government monitored local Head Start grantees and provided some manuals for program guidance, programs did not really have to meet any articulated set of standards. Harmon and Hanley sum up the situation well: At the end of almost five years of operation, "Head Start administrators really had no accurate data as to how many children were served, or even what services were actually provided at what cost or benefit to those reported as enrolled...."[4]

In short, there was no mystery behind the highly uneven quality of the Head Start programs in 1970. Despite the flaws in the Westinghouse report methodology, I doubt that any national impact evaluation at that time would have showed that Head Start had long-term educational benefits. Even if, as I suspected, a third of the programs were wonderful, their effects would most likely have been canceled out by an equal fraction of programs that were poorly operated.

So, for reasons both political and substantive, it was imperative to develop some management controls. Far from posing a threat to Head Start's federal-to-local delivery system, the introduction of such a management system was the key to preserving it.

As a first step toward a quality monitoring system, we launched a survey of the 150 largest Head Start grantees around the nation. The idea was to find the best of those programs serving the majority of the children in Head Start, and to generate best practice standards by which to evaluate all the others.

From there, we began a task force in late 1971 to develop program performance standards. The task force was under the direction of Harley Frankel and Raymond Collins. I had initially hired Frankel to implement child care policy under the ill-fated Child Development Act. A Harvard-trained MBA, he combined the best in modern management training with a strong social conscience. Raymond Collins, as Saul Rosoff once put it, could turn an idea into a program in the space of 10 minutes.

This task force developed the Performance Standards with the help of two highly skilled national Head Start administrators, Clennie Murphy and Henlay Foster, who also had experience with the program at the regional and local levels. The standards were at once very precise on the level of health and other comprehensive services expected, and yet they were not overly prescriptive on program design. For example, the standards, which are still in effect, mandate that every family receive at least two home visits by educational staff, but they do not prescribe when the visits should take place or exactly what level of staff should make them. Similarly, the standards specify that health screenings must include growth assessment, vision and hearing testing, hemoglobin or hematocrit determination, immunization status, and so on, but they do not mandate where or how these screenings should be provided.

As for parent involvement, the 70.2 policy finalized during my first year at OCD was inserted as is in the final Performance Standards document. We wanted to make clear that programs were intended both to involve and empower parents.

There were a couple of unfortunate omissions from the Performance Standards. The standards do not specify either staff-child ratios or class size. OCD deliberately left those out on the grounds that Head Start had better staff-child ratios and class sizes than most child development programs, and it was feared that we might lose the effort to get them into the regulations. As a result, there has been some deterioration in staff-child ratios since the early 1970s, from a ratio of 1:5 at that time to between 1:8 and 1:10 today.

Writing the standards, however, was only part of the battle. Once we developed the standards, we had to make it possible to implement them. Since Head Start clearly did not have the budget to finance all of the comprehensive services mandated, Frankel and Collins spent long hours working out interagency agreements. The most costly services were those pertaining to health care, so they concentrated on this area. One collaborative effort they fashioned was between Head Start and the Early Periodic Screening, Diagnostic and Testing (EPSDT) program, a part of Medicaid. The agreement was first implemented as a demonstration project in 1974. Two hundred Head Start centers in 42 states were selected as Head Start/EPSDT Collaborative Projects. After two years, the collaborative approach was then integrated into all Head Start programs, and a handbook was disseminated showing Head Start programs how to make use of EPSDT.[5]

We reached another agreement with the American Academy of Pediatrics, whereby they agreed to make doctors available, particularly in rural areas. "It was the best $1 million we ever spent," as Frankel puts it. Finally, he and others worked out an arrangement with the Department of Agriculture whereby they agreed to subsidize food for the Head Start program.

In conjunction with the development of the Performance Standards, we also began requiring grantees to evaluate their own performance on an annual basis in relation not only to program standards but also to a community needs assessment. The self-assessment instruments were clearly an attempt to get people at the local level to think about what they were doing, according to Rosoff. It was not so important how they scored as that they understood what was expected.

As part of our monitoring strategy, the self-assessment evaluation instrument was accompanied by a brief annual visit from a federal regional official of HEW, and every third year there was to be a full-scale evaluation by a multidisciplinary monitoring team.

Finally, we tried to develop the capacity of the regional HEW offices to provide meaningful technical assistance and to hold programs accountable to the Performance Standards. Jenni Klein, an expert in early childhood education and special education who had joined Head Start's national staff in 1969, provided outstanding leadership in the educational component. She fought for every region to have early childhood specialists. Without her expertise, the regional offices would not have commanded the respect of the Head Start grantees they were charged with monitoring.

All of this effort to develop an accountability strategy was part of the same improvement package. It was designed to improve services for children and families. It also conveyed the message to Congress and the administration that we cared about the program we were managing, that we were not just handing out taxpayers' money with no regard for how it was spent. In the early 1970s, Head Start clearly did need tighter management.

In one center I visited, the teacher resorted to a bizarre form of punishment. She lined up the children, and made the first one say, "I'm bad." Then each child was forced to repeat the same refrain, until it sounded like a chorus of self-repudiation. And the exercise gave the children a head start on nothing but poor self-esteem.

I also recall a center in Puerto Rico, located in a metal quonset hut; it was like a steam bath. I wondered how the children could even exist there. "Dr. Zigler, we've tried to get air conditioning many times, but we can't get it approved," the director said. "You will get air conditioning," I said, placing the order before I left the island.

On my way to the center I had been depressed to see little children playing in the mud outside their homes, which had been put together with scrap lumber. But I suspected that at least the children were cooler there.

Diversifying Head Start

Concerned about the lack of quality control and the fact that there were a lot of mediocre Head Start programs, I was equally troubled by the fact that Head Start seemed to be too set in its ways, too focused on a half-day, center-based preschool program. I thought we should diversify. Again, my reasons were both political and substantive.

Head Start, after all, was a Johnson administration product. If it was going to survive the Nixon administration, the program had to develop new initiatives for which the administration could take credit. Beyond this strictly political observation, I thought that poor people were as heterogeneous as any other income group, and that they should be given a choice of program options to suit individual family needs.

Head Start's founders had intended the program to be an open experiment, and in its early years there had been two important spin-offs from the initial preschool model. Both of them still exist to this day. The Parent and Child Centers, launched in 1967, were set up in 33 communities to serve families with young children from birth to age three. The Follow Through program, also initiated in 1967, was designed to extend comprehensive services to Head Start children when they entered kindergarten through grade three of elementary school. But by 1970, Head Start was basically in a defensive posture and had lost some of its initial vitality.

OCD therefore began to initiate a series of new program options. Some were rather quickly abandoned, some were eventually incorporated into virtually all Head Start programs, and some were picked up by the early childhood education and family support service fields as part of their overall strategies. Under the direction of Raymond Collins, the program development division of Head Start's "R & D" unit at its peak had a budget of $12 million and a staff of 25 superstars, a relative size and strength we have never seen again.

Health Start, the first new demonstration project, was the shortest lived. Health Start actually grew out of the Westinghouse/Ohio report. The one finding in that study with which I totally concurred was that the summer Head Start program was simply too brief in duration to be of much value. At the same time, Representative Carl Perkins, chairman of the powerful House Education and Labor Committee, had ordered me not to stop the summer program. It provided summer jobs for too many of his strongest supporters, namely school teachers.

What then could we realistically accomplish with a six-week summer program that might be of some benefit to children and families? I decided that, at the very least, we could provide the health screenings and services many of these children so badly needed.

In 1971 OCD funded 29 Health Start demonstration projects across the country. Health Start was intended to provide "Head Start–like health services" to children enrolled in summer Head Start programs and their younger siblings.[6] Children received medical and dental checkups and referrals for treatment. A health coordinator was to ensure that the children received follow-up services after the summer program.

Unfortunately, Health Start had the same drawback as the summer Head Start program: it didn't last long enough to accomplish much, and the follow-up treatment was frequently not provided. For that reason, the Health Start projects were discontinued in 1974. Many local health departments have since picked up the ball and now provide physicals and immunizations to poor children shortly before they enter school. However, the importance of providing these services to younger children has yet to be widely recognized, in part because of our society's taboo against assuming any responsibility for children before they reach the magical years of school age.

Home Start was one of our more successful innovations. Designed by Ann O'Keefe, the program provided essentially the same services as Head Start, but in a home rather than a center setting. Home visitors, usually community residents with some training in child development, worked on a variety of parent-child interaction and learning experiences.

The philosophy behind Home Start was that since parents are the first and major educators of their children, they should be the primary target for intervention efforts. Although Home Start children did not receive as many immunizations and dental checkups as did their peers in center-based programs, overall an evaluation showed that Home Start was just as effective in improving the developmental progress of children.[7] Furthermore, Home Start was found to be particularly well suited to children in rural areas, where center-based programs might not be feasible because of transportation difficulties and resource scarcities. Learning from the experience, Head Start now makes a home-based option available to all of its grantees. Since 1972 when 16 Home Start projects were begun, 400 grantees now use home-based programs for at least some of their children.[8]

The *Child Development Associate Program,* of the many new programs OCD initiated during the early 1970s, was probably the most innovative. The need for such a program grew out of the practical problem that there was no way that the nation could afford to provide a teacher with a bachelor's degree for every five children in Head Start or any other early childhood program. We needed a cadre of trained caregivers who knew how to meet children's developmental needs and who were at the same time affordable. Just who first had the idea for a competency-based credential for early childhood teachers is difficult to say. I trace my own first thoughts about a competency-based credential to a conversation with Bettye Johnson, wife of the governor of American Samoa. Johnson had decided that she wanted to run some Head Start–like programs on the island, and she had found another woman who had some experience teaching young children. They advertised on television for people who might be interested in receiving a week or two of training in child development. After the training was completed, Johnson and the other woman would watch the new teachers in the classroom.

"If the teacher was doing okay, she would be hired," Johnson told me. "If not, we'd take the teacher aside and say, 'You're a wonderful person, but you are not cut out for this sort of work.'"

"How did you know who was and who wasn't?" I asked Johnson.

"Oh, Ed," she said with a nudge, "you know."

Bettye Johnson made me realize that some people really do have a way with children and that these were the people we needed in preschool classrooms. They didn't have to go to college to prove their ability. What we needed was some type of credential based on direct observation of teachers in early childhood classrooms.

Jenni Klein had similar thoughts. She believed that training was the key to improving Head Start's quality. No matter how many performance standards we set up, she felt change would not come about by edict. If Head Start staff were to implement the standards, they would have to begin to believe in them. And the only way that would happen, she thought, was through training.

Klein thought a new model for early childhood education was needed. At the time the only badge available was a college degree. Head Start employed many college-trained teachers, but much of its staff was comprised of parents and other community members who were dedicated and by this time quite experienced. Yet besides being poor, the majority of these people had children to support, and the traditional college degree program was not open to them. Klein thought that we should make the training field-based, and set up competencies for assessing their performance.

Klein's real hope was that trainees would be placed in programs where there was a master teacher. However, we couldn't take people away from their jobs, and there simply were not enough master teachers. Many battles, or what Klein calls her "CDA ulcer," lay ahead in establishing the program. First, she had to convince the early childhood education establishment that competency-based training was valid. Many of these people had fought for years to set up B.A. programs in early childhood education in colleges, and the CDA seemed to them to be undercutting what they had fought so long to achieve.

At the same time, some black paraprofessional staff members thought the CDA should lead to college credits. As Klein recalls, they would say, "Look at you people. You all have advanced degrees, and you want to set up a lower tier for us." That's when she set up a plan where those who wanted to could obtain college credits while working for the CDA. This was the perfect compromise, we thought. Neither Jenni nor I had ever thought of the CDA as the ultimate goal for training, but rather one of the first steps on a career ladder. We always thought the staff who obtained the CDAs should be encouraged to pursue college education.

In January 1971, OCD sponsored a meeting to address the need for qualified personnel in Head Start and other early childhood programs. The meeting was chaired by Barbara Biber, a well-known scholar in the early education profession. We split into task forces, with one group working on how to measure competencies, and another working on training. A third group was assigned to recommend who would be in charge of the CDA effort.

We approached Marilyn Smith, executive director of the National Association for the Education of Young Children (NAEYC), to do a feasibility study on how to administer the Child Development Associate Project. The study recommended that a consortium be formed from 10 organizations, including the American Association of Elementary Kindergarten-Nursery Educators, the American Home Economics Association, the Association for Childhood Education International, the Black Child Development Institute, the Child Welfare League of America, the Day Care and Child Development Council of America, NAEYC, the National Committee on Education of Migrant Children, the National

Indian Education Advisory Council, and Mexican American Systems.[9]

The most difficult decision was whether to accredit schools to conduct training and allow them to award the CDA credential, or whether the consortium itself would form field evaluating teams to assess competencies and award the credential. We chose the second option in order to separate the training from the certification, according to Smith, but 20 years later we still aren't sure we did the right thing. "It might have been better if we had gone the other route," Smith said recently. "There might have been a better chance for the development of a real career ladder."

While some issues were unresolved, we proceeded rapidly. The CDA program was formally launched in 1972, and in 1973, 13 CDA pilot projects were established to work on methodology and to develop a CDA curriculum.[10] In the spring of 1974 and winter of 1975, two field testings of the assessment procedure were conducted. By July 1975, the first CDA credentials were awarded.

There have been many ups and downs in the implementation of the CDA program, with administration at one point being shifted from the consortium to the Bank Street College of Education and then finally to its present home with the Council for Early Childhood Professional Recognition. This organization began as a subsidiary of NAEYC, but is now a separate entity.

There has also been a long struggle to win recognition for the CDA credential, and to make it or some form of training in child development mandatory in Head Start. From 1973 on, whenever the national Head Start staff wrote policy, Jenni Klein recommended that every classroom should have at least one CDA. However, this policy recommendation would always get stopped in the higher levels of the Department of Health and Human Services.

Finally, however, the CDA has come of age. According to Carol Phillips, executive director of the Council for Early Childhood Professional Recognition, 49 states now recognize the CDA in their state licensing requirements as a valid credential. Furthermore, the Head Start Expansion and Quality Improvement Act of 1990 mandates what Jenni Klein fought so hard to achieve: by 1994, every Head Start classroom of 20 children must have one teacher with at least a CDA or an associate degree in early childhood. With Head Start now expanding and the demand for child care soaring, hopefully the CDA program can finally fulfill its initial promise to relieve the shortage of quality caregivers.

Services to Handicapped Children eventually became one of Head Start's most commendable features. From the outset, the Planning Committee had been concerned about the prevention of disabilities, and yet we had not included handicapped children among the original program participants.

Soon after becoming director of OCD, I remember Senator Walter Mondale asked me why Head Start did not serve children with disabilities. I had no satisfactory answer. So I asked Ray Collins to begin trying to mainstream some handicapped children into Head Start, and we started some special pilot projects. Then, in 1972 Congress mandated that at least 10 percent of Head Start's national enrollment consist of handicapped children.

Every change that we proposed in Head Start met with great resistance at both the federal and local level, but later people came to adopt the idea as their own. This time the idea we had been toying with suddenly became a requirement, long before we were ready to operationalize it. With virtually no experience serving this group, we thought we were very bold to be doing demonstration projects, much less trying to serve children with special needs in every Head Start program. But it became the law.

So the pilots we had begun became the nucleus of 14 Resource Access Projects. These so-called RAP programs, funded jointly by Head Start and the Office of Education's Bureau of Education for the Handicapped, provided training and technical assistance to Head Start teachers working with handicapped children. OCD staff also worked with the professional associations representing people with disabilities, and we developed manuals.

Under Collins's direction, OCD did a survey, which later became an annual report, to find out how many handicapped children were enrolled. Initially, the Head Start staff were traumatized at the idea of serving children with disabilities. The irony is that Head Start has been more successful in mainstreaming children with disabilities than have the public schools. As Collins points out, the schools have never really been forced to adopt a mainstreaming strategy. But Head Start did not have the option to place children with special needs in a classroom by themselves down the hall. "Ducking the issue was not an option," says Collins. "So we simply stole the best of the state of the art, and it worked."

Indeed, Head Start's success serving disabled children eventually inspired the 1986 Amendments to the Education of the Handicapped Act, or Public Law 99-457. The law essentially requires states to provide "a free appropriate public education" to handicapped children between the ages of three and five, and provides grants to states wishing to serve even younger children. The mandated services are clearly borrowed from Head Start, particularly those concerning parental involvement and family support.

Education for Parenthood was probably the most controversial program initiated by OCD during the early 1970s. The purpose was innocuous enough, namely to teach the fundamentals of the child development process to teenagers before they become parents. In part, the curriculum was designed to prevent child abuse. If parents only knew some of the factors behind the "terrible twos," or that it is impossible to toilet train a six-month-old, perhaps many incidents of abuse could be avoided. I also thought that the program might help prevent teen pregnancy, and that the curriculum might be good initial preparation for teenagers considering work in child care.

While the Education for Parenthood program eventually spread to 3,000 schools and cost less than $1 million, it became a target of criticism.[11] Some people saw it as yet another infringement by government into private family life. Another critic charged that, as a cost-saving measure, I ultimately intended to substitute Education for Parenthood for Head Start.[12]

If I had it to do over again, I would make some changes in this parent education program: I would introduce it much earlier, perhaps as early as first grade; I would also find a way to evaluate the program's effectiveness. But the idea that it was ever intended to be an inexpensive substitute for Head Start, as opposed to a cost-effective supplement, is absurd. This type of criticism seemed to result from OCD's being part of the Nixon administration; if Nixon or any of his agencies had anything to do with something, many people figured it must be bad. Things I had believed in for years were suddenly suspect. Yet in reality I was just trying to show the country that OCD was worth having, that we were producing programs of benefit to all children and families, not just to those who were economically disadvantaged.

"Sesame Street" was one program "option" under consideration while I was director of OCD that did pose a threat to Head Start. While this proposal never became a reality, I think it helps illustrate the narrow tightrope I was walking. I was trying to improve Head Start as an experimental program, but there were some people willing to end the experiment and replace Head Start with a far less costly venture.

The television program "Sesame Street" had recently come along and been a smash hit. Sid Marlin, Commissioner of the Office of Education, put together a meeting involving the department's power structure, including the HEW deputy secretary. They were impressed with "Sesame Street" and dwelled on the fact that it was so inexpensive. "We can get 'Sesame Street' to reach poor kids by spending sixty-five cents per child," they said. "Why should we spend over a thousand dollars per child on Head Start?"

The group wanted me to take money out of the Head Start budget to help sponsor production of "Sesame Street." I told them Head Start had no money to spare. Finally, as they kept pressing, I said I would give Head Start money to "Sesame Street" if they could answer this question: How long would a poor child have to watch "Sesame Street" to get his or her teeth filled? When nobody could answer, that was the end of the meeting.

"Sesame Street" deserves credit for entertaining and teaching millions of children both rich and poor, but it could never substitute for what Head Start has given to preschool children and their families.

The *Child and Family Resource Program* (CFRP) was perhaps the most farsighted program option created during this period. It really amounted to the nation's first family support program. OCD created experimental CFRPs in 11 locales. These projects were designed to make community services available to families with children from the prenatal period through age eight. Services included health care, nutrition, early education, assistance with housing and employment, marriage counseling, treatment for alcoholism, and other family supports. Instead of just focusing on the child, the whole family enrolled in the CFRP. The basic principle was that children cannot develop optimally in the presence of serious unresolved family problems.

An important part of CFRP was the home visitor or family advocate, who attempted to build a trusting relationship with each family and also served as a broker for them in obtaining various community services. Another key element was family choice. That is, families had freedom to choose from an array of services those that they needed or wanted. This "cafeteria-style" plan enabled the program to fit participating families instead of the other way around.

Even the U.S. General Accounting Office, whose usual pattern is to delineate what is wrong with programs, released a very favorable report on the CFRP model.[13] The documented benefits included better preventive health care for young children, rapid assistance to families during crises, and aid in addressing inadequate housing. Nevertheless, the Reagan administration terminated the CFRPs in 1983. The idea, however, has gained momentum rather than being forgotten.

While the Child and Family Resource Program no longer officially exists, it inspired the development of the family needs assessment in use by most Head Start programs. Furthermore, the CFRP influenced many of the family support programs that developed during the 1980s. Most recently the concept has been reincarnated in the form of Comprehensive Child Development Centers. I still cannot decide whether to be baffled or amused that the CCDCs were authorized as *demonstration* projects, when their value had already been confirmed so many years ago.

The Role of Research and Evaluation

As a research psychologist, I would never have accepted the leadership of OCD without a mandate for the office to pursue research on various issues of importance to the nation's children. In fact, while at OCD I even maintained my own lab at Yale for the study of mental retardation. On the advice of Harry Gordon, dean of the Albert Einstein School of Medicine, I went back to New Haven on weekends to meet with my staff and graduate students. It would be good therapy, Gordon said, and a real respite from Washington.

There were times, however, when science and politics made an explosive mix. One of the most difficult days in my life occurred when I discussed with the OCD staff whether or not to help finance a careful analysis of the extremely controversial issue of race and intelligence.

About the time I arrived at OCD, Arthur Jensen's monograph, *How Much Can We Boost IQ and Scholastic Achievement?*, had created a public outcry. His analysis of black-white differences in intelligence, and particularly his assertion that nature played a greater role than nurture in these differences, immediately prompted five or six rebuttals. Unfortunately, these rebuttals were weak, and Jensen's response to the rebuttals was if anything stronger than his original paper.

Troubled that the Jensen report might stand, Henry Riecken, head of the Social Science Research Council, approached me and said that what was really needed was a careful analysis of the relationship between race and intelligence. Riecken already had a leading behavior geneticist, Gardner Lindzey, to conduct the analysis. But the Social Science Research Council could not finance the entire project. Riecken wondered if OCD could support the other half of the study.

On the basis of my reading of earlier studies by Spuhler and Lindzey, I was fairly certain how this analysis would turn out— namely, that no case could be made for black intellectual inferiority. I knew that the best way to correct bad science is not silence, but good scholarship. I also thought that OCD might play an appropriate role in helping to fund the project. After all, the White House had already approached HEW Secretary Elliot Richardson about the Jensen report, and he in turn had asked me about its possible implications for Head Start.

As a scientist, I could make an easy call that OCD should get involved in the project. But as the chief of the Children's Bureau whose top lieutenant was black, and whose constituents included large numbers of black children and families, it was quite a different decision.

So I called together my black staff and told them what I was planning. After they held a brief caucus, they said they were 100 percent opposed to the idea. I could understand their point: if OCD contributed funds to the study, it could be interpreted to mean that the federal government was giving credence to the assertion of racial inferiority. There were murmurings of resignations if I pursued the study.

I understood the staff's concerns, but I felt that if OCD did not assist with the critique, the Jensen report would have the last word. The next day I called the staff back together and said that, in the long run, our business was to find the truth. While I would be sad if they quit, I added that they wouldn't be hurting me or Jensen if they did so; they would be hurting black children and Head Start.

No one quit, and we got the critique. The conclusion was clear: the evidence does not support the simplistic view that blacks are inferior to whites in regard to intelligence. The critique did acknowledge the genetic component in intelligence without relating it to race. Minority populations exhibit the same range of intelligence as the white middle class. If black children did not do so well in school, the cause might lie in their social environments or in schools that did not nurture their abilities. Changing those environments and the child's relationship to them is what Head Start is all about.

One evaluation I sponsored during this period almost permanently soured the Head Start community against research. In 1971 I asked Urie Bronfenbrenner, a leading figure in the field of child development and social policy who had served on the Planning Committee for Head Start, to review the longitudinal data then available on the effectiveness of preschool programs. He looked at data from every early intervention program he could get his hands on. Bronfenbrenner came up with the same finding already made by Max Wolff and repeated in the Westinghouse report, namely that any short-term benefits "fade out" once the children spend two to three years in elementary school.[14] Interestingly, Sally Ryan, who mined much of the same empirical terrain, came to a quite different conclusion, namely that early intervention programs had a lasting effect on reading achievement and on social adjustment.[15] But the fact that Bronfenbrenner gave his support to the fade-out theory was seen by many as a serious attack on Head Start.

Bronfenbrenner was a good friend and trusted colleague. His fade-out hypothesis was published just after I left OCD and returned to Yale, only to discover I had a brain tumor. I was still recovering from surgery, but I could not let his hypothesis go unchallenged.

In the first place, I disagreed with Bronfenbrenner because, in a follow-up study of children in the New Haven area, my colleagues, Willa Abelson and Cheryl DeBlasi, and I had found that Head Start did show some long-term benefits.[16] Eighty-two percent of the Head Start children were promoted from kindergarten to first grade, as opposed to 65 percent of the control children. In addition, the Head Start children were absent somewhat less frequently, and, at the end of first grade, they had higher scores in reading and arithmetic. It was not a terribly convincing study, because the children had also received Follow Through services once they entered elementary school. Nevertheless, the study did suggest that it was possible to sustain long-term benefits from early intervention programs. Based on this and the data that other colleagues had shared with me informally, I was simply unwilling to accept the "fade-out" hypothesis as the last word on preschool programs.

Consortium Studies

At my first public presentation after my surgery, I took on the fade-out issue directly. I would quit saying that there were long-term effects of Head Start, I said in an address to the National Association for the Education of Young Children, if others would quit saying that there were none. It was time to stop talking, and start collecting some definitive data.

Frank Palmer, a leading child psychologist, and I talked at the meeting about the fact that many people had longitudinal data on early intervention projects dating back to the early and mid-1960s. These included Merle Karnes's project in Illinois, the Deutsches' project in New York, the Bellers' Philadelphia project, Ira Gordon's Florida project, David Weikart's Ypsilanti project, Frank Palmer's Harlem project, Susan Gray's Nashville project, Louise Miller's Louisville project, and the Seitz, Abelson, and Zigler project. We decided to put together a consortium of these researchers, and Irving Lazar of Cornell University agreed to lead the project.

It was a good idea, but it never would have come to fruition without the assistance of Edith Grotberg, then director of the division of research, demonstration, and evaluation at OCD. Grotberg helped ensure that the Consortium on Longitudinal Studies project received the necessary funding.

The Consortium study was launched in 1976, when 12 investigators collaborated by pooling their initial data and designing a common follow-up study. Each project had been carefully planned, with rigorous staff training, constant program supervision, and periodic evaluation. Since the children's abilities had been measured before each program started, the researchers could compare later tests with baseline data.[17] In addition, the Consortium investigators for the first time looked at some new outcomes, such as whether or not the children were in the right grade for the right age, and whether or not they were enrolled in special education classes.

The stakes were very high. I think the whole future of early childhood intervention programs was on the line. It would be several years before the results would be available, but they would permanently alter the perception of the effectiveness of preschool programs. Research, which almost killed Head Start, would finally help save it.

8

The Carter Surprise

J IMMY CARTER TOOK OFFICE IN 1977, JUST BEFORE WE BEGAN TO RE-
lease the first Consortium studies on early childhood programs. His support for a major budget increase for Head Start
and his choice of a vice president known to be a champion of child
and family legislation made child advocates think we finally had
friends in the White House. But through a convoluted series of political circumstances, Carter turned out to be the president who almost ended Head Start as we know it.

Great Expectations

As senator, Walter Mondale had been one of child care's chief proponents, and he and Representative John Brademas had also championed the first child abuse prevention legislation. During the campaign, Jimmy Carter had given a couple of speeches on family support themes. My coauthor, Susan Muenchow, and I had helped
write one of them. When Mondale visited New Haven during the
campaign, he asked me to take a walk with him on the downtown
green. Once again, he made a number of commitments on chil-

dren's issues. I figured that child advocates would get every program they had ever wanted for children and families.

Yet I got one indication, even during the campaign, that the reality might not measure up to the expectations. At a party for Mondale, where I expected to discuss child care issues with him, I was a little surprised when the first question he asked me was, "What do you think about the Panama Canal?"

Admitting that I didn't know the first thing about it, I also began to realize that the vice president is the president's assistant, and if a candidate for president is concerned about the Panama Canal, that's what the candidate for vice president is concerned about. Mondale as vice president would probably have less influence on domestic policy than he had had as senator.

Research Findings Turn into New Dollars

The Carter administration's first move on Head Start was a positive one. Just as the president came into office, the initial findings from the Cornell Consortium studies on the long-term effects of early childhood programs were being released. While Carter officials were finalizing the budget for fiscal year 1978, HEW sent a memo to the White House on the Cornell studies. Unlike the Westinghouse report, the new research showed that early childhood intervention programs did, indeed, have lasting effects.[1]

About the same time, OCD released the George Washington University report, a synthesis of some 150 research studies on Head Start.[2] Dennis Delouria, chief of evaluation at OCD, had commissioned this report because he was tired of responding to constant letters from Congress on the question of whether Head Start worked. The synthesis report put all the existing research together and concluded that Head Start had a positive impact on cognitive development, child health, the family, and the community.

Harley Frankel, who had been one of my top assistants at OCD and who was by this time a lobbyist for the Children's Defense

Fund, made a hundred copies of the George Washington findings, and was always asking OCD for more. He began what he calls "the Battle of the Hill," blanketing congressional offices with the research summaries. Head Start had not had a substantial funding increase for over a decade, and now advocates finally had the justification to support a major expansion.

The National Head Start Association, established in 1973, also fought hard for the increase. The NHSA held a meeting in Washington soon after Carter took office, and visited all the legislative aides of the Appropriations and Budget committees. Copies of a *Denver Post* article on the Cornell Consortium findings were sent to all the committee members. When the increase seemed to come in jeopardy, NHSA members sent thousands of letters from every state.

All of this effort and support paid off. In 1978 Head Start received a $150 million increase, the first of any magnitude since 1967. In addition, the Economic Opportunity Act Amendments of 1978 required that henceforth all Head Start programs be operated in accordance with performance standards no less comprehensive than those in effect on the date of the enactment. Now there was not only money to improve quality, but also there was a law to enforce it.

Proposed Transfer to Department of Education

On the heels of this important budget victory for Head Start, however, the administration took a stance that shocked Head Start advocates: President Carter supported the program's transfer to his proposed new Department of Education. This announcement was viewed as a betrayal not only of Head Start, but also of Carter's many black supporters.

To understand why Head Start advocates would so strongly oppose the Head Start transfer proposal, we have to go back to the program's early days. From the beginning, there was always tension between Head Start and public education agencies. In fact, it has long bothered me that the easiest way to get a round of applause from a Head Start audience is to say something derogatory about the schools.

Head Start's distrust of the schools stems from its roots in the civil rights movement and the Community Action Program. In the mid-1960s, the United States was still an extremely segregated nation. During Head Start's first year in Mississippi, there were three times as many black children participating in Head Start as there were enrolled in first grade.[3] At the local level, minority parents and staff feared they would have no voice in a Head Start program run by white-dominated school systems. At the national level, administration of Head Start by an educational agency was viewed as a threat to the program's comprehensive services and parent involvement.

Sargent Shriver, a former head of the Chicago school board, viewed Head Start as a way to overcome poor, minority parents' alienation from the public schools. He wanted Head Start to draw parents into the schools as early as possible in hopes of improving both their own and their children's attitudes toward education. However, Shriver's Community Action Program staff wanted to empower the poor to set up a parallel power structure outside the schools. They thought that only from this position of strength would poor people be able to change the schools or any of the institutions that had failed them.

Ironically, over 80 percent of the first summer Head Start programs were sponsored by local school systems,[4] and to this day nearly a third are administered by schools. Nevertheless, the basic notion that poor, minority parents need their own power base from which to launch a self-help movement for themselves and their children endured. Even in those localities where school systems administer Head Start, federal officials retain the authority to make sure programs comply with Head Start parent involvement and comprehensive service policies. Had Head Start been located in the federal education agency, which delegates administration to state departments of education or school districts, this oversight function would have been far more difficult to maintain.

First Transfer Efforts by Republicans

Carter's plan to move Head Start to the proposed Department of Education was all the more surprising because the program's advocates had successfully fought back several previous transfer efforts by Republicans. For example, in 1967 Peter Dominick, Republican senator from Colorado, had introduced a bill to transfer Head Start to the federal Office of Education. In presenting the bill, Dominick stressed CAP mismanagement of antipoverty funds in his home state without getting into detail on the benefits of school-managed Head Start programs. In 1968, Dominick tried again, introducing a surprise amendment on the Senate floor that would have literally ended the Head Start program, and provided a lump sum to the states to be used for early childhood purposes. The Senate passed the amendment, which would have left the nature and quality of these programs entirely up to the states.[5]

Dominick's measure was only blocked when Richard Orton, national director of Head Start from 1968 to 1972, alerted a telephone network, originating in his office, that fanned out to each region and spread to local Head Start programs. "Everyone in the office had an assignment should the button be pressed," Orton notes.[6] When word came that Representative Edith Green of Oregon planned to introduce the amendment, Orton was on vacation, but he still managed to activate the network. "The House of Representatives never received more phone calls," Orton adds, "and the lady who allegedly was going to introduce the amendment swore that was never her intention."[7]

OMB Circular A-95

Having defeated these Republican efforts to transfer the program to the states, Head Start advocates never expected they would have to fight the same battle with a Democratic president. Had they known the history of Carter's involvement with Head Start as governor, however, they might not have been so surprised.

In 1974, Congress had passed legislation giving the Office of Management and Budget the authority to create substate planning districts. These districts were to coordinate all the various federal human service funds that went to the states. The administration published a revised version of OMB Circular A-95, explaining the opportunity for states to assume a greater role in the planning of federally funded programs through these districts.

All of a sudden, OMB got a letter from a moderate southern governor who wanted to use the new authority to take control of Head Start in his state. "He was very well intentioned," notes Harley Frankel, then deputy director of OCD, and his name was James Earl Carter.[8]

With support from a Democratic governor, OMB was jumping up and down and doing cartwheels. This was the opportunity they had been waiting for to turn Head Start into the New Federalism and a block grant. Frankel, as well as Saul Rosoff, acting director of OCD, knew that loss of federal control would be the beginning of the end for Head Start. But they were in an extremely difficult political position. After all, they worked for a Republican administration that liked the idea of turning programs over to the states.

How Rosoff and Frankel fought—and won—the internal battle to block Governor Carter's request reveals a lot about the inner workings of government. First, Frankel persuaded the assistant general counsel in HEW that the OMB circular did not apply to Head Start because it was not a federal-to-state program. Then Rosoff sent out a daring memo to the regional HEW offices that flatly declared that Head Start was excluded from substate districts.

Although Rosoff and Frankel won their case with some of the upper levels of HEW, they knew their real battle was with OMB. Officials in this agency, which controls the budgets of all other agencies in Washington, were furious that HEW was not going along with their opportunity to send Head Start to the states. OMB called a meeting on its own turf to decide the issue once and for all.

"We knew we had to surround OMB, or we would lose," said Frankel. So he and Rosoff developed an elaborate strategy that eventually gave not only their friends, but even their worst enemies, reason to support them. Marian Wright Edelman, director of the Children's Defense Fund, was asked to seek help from Senator Walter Mondale. Mondale then approached Senator Edmund Muskie, the chief sponsor of the bill that had given OMB the authority to issue the circular. Muskie informed OMB that if they overstepped their bounds on the Head Start issue, they might jeopardize their authority to create any substate planning districts.

Before the meeting, Frankel and Rosoff also secured the backing of an unexpected supporter, HEW Secretary Caspar Weinberger, who agreed that the circular did not apply to Head Start. As Frankel sums up, "So here we have Cap-the-Knife Weinberger, of all people, fighting OMB on the New Federalism!"

Unsung Heroes

Although Weinberger was a proponent of block grants, he made an exception for Head Start. "In the case of Head Start, I wanted to be assured that the money would go where it was intended," he said recently. "I didn't want the schools to spend money for Head Start on vocational education or some other activity."[9]

Weinberger felt the same way about Head Start that he did about health screening under the Early Periodic Screening, Diagnostic and Testing Program. These were prevention programs to detect if children needed eyeglasses, or had diseases or other conditions that would be potentially disabling if they went untreated. "I felt that an additional boost was necessary to get these poor children to the starting line," said Weinberger, "and that the effort did need federal direction."

Weinberger's support for Head Start seemed to rest partly on his personal assessment of the program's effectiveness. Shortly after becoming HEW secretary, he visited a Head Start program in the mountain region of Kentucky. Sylvia Pechman, who was in charge of Parent and Child Centers for OCD, was initially reluctant to accompany Weinberger on the trip. "My husband, Joseph Pechman, then director of economic studies for the Brookings

Institution, was on Nixon's enemy list," she said, "and he was proud of it."[10] But Saul Rosoff pointed out to her that she was not a political appointee but a civil servant, and as the person in charge of the program division she was the logical person to go.

When Pechman met Weinberger at the airport to leave for the trip, the first question he asked her was, "Aren't you Mrs. Joseph Pechman?"

"I'm Sylvia Pechman, and I'm a civil servant," she replied.

"I get the message," Weinberger told her. "I'll never ask that question again."

"Once we got to the center, he was amazing," according to Pechman. "He watched everything I did. If I played with blocks, he did. He listened to the way I talked to the kids, and he emulated me."

Based on his experience with the program, Weinberger also had little patience with the fade-out critique of Head Start. "There was opposition to Head Start from people who thought it was unwise to give these children a head start because it couldn't be kept up when they entered school," he said in a recent interview. "I thought this was sheer nonsense."

Campaign Promises

If Head Start advocates did not sufficiently appreciate Weinberger, we also did not pay enough attention to Carter's pronouncements during the 1976 campaign. Candidates Carter and Mondale both endorsed a separate cabinet-level Department of Education, and as a result received the first National Education Association (NEA) endorsement ever given a presidential and vice presidential candidate. The summer before his election, Carter also made a campaign pledge for a "Department of Education that would consolidate the grant programs, job training, early childhood education, literacy training, and many other functions scattered throughout the government."[11]

A few months after Carter's inauguration, the NEA started pressuring him to make good on his promise. Terry Herndon, executive director of NEA, informed the president that NEA was losing dues because of its support for his candidacy. Herndon also complained that Carter's appointees were showing no interest in following up on his pledge to establish a Department of Education. "Many fears and anxieties would be quelled," he added, if Carter would reaffirm his promise and announce a specific schedule for fulfilling it.[12]

Despite the pressure, Carter took his time endorsing the bill Senator Abraham Ribicoff had introduced in March 1977 to create a broad-based Department of Education that included Head Start. Ribicoff thought the huge HEW was totally unworkable. When he served as HEW secretary, he said his only real accomplishment was the installation of an elevator that ran nonstop to his office on the top floor. Seeing the labyrinth created by having all health, education, and welfare services in one place, Ribicoff had been sponsoring legislation to create a separate Department of Education since 1965.[13] However, this time, he had more than half the members of the Senate as cosponsors.

The president's "Reorganization Project," based in OMB, wanted time to study the issue. After examining the pros and cons of establishing a Department of Education for over six months,[14] the OMB reorganization team finally completed its report.[15] Essentially, OMB recommended the creation of a broad-based Department of Education and Human Development that would include virtually all of HEW except Aid to Families with Dependent Children, Medicare, Medicaid, and Social Security. Not only did OMB think this new department should include Head Start, but it also recommended that it oversee child day care, job training, delinquency prevention, food and nutrition programs, the Bureau of Indian Affairs schools, the Community Services Administration, and possibly even maternal and child health. The team envisioned that "the new department, by grouping service programs that support people, could be the organizational focus of a comprehensive family policy."[16]

Summarizing the case for and against moving Head Start to the proposed new department, OMB emphasized that it only recommended Head Start's inclusion if other human development programs were transferred as well. The team opposed the transfer of

Head Start to a narrowly based Department of Education, because they thought such a move would convert the program into "a preschool education program run by educators in school facilities rather than a community development tool, and its opportunity to stimulate change in the educational system would be lost."[17] In fact, the OMB team opposed the creation of a circumscribed Department of Education, on the grounds that it would increase the insulation of education from other human services and be too oriented toward the education establishment, such as administrators and teachers. In short, OMB wanted a broad-based Department of Education *and* Human Development or no Department of Education at all.

OMB's plan was logical and well-intentioned, but it was politically naive. The report never addressed the central issue of whether federal funds would all flow through state education agencies, or whether some funds would continue to go directly to community-based agencies. After extolling the prospects for coordination at the federal level, OMB had no real plan for how it would lead to restructured schools or linkages between education and human service agencies at the state and local levels. The whole idea was something like the mouse that roared: Head Start was to be included in the new educational agency in hopes that it could change the schools, making them more open to parent involvement and more sensitive to the relationship between education and health and social services. But no one ever explained how a little program like Head Start was to revolutionize the nation's entire public school system.

From the outset, even OMB noted that its proposal for a broad-based educational agency would spark controversy. Organized labor would probably oppose the movement of job training programs to the new department, and poverty groups would most likely line up against the transfer of Head Start and other human development programs. With the exception of Senator Ribicoff, whose own bill called for an expansive department, there were also few strong proponents in Congress. Indeed, support for a Department of Education in Congress was said to be a mile wide, but an inch deep. Finally, as OMB conceded, "Almost all agency heads with whom we talked endorse the restructuring of Federal education programs in general, but argue that the virtues of consolidation do not apply to their own programs."[18]

Stuart Eizenstat, the president's chief domestic counselor, opposed the inclusion of social services, such as Head Start, in the new department on two grounds. First, he thought it unwise to separate the services from welfare, Social Security, and Medicaid. Even more important, he didn't want to burden the Department of Education with the opposition of social service and minority advocates.

Despite these voices of caution within his own administration, President Carter finally indicated his general support for a broad Department of Education after the Reorganization Project released its report. Carter's decision to include human development programs was sent to OMB director James McIntyre. However, Carter indicated in the margin of the memo to McIntyre, "Be general—not specific," regarding the particular social service programs to be included.[19] Thus, while the president announced his support for the Department of Education in his 1978 State of the Union address, even his closest advisers were left wondering exactly which programs the president wanted to include.

The National Head Start Association began trying without success to determine the president's position on the transfer of Head Start. Hearings on the Ribicoff bill were scheduled for mid-April, and by late March the president had yet to decide which programs would be included. A coalition of civil rights leaders, including Coretta Scott King, Vernon Jordan, Joseph Lowery, and Jesse Jackson, sent a telegram to the President's Reorganization Project. They strongly urged the administration to reject the inclusion of Head Start in the Department of Education proposal.

"Over the last decade we have successfully defended Head Start's independence against segregationists in the South and the machinations of its bureaucratic foes in Washington," they wrote. Narrow established interests, meaning teacher unions and school administrators, would inevitably dominate Head Start's minority leaders in the proposed Department of Education. "To threaten the integrity of Head Start at this time," they added, "could only be viewed as a betrayal by many of the poor who have found hope in its reality and faith in the promise of this administration."[20]

The aversion of Head Start leaders to a takeover by the schools becomes more understandable in light of experiences in places like Lee County, Alabama.

When the county was about to close a formerly all-black school there, largely because white parents refused to allow their children to attend it, Head Start parents asked if they could have the building. With a little work, they thought, the school would make the perfect setting for early childhood programs.

The school board not only rejected the Head Start parents' request, but added insult to injury by announcing they would sell the school for a dollar to a man who was starting a segregated white academy. Only under threat of a lawsuit by the local Head Start director, Nancy Spears, herself a white Southerner, did the school board reverse itself and allow Head Start to have the building. Head Start parents, together with local college students, then donated their time to renovate the school, which now serves over 250 Head Start children.

Relations between the schools and Head Start have improved greatly in Lee County since this incident in the early 1970s. Nevertheless, Spears feels strongly that Head Start should remain independent of the state and federal educational establishment.

Concerned that Carter might include Head Start in the new department, Marian Wright Edelman called HEW Secretary Joe Califano and Vice President Mondale to convey CDF's objections. Califano had already made it clear that he opposed the whole idea of a Department of Education, and he had also recommended that Head Start not be moved. But Mondale made no promises. "I realize now how dependent they were on the NEA for election," said Edelman recently.[21]

Two days before OMB director McIntyre was scheduled to testify before Senator Ribicoff's committee on the proposed Department of Education, President Carter had still not decided which programs to include. On April 12, McIntyre and Eizenstat sent a memo to the president in effect begging him to make a decision before they had to appear in Congress.[22]

A few hours before the scheduled testimony, the decision memo came back. "Carter had checked the wrong box," said Frankel. "He wanted Head Start in the department." OMB, which had apparently been assuming that the president would decide not to include Head Start, had to change all its testimony and graphs and charts to support the president's position.[23]

Carter's reasons for including Head Start in the proposed department remain an object of speculation. One theory is that the president may have needed Senator Ribicoff's support for a major arms sale of F-15s to the Saudis and Egyptians. Ribicoff was the only Jewish senator who supported Carter on this sale.

But it is equally likely that the president simply bought OMB's vision of a broad-based education department. He thought the broader the department, the more difficult it would be for special-interest groups to control it.[24] Furthermore, Carter's first elected position had been to a school board. He did not see anything wrong with education officials administering Head Start programs.

On April 14, 1978, McIntyre testified before the Senate Governmental Affairs Committee, recommending the inclusion of Head Start in the proposed Department of Education. On the same day, he wrote a memo to Carter urging that the president call Marian Wright Edelman and Coretta King to try to defuse their opposition. The president might tell them, McIntyre wrote, that early childhood programs would report directly to the Secretary of Education, and that Head Start grants might still be awarded to a range of community organizations other than schools.[25]

"Fritz, do this," Carter wrote on the top of the McIntyre memo, referring to the calls to Edelman and King.

Such are the pleasures of being vice president. Mondale, already well aware of the two women's views on the issue, was no more eager than Carter to place the calls. The following week he left for Asia, leaving the task to his assistant, Bill Smith. Smith called Edelman and reported that "Marian will fight the transfer with every resource at her command."[26] Then he passed the buck to Stuart Eizenstat to call Coretta King. Eizenstat put the call off another week. Finally, after another request from the president, Eizenstat called her. "Hopes Head Start can keep its special characteristics and appreciates the concern voiced by the call," he reported she said, in a more tactful reiteration of Edelman's response.[27]

"You're Going to Lose"

Edelman and Frankel were in a state of shock over the president's decision to transfer Head Start to the new department. They knew they would have to conduct an all-out fight.[28] But with the president championing the issue, the chances of excluding Head Start did not look good. "The NEA was against us, the administration was against us, and senators Ribicoff and Percy from the Governmental Affairs Committee both wanted Head Start in the department," said Frankel. "I sat down with a very progressive friend who said, 'You're going to lose this one; you haven't got a chance.'"

However, CDF and the rest of us who opposed including Head Start in the new department did have two things in our favor. First, as Frankel puts it, we firmly believed we couldn't afford to lose. Whatever OMB's vision of a broad-based department, we thought it would be dominated by teacher unions and administrators, and that the federal voice for comprehensive services and parent involvement would be lost. Second, the people for the new Department of Education wanted it so badly that the last thing they needed was something so controversial that it could jeopardize the legislation.

CDF's strategy to oppose the transfer was thus straightforward: they made it clear, albeit nicely, according to Frankel, that if Head Start were included in the proposed department, the bill wouldn't have a chance. Since Head Start was viewed primarily as a program for minority children, the proposed transfer would be seen as a civil rights issue. The last thing the proponents of the Department of Education wanted was to be called anti–civil rights.

At this point, the National Head Start Association also proved itself a powerful force. NHSA did not yet have a paid lobbyist in Washington, but it did have Nancy Spears, director of Head Start in Lee County, Alabama, and NHSA public affairs and education committee chair. She never quit until she called all the legislative aides in Washington. The NHSA budget that year was less than $8,000, collected from member dues, plus some additional support from CDF. In these days before facsimile machines, almost everything NHSA did was by telephone or mailgram alerts or letters. Spears's own board paid a quarter of her salary so she could work on national legislative issues for Head Start.

Spears, joined by Aaron Henry from Mississippi, took some time off from her position in Alabama to go to Washington to talk with legislators and staff. In every office they visited, Henry would ask, "What is going to happen to black children if Head Start is put into the schools?" And in every single office, they would also encounter the lobbyist for the NEA.

Meanwhile, Harley Frankel was working on securing the support of Texas Democratic Congressman Jack Brooks for removing Head Start from the Department of Education bill. CDF asked former president and Head Start founder Lyndon Johnson to enlist his help. Brooks went to the White House and offered to carry the bill for the Carter administration in the House Governmental Operations Committee if Head Start were not included.

I also got involved by calling Senator Ribicoff, a personal friend who was from my own state of Connecticut. I pleaded with him to leave Head Start out of the bill. Ribicoff told me he was sorry, but he couldn't help me on this one. He said he was "carrying the water for the president" on this legislation, and that he couldn't change his stand.

A short time later, however, some more skillful lobbyists began pressuring Ribicoff. A group of Head Start mothers got on a bus in Hartford, Connecticut, about 3 A.M. They picked up some more parents an hour later in New Haven, and they rode that bus all night to Washington. Then they went to Ribicoff's office and talked to him personally. They achieved what I had been unable to do: they changed the senator's mind.

Shortly after their visit, Ribicoff joined the rest of his committee in a 14–0 vote to delete Head Start from the Department of Education bill. The committee recommended that Head Start remain in its current location in the Administration for Children, Youth and Families (Carter's new name for the Office of Child Development), and not be moved to any organizational structure where it would be administered by state education or welfare-oriented agencies. A few days later in the House, Congressman Brooks introduced the administration's bill minus Head Start.

"Fundamentally, the victory of keeping Head Start out of the Department of Education belongs to Head Start parents," said Bambi Cardenas Ramirez, who served as director of ACYF during this period, and who did all she could behind the scenes to oppose the transfer. "All of the rest of us played an important role, but they are the people who got the message across. It's a miracle that the least empowered parents took on a president of the United States they liked and won."[29]

By the time the Department of Education bill was finally enacted in February 1979, not only had Head Start been deleted, but so had the Bureau of Indian Affairs schools, child nutrition programs, and most of the other human development programs that had been proposed for transfer. President Carter kept his promise to establish a separate Department of Education, but it was not the broad-based agency that either he or his administration had originally proposed.

Another Budget Increase

Given Harley Frankel's role in opposing the Carter administration's plan to transfer Head Start, it may seem surprising that a few months later some of his former adversaries offered him a job in the White House. From November 1978 until the end of the Carter administration, Frankel served as deputy director of personnel.

From that position, Frankel, with the help of Eizenstat, began working on another significant budget increase for Head Start.

Eizenstat had from the outset of the administration been very supportive of Head Start. "OMB's job is always to say no," said Eizenstat. "I pushed OMB and ultimately the president for increases for the program." Eizenstat was primarily influenced by the research and by a cost-benefit analysis indicating the effectiveness of Head Start. Frankel recruited Peggy Pizzo, then special assistant to the Commissioner of ACYF and a highly respected child advocate, to join Eizenstat on the White House domestic policy staff. Pizzo was charged with the responsibility of developing a proposal for another substantial budget increase for Head Start. The domestic policy staff's first task, in pressing for the increase, was to get the president on their side. So they planned a White House birthday party for Head Start to celebrate its 15th anniversary. Eizenstat would emcee the event, and Mrs. Lyndon Johnson would be the guest of honor. They thought this would be the perfect time and place to have President Carter go on record in support of a major raise for Head Start.

At the birthday party, the president delivered the speech, which had been written by Frankel and Eizenstat. As Carter proceeded, Frankel kept waiting for the line that committed him to the budget increase. When the president reached that section, he started ad-libbing about his feelings for Head Start when he had served on the school board in rural Georgia. Carter moved the assembled guests with his account of how, at the time, Head Start had been the only fully integrated program in that southern state. Those of us in the audience loved it, but Harley was growing increasingly anxious that Carter was going to omit the most crucial part of the speech.[30] Finally, the president looked down, read the rest of the speech, and made the oral commitment to a substantial increase. The domestic policy staff expressed a collective sigh of relief.

The president then announced another idea of Frankel's—the appointment of a blue-ribbon committee to develop recommendations for how to maintain and strengthen the quality of Head Start. By 1980 inflation was seriously eroding the quality of the program. I was asked to chair the committee, and my coauthor wrote the committee's report. This report, completed that summer, further supported the request for a budget increase, and particularly the need for improvements in staff salaries and cost-of-living adjustments (problems that unfortunately had to be repeated in a report issued a decade later for Head Start's 25th birthday).

With the signal from the president on behalf of a major increase, the question became not whether, but when and how much. Eizenstat, Frankel, and Pizzo wanted to ensure that the request would be so large that even if Carter lost the election, it would be difficult for the next administration not to provide some increase for Head Start. They tried to get Carter to announce prior to the election a $300 million increase for Head Start in FY 1982. OMB director McIntyre didn't like pre-election requests, but agreed to write a memo recommending that the president ask for $125 million to address quality concerns as well as the need for expansion. Meanwhile, the domestic policy staff proceeded with a separate memo recommending that the president ask for the larger increase.

The president received both memos on the day of the presidential debate in Cleveland, in which he alluded to his daughter Amy and nuclear war. After this debate, generally regarded as one of the turning points in the election, Carter apparently had no enthusiasm for jumping the gun on the normal budget request process. The domestic policy staff received its memo back with no decision. OMB got its way, proceeding with the smaller $125 million budget increase request.[31]

A Turning Point

Although Head Start's budget nearly doubled during President Carter's four years in office, Head Start advocates often remember him as the president who tried to transfer Head Start to the schools. In retrospect, however, the Carter administration represented an important turning point for Head Start. While the Reagan administration would try to include Head Start in a block grant, no president since Carter has dared to recommend a transfer of Head

Start to the Department of Education. Head Start parents and other advocates made their case that Head Start was more than an education program, and that the decision of who should administer Head Start locally should not be made by state chief school officers.

Actually, in some cases schools *do* make the best grantees, and collaborative efforts between Head Start and the schools are on the rise. With more minorities in leadership positions in the schools, Head Start may have less to fear from school sponsorship today than it did a decade ago.

In a strange twist in the history of Head Start and the public schools, the Community Action Program director in Broward County, Florida, actually joined with other community leaders to ask the school district to run the program.

CAP officials were tired of trying to beg and borrow space to house Head Start. "We were located in churches from every conceivable denomination," says Willette Hatcher, who has been with Head Start for 21 years and now directs the program. "There was the Abiding Savior Church, the Church of the Nazarene, the Sanctified Holy Rollers, and, of course, the Southern Baptist. We had to learn some of the doctrine of each in order to get along."

Head Start programs had to disappear on certain prayer days, as well as every Friday, when the staff had to take everything off the walls and put all the materials in boxes to prepare the rooms for Sunday school, only to put it all back up on Monday morning. Sometimes Head Start would just manage to get a space in a church renovated when the church would decide to use it for another type of program.

Faced with these numerous difficulties, in 1976 several of the county's original Head Start advocates, including black leaders like Cato Roach and the white CAP direc-

tor William Stone, petitioned the public schools to take over Head Start's administration. The school system was willing to do so on Head Start's terms, namely that the schools would continue to employ all of the existing Head Start staff. Today Broward's Head Start teachers enjoy a rare commodity—pay equity with their public school counterparts—and every Head Start class has a trained lead teacher.

But there are trade-offs. Some Fort Lauderdale schools are not really set up to deal with preschool children. In one school, in order to avoid going through the cafeteria line with the older children, one group of Head Start children must eat lunch at 10:30 A.M., soon after breakfast, and the other eats at 1:30 P.M., just before going home. The whole setting is a long way from the "family style" lunch recommended by Head Start federal policy. The preschoolers must carry their trays to long tables that seat at least 20 children. Several children play with their food, while another little boy falls asleep, his head in his lunch.

Our position is that the decision of who should administer Head Start locally should be left to communities. Furthermore, collaborative efforts between Head Start and the schools are most likely to succeed with Head Start negotiating from a position of strength, namely its base in a federal agency independent of state education leaders.

In addition to resolving Head Start's relationship to the federal Department of Education, the Carter administration also made another major contribution to Head Start's future. By starting a trend for substantial budget requests and publicizing the program's effectiveness, President Carter put Head Start on a course that would be difficult for the next president to reverse. Even before the Reagan administration coined the phrase, Head Start already had a kind of "safety net."

9

Surviving the Reagan Years

THE ELECTION OF PRESIDENT REAGAN WAS WIDELY REGARDED AS THE death knell for many federally funded programs for children. Federal human service officials adopted a bunker mentality. At the White House, the atmosphere of a prolonged wake prevailed among Carter's domestic policy staff in the last weeks before the Reagan inaugural.

As a symbol of their impending loss of power, the White House staff had no money left for travel. Peggy Pizzo, who had helped develop the administration's last proposal for a Head Start budget increase, was scheduled to attend the National Association for the Education of Young Children conference in San Francisco. A colleague in the Department of Health and Human Services had to pass a hat to buy Pizzo a ticket.

To get free meals, Pizzo decided to hit every reception at the conference. The only problem was that there was nothing but wine to drink. Feeling a bit brave, she bumped into Larry Schweinhart of the High Scope Educational Research Foundation.

"I hear that High Scope has some new research data on the effectiveness of preschool," Pizzo said.[1]

"Yes, and I'm having the hardest time getting Carnegie to hold a press conference on the Perry Preschool data," he told her. The

Carnegie Corporation of New York was convinced that no re-porters would come to hear what had happened to a little over 100 children who had participated in a preschool program many years ago in Ypsilanti, Michigan. All of the children came from extremely poor minority families, and fewer than 20 percent of their parents had completed high school.

Pizzo offered to help. As a former Carnegie grant recipient who worked in the White House, she called key executives at Carnegie on High Scope's behalf. Then she recommended that High Scope tie the Perry Preschool findings to Head Start. If the research had im-plications for Head Start funding, reporters would be interested.

By mid-December, there were editorials all over the country about the benefits of "Head Start–like" programs. The Perry Preschool findings were similar to those of the Cornell Consortium for Longitudinal Studies, which included some earlier High Scope data. But while most of the Consortium researchers had stopped following the preschool graduates after a few years of elementary school, High Scope continued to collect data on them as they be-came teenagers.[2] Thus, the Perry Preschool study was able to show that program participants were more likely to graduate from high school, get a job, and stay out of trouble with the law. Moreover, the High Scope researchers did the first cost-benefit analysis indi-cating the long-term taxpayer savings associated with investments in early childhood education for disadvantaged children. For every $1 spent on the Perry Preschool program, researchers estimated that taxpayers would ultimately save $4 to $7.

While these new data were being circulated, another Carter ad-ministration official who had just taken a job as NHSA's first lobby-ist was laying some other groundwork to protect the program. On the day after President Reagan's inauguration, Harley Frankel, who had served as Carter's deputy director of personnel, placed a call to a telephone extension he knew in the Office of Management and Budget (OMB). Since no secretary had yet been hired in this partic-ular office, one of the new budget director David Stockman's own deputies picked up the phone.

"I know you'll be cutting a lot of programs," Frankel said, de-scribing himself as a former Nixon administration official, and neglecting to mention his more recent employers. "But to avoid bad press, you'll need to save a few, and let me tell you about Head Start: everybody likes it, and it doesn't cost very much."[3]

A week later at the Cabinet meeting, Stockman suggested that Head Start be placed in the "safety net" of social programs that would not be cut. Before anyone spoke, Ted Bell, the new Secretary of Education, said he thought it was a good program and that it should be saved. Caspar Weinberger, Reagan's Secretary of Defense, who had protected Head Start when he served as Secretary of Health, Education and Welfare during the Nixon administration, also spoke on behalf of the program. No doubt there were additional factors that led to Head Start's inclusion among the so-called seven essential human services in the "social safety net," but sometimes Washington works very simply.

While Head Start's budget, almost alone among social programs, remained intact during the Reagan years, its quality was eroded in numerous ways. The administration forced Head Start to serve more children while cutting back on the hours, services, and technical assistance. Stockman did try to turn over the program to the states, and Head Start's national leadership was almost destroyed.

Head Start's survival can be attributed to several factors—the dedicated federal agency staff who remained to administer the program; the increasingly sophisticated organization of Head Start directors, parents, and staff; the resulting bipartisan support in Congress; and the well-publicized research on the effectiveness of Head Start and "Head Start–like" programs.

Inroads on Quality

Despite the substantial increases in Head Start funding during the Carter administration, program quality had already been affected by inflation before Reagan took office. Asked by President Carter to chair a committee to make recommendations for Head Start's future in 1980, I had been especially concerned about the cutbacks in staff, hours, and services. Class size had increased from 15 to 20 children, and the overall expenditure per child expressed in constant 1967 dollars had declined from $835 in that year to $813 in 1980. The average Head Start salary was $6,280, with a large percentage at minimum wage, and low wages were contributing to increased staff turnover. The federal regional staff charged with monitoring local programs had declined by at least 25 percent since 1970, at the very time that the program needed more staff to prepare for its first significant expansion in many years.

That committee's report, written by my coauthor, Susan Muenchow, called for a number of measures to improve Head Start's quality.[4] First, the report recommended that staff-child ratios and class size be restored and specified in the Head Start Performance Standards. It also said that at least one teacher in every Head Start classroom should be required to have a nationally recognized credential in child development, such as the Child Development Associate (CDA). In addition, the report called for salary increments to reflect completion of training, and a reduction in the caseloads of the regional community representatives charged with monitoring local Head Start programs.

The Reagan administration not only dismissed these recommendations, but developed an elaborate rationale for how Head Start could maintain and even expand enrollment without any new money—if only it would operate more efficiently. In a familiar repetition of former efforts, the administration's preferred scenario for improving Head Start's efficiency was to turn the program's administration over to the states. The only difference between the block grant proposal during the Reagan years and that of previous administrations was that this time the proposal had the support of one of the top Health and Human Services (HHS) officials charged with overseeing the program. While prior officials in her position had worked hard to prevent Head Start's transfer to the states, Dorcas Hardy, Assistant Secretary for Human Development Services, seemed prepared to out-Stockman Stockman.

In late fall of 1981, David Stockman floated the block grant plan for Head Start. Fortunately, some key congressional leaders were alerted, and Senator Alan Cranston leaked the proposal to the press right before the holidays. "Just in time for Christmas, it seems we have a real-life, modern-day Scrooge," wrote Dorothy Gilliam in the *Washington Post*.[5] Although Stockman had pledged that Head Start would be forever safe from budget trims, now he was proposing that it be folded into the Community Services Block Grant. As a result of the anticipated savings on federal operation of the program, the 1982 budget request for Head Start would be cut by $130 million. Once the public was informed about these plans for Head Start, the outcry was so great that the administration backed down.

But what cannot be achieved legislatively can sometimes be accomplished administratively. Dorcas Hardy asked the Administration for Children, Youth and Families (ACYF) to prepare a Head Start strategy paper that would respect the changing role of the federal government, and give the states more responsibility for administering the program. The primary goal would be to maintain enrollment, squeezing services for more children out of the same dollars.

The task of writing the new Head Start manifesto fell to a civil servant, John Busa, then serving as ACYF's acting deputy commissioner. "I tried to follow a fine line between doing what Dorcas wanted and keeping bad things from happening to Head Start," he said. "It's sort of the old story of do you spank your own child, or let someone else do it."[6] Given the recommendations floating around to turn Head Start over to the states, Busa thought it was better to do it himself.

Writing the report also gave him an opportunity to describe Head Start's benefits, which would make it harder for the administration to dismantle the program. If the report indicated that Head Start worked, then the administration would be on public record endorsing its effectiveness. By casting the document as a "discussion draft," Busa would be able to circulate it broadly and alert the Head Start community to the administration's plan.

As a result of Busa's efforts, the draft of the report, "Head Start: Directions for the Next Three Years," did place the administration solidly in the position of recognizing the effectiveness of Head Start.[7] For example, while the paper paid lip service to the adminis-

195

tration's goal of increasing program efficiency, it showed the impressive extent to which Head Start already used Medicaid/EPSDT to pay for medical screening and attracted parent volunteers to supplement paid staff. The report also made the point that Head Start teachers were underpaid, that class size had grown alarmingly, and that inflation was cutting into services. Finally, while deferring to the administration's decision to forgo the Carter administration's $125 million increase for 1982 in favor of a more "affordable" increase of approximately $13 million, the draft report put on record ACYF's assumption that a portion of the increase originally proposed would be made available the following year as a "deferred increase." This is bureaucratic damage control at its best.

Nevertheless, the report did make a number of recommendations that starkly illustrated the problems with trying to serve more children with no increase in funding. For example, just as it was being advised that Head Start should offer full-day, full-year services in order to enable parents to work, the ACYF paper said the program should be restricted to six hours a day and eight months a year. Furthermore, although the paper proposed targeting future funding increases to the elimination of classroom overcrowding, it also said that the Reagan administration should consider ways to relax staff-child ratios, albeit "without impairing service quality."[8] In addition, the report called for converting Parent and Child Centers for infants and toddlers to regular Head Start programs, and for withdrawing federal support from the highly acclaimed Child Development Associate program. Transportation costs would be reduced by "route restructuring," a euphemism for route elimination.[9] Research, demonstration, and evaluation activities would be greatly reduced if not phased out altogether.

Once the new Head Start manifesto was released, ACYF was bombarded with hundreds of protest letters. Already wary because of the earlier Stockman proposal, the House Subcommittee on Human Resources, the panel with jurisdiction over Head Start, decided in February 1982 to conduct an oversight hearing. As a result, the administration soon found itself recanting some of its own Head Start manifesto. The newly installed ACYF Commissioner

Clarence Hodges promised to maintain the few existing full-year Head Start programs; to continue federal support for the CDA program for the near-term; and to abandon plans to convert the Parent and Child Centers to regular Head Start programs. John Busa, who had tried to protect the program from within, transferred to bureaucratic purgatory in another agency.

Nevertheless, some of the administration's proposed economy measures came to pass. Perhaps the most damaging policy changes may have seemed the most innocuous. Following up on the report, the administration "decentralized" training and technical assistance (T and TA). Head Start T and TA resources amounting to $27 million had been used for in-depth, on-site reviews of grantee operations, expert guidance to programs, college degree and CDA training programs for Head Start staff, and special assistance on such efforts as incorporating handicapped children into Head Start. This T and TA network had linked Head Start to local colleges and universities, making expertise in early childhood education and home economics departments available to local programs. The Reagan administration largely dismantled the network, turning over the money to local grantees with no real assurance that the T and TA activities would continue with the same level of intensity.

At the same time, ACYF implemented the report's recommendation that federal regional officials no longer be required to conduct full-scale, on-site monitoring of one-third of Head Start programs annually. With severely reduced staff and travel budgets, the regional offices would do little more than desk monitoring of program records for the next decade. While our 1980 report had called for increasing the number of community representatives to conduct on-site monitoring of Head Start programs, the Reagan administration virtually eliminated the practice.

---

*The farther from the federal regional office a Head Start
program was located, the less likely it was to be monitored
during the Reagan years. For example, the Head Start
program in Fort Lauderdale, Florida, is located nearly
700 miles from the regional HHS headquarters in Atlanta.*

As a result, in a visit to the program in early 1991, we found that the grantee was about to receive its first monitoring by federal officials since 1983. No wonder no one was upset that the program no longer had enough social service staff to make home visits, except on an emergency basis. This is an outstanding Head Start program from an early childhood education standpoint, but at the time we visited, the social services unit was severely overtaxed. The program had placed parent involvement under the social services coordinator. She in turn supervised five community workers, each of whom had a caseload of 148 families.

Similarly, by the time federal officials from Boston closed down the Head Start program operating in New Haven, Connecticut, in June 1989, it was suffering from serious neglect. Many people, including myself and the original education director, Jeannette Galambos Stone, knew that the program had been going downhill for years. Finally, there were rumors that the children were not even receiving the required immunizations, and that, worse yet, program administrators were lying, maintaining that all the inoculations were up to date. Only then did federal officials intervene, encouraging the school system to take over the program and completely revamp it.

In short, while Congress had rejected the idea of turning over Head Start to the states, the executive branch decided it would no longer assume the responsibility for program oversight. HHS would in effect "block grant" Head Start dollars to the more than 1,200 existing grantees, with no one responsible for monitoring them.

"RIF": Reductions in Force

Not surprisingly, ACYF's top leadership is evasive on the exact reduction in staff responsible for Head Start during the Reagan years.

They stress that the office was reorganized, and that it is not so easy to compare the numbers of staff responsible because functions changed.

But civil servants in the agency indicate that the national office staff was cut by about half, and regional directors acknowledge privately that they lost about two-thirds of the staff responsible for Head Start. Not only was the staff reduced in number, but there was also a deliberate effort to eliminate some of the most experienced members. These were not political appointees, but civil servants with strong expertise in program areas. As these specialists fell as victims of "RIF"—Reductions in Force—they were frequently replaced by people from completely different fields with no expertise in the area of early childhood.

Jenni Klein, who had a doctorate in special education and was nationally recognized for her role in developing the Child Development Associate program and Head Start's early childhood education component, quit rather than accept a part-time, lower level job.

Edith Grotberg, a former American University professor who served as Head Start's research director, was also forced to leave. The entire research and evaluation unit was dismantled. Grotberg had commissioned the highly acclaimed Cornell Consortium study that helped save Head Start, and her reward was being fired. The Reagan administration officials in HHS refused even to hold a retirement dinner in Grotberg's honor. So the National Academy of Sciences had a party for her, and I gave a speech.

At the top level of ACYF, positions were left vacant or with persons serving in an acting capacity. It was as if there were a deliberate attempt to cripple the agency, dislocating the staff so it could no longer function as an effective unit.

Loyal Protectors

Fortunately, some key experienced staff stayed on and managed, against all odds, to hold the program together during the Reagan years. Many of the strongest leaders among the remaining staff were black, and had started out with the War on Poverty. These people had seen it all. Administrations would come and go, but they were determined that Head Start would survive.

Up to this point, Head Start had benefited from a series of strong national directors—Dr. Julius Richmond, the pediatrician who championed comprehensive services; Jule Sugarman, the administrative wizard; Richard Orton, who protected Head Start from an attempted transfer to the states; and Jim Robinson, who encouraged Head Start parents and staff to organize and helped put the program in Caspar Weinberger's good graces.

The two Head Start directors during the Reagan years were no exception to this tradition. Henlay Foster, national Head Start director from 1980 to 1982, was very realistic about his task: it was, he said, to maintain the status quo. Foster had started out with the antipoverty program in 1965, then became assistant director of the St. Louis Head Start program in 1970, and then entered the federal civil service as a community representative in the Kansas City regional office responsible for monitoring local Head Starts in the state of Missouri. He joined the national Head Start staff in 1972.

Foster's biggest challenge was maintaining the Head Start Performance Standards, the basic framework we had worked so hard to establish to protect the program's quality. When the Reagan administration came in, newly appointed officials wanted to revise and relax these standards.

"I cooperated as a civil servant," said Foster, "but I expressed my opposition to what they were doing. Not only was the climate not conducive for changing the standards, but any reduction in the scope of the Performance Standards ran contrary, in my view, to the law and legislative intent."[10]

The effort to revise the standards proceeded, but there were many complaints from the field. The revised standards finally reached HHS Secretary Richard Schweiker's desk. To our relief, he refused to approve them.

Foster said he viewed his two and a half years as national Head Start director as a dual job. "It was to be the quintessential civil servant, and to do what I have always done—implement the policies and procedures of the administration, and try within those parameters to make sure the program did not deteriorate," he said.

Following Foster, Clennie Murphy, who had worked in the Head Start bureau since 1969, took on the federal direction of the program. Murphy served as acting Head Start bureau chief from August 1982 until March 1989. The Bush administration then appointed him as associate commissioner of ACYF, a position he held until his retirement in summer of 1991.

Murphy had worked in the Peace Corps, and his diplomatic experience showed. He acted as the administration's ambassador to the Head Start directors, parents, and staff. "My real struggle was to represent the administration," he said. "There was not one federal official I've known who wanted to hurt Head Start; even Dorcas was supportive. But I asked her to tell me if she was going to do something, so that I did not first learn about it in the newspaper."[11] As a result, when administration policies conflicted with what he knew were the wishes of local Head Start leaders, Murphy was at least in a position to negotiate the differences.

At the same time, Murphy's many years as regional liaison had earned him the respect of Head Start directors, staff, and parents. "If I said, 'Don't take on that fight,' they wouldn't." Murphy said he worried sometimes, when an issue did not go the way the Head Start Association wanted, that he had injected himself too much in the process. But for his skill in negotiating and his ability to smooth things over, Murphy was dubbed, "Mr. Kissinger."

Perhaps the best measure of Murphy's talent is that while the Reagan administration proposed level budgets for the Head Start program throughout the 1980s, the president never opposed the much more substantial increases appropriated by Congress.

National Head Start Association

The staff trying to protect Head Start from within ACYF would have had far less success, however, were it not for the increasingly sophisticated organization of the National Head Start Association (NHSA).

"I had worked to build up the Head Start Association," said Jim Robinson, director of the Head Start bureau from May 1972 to May 1980. "I first raised the idea of establishing a national office in 1978, and discussed it again in 1980 just before I left. I said it was important for an association with several thousand members to have an office in Washington to be their eyes and ears, and to understand how legislation is put together."[12]

The NHSA went to work cultivating support in Congress. They drew up a contact list with NHSA representatives from each state who could testify on behalf of Head Start issues. Perhaps most surprising, NHSA members made friends with some of the most conservative members of Congress. Republican Senator Jeremiah Denton of Alabama was viewed as a Moral Majority leader. But when he became chairman of the Senate Committee on Labor and Human Resources, Subcommittee on Family and Human Relations, fellow Alabaman Nancy Spears went to see him. Spears, chair of NHSA's education and information committee, had no trouble securing Denton's support for Head Start. "Denton was a family man all the way," said Spears, "and he saw Head Start as a family program."[13]

Senator Orrin Hatch, Republican from Utah, another New Right leader, also quickly became a Head Start convert. Noting Head Start's success in attracting local volunteers and in highlighting "the role of parents as the prime educators of preschool children," Hatch pledged his support for an "expeditious enactment of reauthorization legislation continuing the goals and objectives of the Head Start program."[14]

The NHSA, working closely with Helen Blank, who has served as CDF's chief lobbyist for Head Start since 1981, managed to stave off a number of the Reagan administration's attempts to dilute the program's quality. The 1984 Head Start reauthorization bill was carefully drafted to ensure that a specific amount of funds would be continuously available for training, that the administration's plans to eliminate funding for the national Child Development Associate program would not succeed, and that Head Start's performance standards would be maintained. When it appeared that Congress might adjourn before completing the reauthorization, CDF placed an ad in the Washington Post which pictured young children over the caption: "400,000 Head Start children are looking for one good senator." Senator Hatch offered to be the senator, and with the help of Senator Stafford the bill was brought to the Senate floor just before congress adjourned.

As a result of the continuing efforts of NHSA and CDF, in 1984 Congress appropriated over an $80 million increase for Head Start. In 1988 congress approved a $50 million set-aside for Head Start salary improvements, another long sought-after NHSA goal. "Then we sent thousands of thank-you letters," said Spears, "because most of the time Congress only hears from you when you want something."[15]

Throughout the Reagan years, NHSA officers also cultivated even the most intransigent of administration officials. By 1986, even President Reagan himself was willing to pay tribute to the program: "Head Start has demonstrated its worth and effectiveness over the past two decades," he wrote in a message to participants in a national conference.[16]

But the Reagan administration was trying to limit all children to one year of service. In this way, for the same amount of money, a larger number of children could participate in Head Start. But NHSA President Sarah Greene pointed out that many children, especially handicapped children, required a second year of Head Start to reap any significant benefits. In addition, she said, many parents only began to participate in the program after the first year.

Federal law explicitly stated that local programs had the right to provide more than one year of service to eligible children from age three to the age of compulsory school attendance. But despite assurances to the contrary, the administration continued to play the numbers game, covertly encouraging federal regional officials to limit services to one year in order to expand the total enrollment.

Finally, Nancy Spears, NHSA's education and information committee chair, got tired of hearing the administration deny that it was trying to stop the multiple years of service. She sent out a survey to Head Start grantees. In response, two-thirds of the grantees said they had received some pressure from regional HHS offices to restrict the enrollment to one year of service. Spears collected these regional directives and brought them to the attention of Congressman Dale Kildee, chair of the House Committee on Education and Labor. As a result, although the battle is ongoing, NHSA was able to stop, at least temporarily, the administration's effort to restrict Head Start to a one-year program.

A Program that Works

Head Start's survival during the Reagan years must also be attributed to the growing perception that the program works. While Head Start is far from a panacea for poverty, there is ample evidence that it and other quality preschool programs make both immediate and lasting improvements in the lives of many disadvantaged children.

Head Start's immediate benefits are indisputable: children's health is improved; they receive dental care; they have higher self-esteem and motivation; they score higher on academic tests; and many of their parents receive education and become involved both as volunteers and employees.[17]

As for the long-term effects of Head Start and other preschool programs, the Consortium for Longitudinal Studies offers probably the cleanest data. The 1978 follow-up research on 12 preschool programs (two of which were strictly Head Start and Head Start/ Follow Through) showed that early intervention significantly reduces placements in special education and grade retentions. For example, a follow-up study on the Harlem Training Project found that the children were twice as likely to be in the right grade for the right age as were their peers who had not had the benefit of preschool.[18]

The High Scope Foundation's Perry Preschool study found that disadvantaged children who participated in the program fared much better than a control group who had no preschool experience. By age 19, the preschool graduates were almost twice as likely to be employed or in college or vocational training. Their arrest rates were 40 percent lower and they were also less apt to get pregnant as teenagers.[19]

Critics rightly point out that most of the above studies focused on early intervention efforts that were not Head Start programs, but that were in many cases more expensive projects operated under laboratory conditions. However, a 1987 study of more than 3,500 children who had been in Head Start programs in Philadelphia came up with similar, although somewhat less dramatic, findings as did the Cornell Consortium and High Scope.[20] While, like earlier studies, the Philadelphia data showed no lasting effect of Head Start on achievement scores, children who had been enrolled in the program were more likely to participate in school. Even as late as eighth grade, Head Start children seemed more likely than their peers to be in the right grade for the right age. Most of these children were far from honor students, but the main point is that they were more apt to attend school regularly and to show up for the tests. Given this nation's concern with dropout prevention, that finding should not be minimized.

Similarly, a subset of longitudinal studies in a 1985 review of 210 studies—limited strictly to research on Head Start itself—documents that Head Start graduates fare better than their peers on such measures as being kept back in school and being placed in special education.[21]

There is even some indication that the management and quality improvements we made in Head Start during the 1970s, such as the introduction of the Head Start Performance Standards and the conversion of summer programs to full-year schedules, led to better outcomes for the children enrolled. When researchers compared long-range cognitive effects on Head Start children in studies before and after 1970, they found that the gains were greater among children who entered the program after 1970.[22]

Yet we must be careful not to oversell the effectiveness of Head Start. There is a classic design in most research on Head Start or other early intervention programs: a researcher looks at a group of children participating in a program, and at a control group of similar children who are not enrolled, and follows the two groups to determine if there are differences in outcome. Viewed from this perspective, Head Start and many other early intervention programs clearly "work."

If Head Start children are compared with their middle-class

peers, however, we begin to see early intervention programs in a more realistic light. In a Montgomery County, Maryland, study, for example, there were three groups of children—Head Start children; non–Head Start children from similarly deprived circumstances; and middle- to upper-middle-class children. Compared to poor children not enrolled in Head Start, the Head Start children fared significantly better. But compared to their wealthier peers, the Head Start children still were disturbingly behind. Indeed, as a general finding in studies on the effects of quality preschool programs, a substantial portion of the participants still require remedial education, and/or get held back a grade or more in school. Head Start cannot by itself compensate for all the bad housing, substance abuse, violence, and lack of jobs in many communities. Head Start is merely one important tool for better preparing children and families to deal with a difficult environment; it does not inoculate them against all the social ills threatening America's children and families.

Substance abuse makes it much more difficult to help the children and families in Head Start. There are the indirect effects. In New Haven, a Head Start child told her teacher that she had to sleep on the floor at night and be careful not to raise her head. Living in a housing project where drug gangs fight nightly, that was the only way the little girl could protect herself from the bullets that are regularly fired through the project walls.

And there are the direct effects, such as the 150 children in the Dade County program who have behavioral problems resulting from their exposure to drugs before birth. Even when these children have therapy, they "act out" so much that they disrupt the environment for the rest of the children.

Fear that the children will be lured into the drug world themselves always looms in the background. "All we can do is constantly teach them about drugs," says Christine Johnson, director of the Coconut Grove Elementary School

Head Start Center. Johnson adds that she "prays to God every night" that her own grandson, now a star pupil in second grade, won't get drawn into drugs as he gets older.

We must also guard against the impression that any one- or two-year program can, by itself, rescue a whole generation of children and families. Early childhood educators are re-discovering what was really clear from the outset of Head Start: the program is far more effective when it is followed up by projects designed to ease the child's transition to elementary school. Like Head Start, these transitional projects should emphasize parent involvement and health and social services, and continue through at least the first three years of school.

While recognizing Head Start's limitations, I think there is no longer any question that the program has both short-term and lasting benefits. The more important questions are, What are the dynamics that produce the benefits, and how can we maximize them? There are three main hypotheses.

The first is the snowball hypothesis. According to this theory, advanced by the High Scope group,[23] early intervention gives disadvantaged children a "head start" on getting along well with their teachers. As a result, preschool graduates interact a little better than their peers with their kindergarten teachers. One positive experience in turn leads to a better one at the next grade level, and the accumulation of slightly better experiences results in a child's completing school.

The second hypothesis is that Head Start makes the parent a better socializer and advocate for the child. Through participation in the program, parents receive education that helps them do a more effective job of childrearing. Head Start's benefits endure, not only because of the time the children spend in the program, but more importantly because the parents' relationship with the child has been permanently improved. This hypothesis is consistent with Bronfenbrenner's ecological view of child development.[24] It is further supported by findings that parents who participate in Head Start appear to have higher self-esteem, which probably carries over to their children as well.[25]

Dina and her son Rahim illustrate the benefits of early intervention. Although Rahim was born while Dina was still in high school, she managed to graduate and is now taking some college classes. Dina attributes her success both in school and in childrearing to the teen parent program she attended, and to the new Head Start program administered by the New Haven school system.

Dina makes a point of accompanying Rahim every morning to Head Start. They sit down at a table together, and he begins to trace a circle from the bottom of a cup. "Look, I know how to draw a circle without that," he tells her, confidently proceeding to draw several more circles free-hand. Then Rahim starts on a house, describing its every feature to his mother as he draws: "Those are snowballs, and here's a door and doorknobs, and there's a chimney." The only indication that this highly verbal child is from inner-city New Haven is that he draws bars on the windows of the house.

If it is the changes in the parent that account for the lasting effects of early intervention, then the siblings of Head Start children should benefit almost as much as the children who are directly enrolled. In a study by Victoria Seitz of an early intervention project in New Haven,[26] the siblings of children enrolled in the program did show some of the same positive outcomes as the children who directly participated. The children's achievement scores were not very impressive, but the parents liked their children and felt proud of them. Sisters and brothers of the children enrolled were not in trouble with the law; they were decent kids. Furthermore, the intervention program had a positive impact on the whole family's quality of life: the follow-up data showed that many of the families had moved to better housing, furthered their education, and obtained jobs. In short, researchers may have seriously underestimated the effectiveness of Head Start. Instead of focusing on the children enrolled, we should have been looking at the effects on the status of the whole family.

The third hypothesis, and one that has long interested me, is the health hypothesis. In a study by Barbara Hale, Victoria Seitz, and me, the one area where Head Start children did seem just as well off as their middle-class peers was in the area of health. They had all the right immunizations, they had regular physicals, and they had no particular health problems. By contrast, the poor children not enrolled in Head Start had received much more irregular health care and were not as healthy children. It may well be that the health contribution of Head Start has long been underappreciated. The fact that children in Head Start are more apt to be healthy may account for why they are more likely to complete school and become employed. Perhaps if we psychologists had stayed out of the evaluation of Head Start, the entire case for the program would have been made on its health benefits alone.

Summing up the verdict on the effectiveness of Head Start, the program has been remarkably successful. Any intervention that can reduce school failure is well worth the investment. Beyond that, Head Start may have benefits that have yet to be evaluated. In the course of writing this book, we ran into countless Head Start "success stories"—an Alabama parent whose six children completed college; a Head Start graduate who's now a top insurance executive in Florida; lots of Ph.D's; and literally hundreds of Head Start parents who have become employed as educators themselves. The fact that not all participants in Head Start enjoy such positive results in no way diminishes the program's importance. It just suggests that more needs to be done to make sure that all 24,000 Head Start classrooms have the dynamics that seem to make a difference—teachers trained to interact with young children, strong health components, and activities to involve parents.

A Bipartisan Consensus

Looking back over the Reagan years, it is clear that Head Start was not only salvaged, but, in many ways, strengthened. The program found protectors within the administration, and cultivated unexpected new friends in Congress. The National Head Start Association, with the help of CDF, became a force with which all politicians must contend. Cost-benefit studies convinced business leaders, including the top officers of Procter and Gamble and AT&T, that Head Start was a good investment. As a result, during a decade when most social programs suffered substantial cutbacks, Head Start's budget continued to grow.

By 1988 Republicans and Democrats were almost in the posture of competing to see who could provide the greatest boost for Head Start. Both party platforms that year called for extending services to all eligible children. A campaign document for one presidential hopeful clearly sang the praises of Head Start: "This program works: George Bush will sharply increase its funding."[27]

10

Head Start: The Next Generation

IN 1990 HEAD START RECEIVED ITS LARGEST BUDGET INCREASE EVER, and both President Bush and Congress pledged "full funding" for the program. Congress authorized a total appropriation of $2.4 billion for 1991, with annual increases that would quadruple the program's budget in four years. The Head Start Expansion and Quality Improvement Act was landmark legislation, the culmination of a 25-year bipartisan success story. As *Newsweek* put it, "Everybody likes Head Start."[1]

While appropriations have lagged considerably behind the authorized levels, Head Start's budget has nearly doubled since President Bush took office. And the program remains on a roll: Senators Edward Kennedy and Christopher Dodd have introduced the School Readiness Act, which would make Head Start an entitlement for all poor children, providing $1 billion–per-year increases until the goal was met. President Bush has also proposed a $600 million increase in Head Start for 1993. He wants to ensure that Head Start is available to every eligible four-year-old so that, "by the year 2000, all children in America will start school ready to learn."

Both President Bush and Congress deserve great credit for championing these major new investments in Head Start. The only problem is that the administration is playing a numbers game. Like many presidents before him, Bush is placing too much emphasis on program expansion at the expense of program quality, even proposing to reduce the funds Congress set aside for quality improvements. At the end of this book, we argue that the emphasis on simple expansion of the existing half-day, part-year Head Start program for preschool children is misplaced. Based on more than 25 years of experience with Head Start and our own visits to contemporary programs, we offer five major recommendations for the next generation of Head Start. Our recommendations build upon those recently offered by the Silver Ribbon Panel of the National Head Start Association.

1. Provide "Full-Quality" Head Start

Our first priority for "full funding" is to improve the quality of Head Start. Without such improvements, the next longitudinal study may well conclude that while high quality preschool programs do indeed produce lasting benefits, too many Head Start centers are not of high quality.

Public support for Head Start expansion has been based largely on the notion that Head Start "works," meaning that it has long-term benefits. As we have shown, there is ample evidence that high quality early childhood programs have the capacity to reduce special education placements and grade retentions. These programs have been found to help children complete school, and even reduce juvenile delinquency.

Yet with the exception of the Philadelphia Head Start study, most of this research was conducted on programs that have far more resources than the typical Head Start program. Consider the characteristics of the program in the most cited study on the benefits of early childhood education, the Perry Preschool. This program, over the long run, was found to save $4 to $7 for every $1 invested by reducing special education placements, grade retentions, delinquency, and welfare dependency. The Perry Preschool was rich in resources. Not only did it have a more favorable staff-child ratio than does Head Start (one staff member for every five children, as opposed to Head Start's range of one-to-eight to one-to-ten), but virtually all of the teachers had post-graduate degrees in early childhood education. While Head Start struggles to provide the federally mandated two annual home visits to families, the Perry Preschool program had sufficient staff to pay a weekly one-and-one-half-hour home visit to every family whose child was enrolled. Finally, simply by being part of a research experiment, the Perry Preschool program received intensive monitoring and technical assistance, practices that are often the first casualty during tight budget periods in Head Start.

Perhaps most telling, the Perry Preschool program spent about $5,000 per child per year, almost twice the $2,803 per child expenditure for the Head Start program in 1990.[2] Indeed, according to the High Scope Educational Research Foundation, the expenditure per child in Head Start in constant dollars actually declined 13 percent between 1981 and 1989.[3]

We are not suggesting that Head Start clone the Perry Preschool program. In some respects, Head Start is a superior program offering more comprehensive services, especially in the area of health and parent involvement. Furthermore, even the High Scope Foundation that administered the Perry Preschool now considers a one-to-five staff-child ratio unnecessarily protective for most preschool children.

But we do think that Head Start must look more like the highly proclaimed models in research projects if it is to be expected to produce similar results on a nationwide basis. Specifically, we recommend that Head Start have the resources to: (a) offer salaries and benefits to attract and retain lead teachers with professional training; (b) enhance comprehensive services for multiproblem families; (c) strengthen health services; (d) reduce class size to accommodate children with special needs; (e) acquire permanent space especially designed for young children; (f) provide federal monitoring and technical assistance; and (g) allocate the full cost of quality. Moreover, funding for these quality improvements should not be contingent on appropriations for program expansion.

IMPROVE SALARIES AND BENEFITS

Head Start is making major strides in requiring professional training for its teaching staff. By 1994, every Head Start class must have at least one teacher who has a Child Development Associate (CDA) or other appropriate early childhood degree or credential. In an effort to attract state prekindergarten funds, some Head Start programs are attempting to recruit teachers with bachelor's-level training and certification.

Unfortunately, Head Start still does not offer salaries commensurate with professional training. In 1988, 47 percent of Head Start teachers earned less than $10,000 per year.[4] Even Head Start teachers with a B.A. in early childhood education had an average starting salary of $11,518, which is only 63 percent of the average beginning salary for a public school kindergarten teacher. Is it any wonder that nearly one in every five Head Start teachers left each year?

As a result of the Head Start Expansion and Quality Improvement Act, Head Start salaries are improving. Congress mandated that at least half of the $194 million appropriated for quality improvements in 1991 be designated for salary increases, and programs were given the discretion to use virtually all of the funds for that purpose. Head Start programs are also making progress in establishing career paths, with incentives for educational attainments.

Progress toward offering Head Start staff standard employee benefits is slower. Head Start programs have begun to offer them, but the scope and level of the benefits vary widely. When Fran Collins became director of the Head Start program in Cambridge, Massachusetts, six years ago, the staff received no pension. "This was ridiculous," said Collins, who also chairs the statewide Head Start Directors' Association. "People were retiring after 20 years of service with no pension."[5] So Collins proposed a retirement plan, with a 3 percent contribution by Head Start.

In an effort to help narrow the gap between Head Start and public school salaries and benefits, some states are supplementing federal allocations for Head Start. According to the Education Development Center, 13 states now make specific appropriations for Head Start amounting in all to a $38 million supplement to the program's budget.[6] For example, prior to the passage of the Head Start Expansion and Quality Improvement Act of 1990, the Massachusetts legislature allocated $1.5 million to raise Head Start teacher salaries. Head Start also benefits from an as yet unidentified portion of the estimated $443 million spent on state-funded prekindergarten initiatives, which are sometimes subcontracted with Head Start. In 1991 Florida's commissioner of education set aside over $6 million in state prekindergarten funds to help close the gap between the state's per-child expenditure for its prekindergarten early intervention program and the federal per-child expenditure for 1,650 new children to be admitted to Head Start. Some counties and local school districts also contribute funds to Head Start over and above the 20 percent local match requirement.

These state and local initiatives are based on an important recognition: Head Start is a school readiness program, and schools benefit from having children attend well-staffed Head Start programs, regardless of who administers them. The extra state and local funds can make a major difference in the quality of those Head Start programs fortunate enough to receive them.

While welcoming the state and local supplements for Head Start, we think it is the federal government's role to ensure that every child in Head Start receives a quality program. The federal government should establish a regional cost per child for Head Start that takes into account local labor market conditions and enables the program to pay salaries and benefits commensurate with those for similar services. Where states or localities have provided funding supplements for Head Start beyond the local match requirement, these funds could then be used to expand the number of children served, including those slightly above the federal income eligibility guidelines for admission to Head Start.

In addition, federal administrators in Head Start should provide technical assistance to Head Start grantees on how to develop benefit packages and set up insurance pools. Half of any funds appropriated for quality improvement in Head Start should continue to be designated for improving compensation, including both salaries and benefits, until Head Start reaches equity with similar preschool programs.

Since 1986, Head Start teachers in Broward County have been on the same salary schedule as their public school colleagues. Although the school district's requirement that Head Start be staffed with certified teachers has contributed to a modest decline in the percentage of minority teachers in the program, a serious effort has been made to help the original Head Start staff move up the school's career ladder.

Consider Mary Barner, who started out as a Head Start parent and has held every conceivable position in the program, from bus driver to classroom volunteer to parent coordinator. When her daughter went to college, she went back to school as well, and now she is a certified teacher in Head Start. Barner is particularly grateful for the school system's benefit package. "For ten years, I worked for Head Start with no retirement plan," she said. "Where would I be now without one?"

ENHANCE COMPREHENSIVE SERVICES TO MULTIPROBLEM FAMILIES

Head Start's greatest strength is its comprehensive services and parent involvement. Yet both national program data and our own visits to Head Start programs confirm that Head Start's social, health, and parent involvement components have often not kept pace with the changing needs of Head Start families. Without attention to these components, there is a real danger that Head Start will no longer be able to do what it has done best—help children in a family-centered context.

Caseloads for health and social service staff have become unmanageable. While a recent Department of Health and Human Services task force recommended a caseload of 35 families per social service worker, 71 percent of Head Start programs nationwide had an average social service caseload of 61 families per worker. In one program we visited, there was only one social worker for every 270 families.

As a result of rising social service caseloads, Head Start staff are increasingly unavailable to make more than the two annual home visits required by the Head Start Performance Standards, except on an emergency basis. Nor are home visits the only casualty of rising social service caseloads. Family needs assessment has been one of the practices that distinguishes Head Start from other early childhood programs. However, too many Head Start programs limit the family needs assessment process to the initial enrollment period, before families have had enough time to develop the trust in the staff necessary to share sensitive information. Furthermore, while federal law now mandates at least one teacher with a CDA credential for every 20 children in Head Start by 1994, there are no comparable educational qualifications for social service and parent involvement staff. Finally, there is as yet no equivalent to a competency-based credential for social service or health service personnel in Head Start.

Meanwhile, Head Start's need for trained staff in the areas of health, social service, and parent involvement is greater than ever. Staff need training to deal with a growing number of dysfunctional families, according to a 1989 report by the Inspector General of the Department of Health and Human Services. The major family problems encountered by Head Start staff are substance abuse, child abuse, domestic violence, lack of parenting skills on the part of teenage parents, and crime-infested, inadequate housing.[7] About 84 percent of the Head Start grantees reported increased demands on staff time for such activities as one-to-one counseling, assistance to families, and dealing with troubled children in the classroom. Summing up the changing needs of Head Start families, Don Bolce, former information specialist for the National Head Start

Association, says, "We look back to the poverty of the early 1970s as the good old days. Poverty is getting uglier."[8]

Because of its commitment to provide comprehensive services in a family-centered context, Head Start has more potential to serve dysfunctional families than any other early childhood program. However, lack of resources is limiting Head Start's ability to serve these families. The administration should follow the recommendations of the Silver Ribbon Panel: Head Start should increase the number of family support staff to meet the 35:1 ratio; funds should be allocated to hire at least a coordinator with professional social work credentials; a social services competency-based curriculum should be developed to train paraprofessional staff; and a career ladder with salary increments should be established to provide incentives for training.

STRENGTHEN HEALTH SERVICES

Head Start's health component, which has long been one of the program's strengths, also needs revitalization. At a time when immunization rates are declining among young children, every Head Start program needs a trained health coordinator. In Dade County, Florida, for example, a new health coordinator with extensive public health experience has increased the immunization rate from 85 to 98 percent in Head Start. By training nurses to follow up referrals, he has also greatly reduced the time between referrals and actual treatment.

With increasing numbers of children with special needs in Head Start, staff with nursing backgrounds fill a very important function. Families look up to nurses as an objective, nonstigmatizing source of help. Ideally, Head Start should provide an on-site nurse for all of its large multiclassroom programs, and the nurse should be part of a multidisciplinary team including social service and parent involvement staff, that reviews family needs assessments.

Head Start staff also need far more access to mental health services for children and families. Aside from a provision in the Head

Start Performance Standards that a mental health professional be available at least on a consultation basis, there are no real staffing requirements in this area. The need is not just for one-on-one counseling for children and families, but for expert training for Head Start staff in how to deal with disruptive children in a mainstreamed setting.

One promising development is that the American Psychological Association has recently established a network of 500 psychologists to volunteer their services at Head Start centers across the country. Psychologists will be called upon to screen and diagnose developmental disabilities, conduct parent support groups, and train project staff on dealing with such problems as substance abuse and family violence.

The Administration for Children, Youth and Families should also assist local Head Start programs in improving health service coordination by taking advantage of changes in the Medicaid program that allow some flexibility with respect to the type of providers who qualify for reimbursement. According to David Chavkin, an attorney who specializes in health and poverty law, and early childhood educator Peggy Pizzo, Head Start programs can apply for Medicaid funds to help finance the salaries of health and social services coordinators who help Medicaid-eligible families gain access to needed medical, social, and educational services.[9] Head Start may also be able to use Medicaid funds to pay a licensed psychologist or physical therapist to provide necessary services to eligible families.

"We need more help with the Michael's in our classrooms," explains Gretchen Ahern, health coordinator in the New Haven Head Start program. Michael is a child who consistently demands attention, and often takes his aggression out on other children.

But he also cries about not being able to behave. Recently Michael couldn't sit still long enough to have his vision tested, even though he desperately wanted the stick-

ers that were promised him as a reward for completing the test.

Because he has no cognitive deficit, Michael does not qualify for special education programs. In order to keep children like Michael in a regular Head Start class, Ahern thinks the program needs a mental health coordinator who can at least give teachers suggestions on how to handle them.

REDUCE CLASS SIZE TO ACCOMMODATE SPECIAL-NEEDS CHILDREN

Head Start seems to be managing well with two adults in charge of a maximum class of 20 (minimum of 17). However, programs need the flexibility to have smaller classes and additional staff in order to accommodate children with special needs.

At times, federal Head Start policy requiring that every classroom have at least 17 children poses a potential barrier to partnerships with state agencies that might be able to share the costs of the additional staff. In Massachusetts, where state policy requires that classrooms integrating special-needs children have a maximum class size of 15, the Head Start program in Cambridge was fortunate to obtain a federal waiver on the minimum size. As a result, "the schools are paying for a third teacher in some of our classrooms," says Head Start director Fran Collins. "It's what every integrated classroom should be."

Smaller classes and more staff may also be needed in order to serve younger children. When Head Start began in 1965, many states did not yet have kindergartens, so the program served a good many five-year-olds as well as four-year-olds. At that time, there was one adult for every five children. Today, when 92 percent of the children served are under five, programs have to manage with half as many teacher aides, and the typical class size has risen from 15 to 20. Given the fact that younger children usually require more attention, programs need the flexibility to adjust class size and teaching loads accordingly.

ACQUIRE PERMANENT FACILITIES

Twenty years ago, it was clear to a bipartisan group in Congress supporting child development legislation that program facilities were an important component of program quality. The Child Development Act of 1971, which was passed by Congress but vetoed by President Nixon, would have allowed local communities to obtain federal grants or low-interest loans for the construction of facilities, provided that not more than 15 percent of the total financial assistance provided to a prime sponsor be used for construction.

Unfortunately, federal law currently prohibits Head Start programs from using grant funds to purchase or construct facilities. As a result, Head Start is forced to rely on rented or donated facilities, which are increasingly difficult to obtain. According to the Silver Ribbon Panel report, some public schools have taken back space that they had given or rented to Head Start in the past.[10] This is especially troubling, the Panel concluded, because the General Accounting Office estimates that 29 percent of Head Start programs are located in public school buildings. Even when schools or other landlords continue to allow Head Start to have space, they are often no longer willing to do so on a rent-free or low-rent basis.

Not only are Head Start programs having increasing difficulty finding affordable facilities, but many of the existing program sites need to be replaced or extensively renovated. According to the Silver Ribbon Panel, a survey by the Mississippi Head Start directors showed that 25 percent of the centers needed to be replaced.[11] Our own visits to Head Start programs found many in public housing projects and buildings that formerly served as schools that had been in need of extensive repairs for years.

The argument for not allowing federal funds to be used for the purchase of Head Start space and facilities has been that it would be too expensive. However, federal funds are already being used for costly rent and renovations, and this practice often amounts to a total waste of federal tax dollars. Frequently Head Start programs complete payments for renovating a rented building only to be forced to vacate the structure. The National Head Start Association estimates that taxpayers lost nearly $13 million on renovations of now vacated facilities between 1987 and 1990. Unless Head Start is allowed to use federal funds to help purchase facilities, the program is likely to throw away far more tax dollars on the renovation of rented facilities.

After 25 years, Head Start is no longer a temporary program, and it should be housed in permanent quarters. A number of approaches should be considered for allowing local Head Start programs to purchase or construct facilities. As proposed as far back as 1971 in the Child Development Act, one option is to provide federal grants or low-interest loans for construction. A more flexible approach is proposed in the School Readiness Act (S. 911), which would allow Head Start agencies to use their basic expansion funds to acquire, expand, or construct new buildings. The bill would also allow Head Start agencies to use federal funds to amortize the costs of the principal and to pay interest on loans obtained through private commercial channels.

Short of allowing the expenditure of federal funds for the purchase or construction of facilities, all Head Start programs should be given information on how to apply for Department of Housing and Urban Development (HUD) loans that can be used for building construction; in 1991, HUD made available $4.8 million for Head Start construction loans. Programs should also be encouraged to conduct capital campaigns for the purchase of permanent buildings.

There is no way we can be entirely objective about the new Edward Zigler Head Start Center in New Haven. Not only is the center named after the first author, but the facility is also state-of-the-art. With eight classrooms and on-site health, education, and social services staff, the center is large enough to avoid the isolation of many self-contained Head Start centers and small enough not to feel institutional.

The majority of Head Start parents in the New Haven area request this center, according to Michael Rudel, its social service coordinator. He adds that they make it

sound like the "palace of Head Start." Perhaps the parents
like the newness and cleanliness of the building, and the
fact that it is located in a relatively safe neighborhood. Or
maybe it's the multipurpose room where they can sit
down for a cup of coffee.

While we remain loyal to the old dictum that the most
important component of an early childhood program is
the quality of the staff, space also matters. Placing Head
Start programs in public housing basements may sound
like a wise policy, because it takes the program to where
many of the families live. In the long run, however, that
kind of environment is not only hard on the staff's morale,
but it also offers no new hope to the children and their
parents.

PROVIDE FEDERAL MONITORING AND TECHNICAL ASSISTANCE

In the 1980 committee report on Head Start requested by President Carter, we pointed out the need to strengthen the federal oversight of the program at both the national and regional levels.[12] Understaffing was particularly critical at the regional level, where the staff assigned to advise and monitor local grantees are the key to assuring that local Head Start programs actually deliver the services mandated by Congress.[13]

With the election of President Reagan, the Carter-commissioned report recommending increased monitoring staff for Head Start was not just put on the shelf—it was put in the wastebasket. Head Start services survived during the Reagan years, but the federal infrastructure for monitoring the program was depleted. Travel funds for staff were virtually eliminated, and many regional offices no longer had even a single child development specialist on the Head Start staff.

Given the reduction in regional staff, it is hardly surprising that on-site monitoring declined significantly. In 1988, the regional offices monitored only 10 percent of Head Start grantees, according to the National Head Start Association. "There are plenty of programs," adds Don Bolce, "that have not seen a federal official in five years." Concerned that lack of monitoring is endangering the program, the NHSA itself is now leading the charge for greater federal oversight of Head Start.

Not only did the regional offices lose staff, but, equally important, they also lost staff with appropriate training and experience. "A generation ago there were people in the regional offices who really served as resources to local Head Start programs," says Bolce. "Now we have people who may never have seen a Head Start program and may not even know the regulations."

With the increased investments in the expansion of Head Start, improved federal monitoring is now of critical importance. In an effort to restore the federal oversight and technical assistance to Head Start, the 1990 reauthorization legislation mandated that one-third of the programs be monitored each year. However, it is not clear that sufficient funds were appropriated to carry out this policy. While ACYF officials said 40 new regional staff were to be hired to monitor and provide technical assistance to Head Start, this is still a fraction of the staff that once provided federal oversight of the program. Furthermore, job specifications and salaries for the new staff may be too low to attract the best candidates, namely persons with experience managing Head Start programs.

Not only have federal on-site monitoring and technical assistance to Head Start declined over the years, but the systems necessary for "desk" monitoring are also underdeveloped. Every year Head Start programs across the nation fill out Program Information Reports (PIR) on such issues as the number of handicapped children enrolled, the number of teachers with degrees in early childhood, and the percentage of children immunized. These PIR reports could be an excellent management tool for improving the program. However, the PIR need to be updated to obtain more information on the changing needs of Head Start families and the programs that purport to serve them.

In addition, the information collected through the PIR should be readily available to the public. When we asked for PIR, the only official data extended to us were 10 annual statistical fact sheet summaries. "There is limited official reporting of the PIR data to the public," according to the Silver Ribbon Panel Report, and "the PIR needs revision, particularly in the area of health and parent involvement."[14] Baseline data on many issues are simply not collected, collated, or disseminated.

In summary, for a program that is scheduled to receive "full funding" by 1994, the national and regional offices charged to guide and monitor this expansion are greatly understaffed. As recommended by the Silver Ribbon Panel Report in 1990, funds should be earmarked to increase qualified staff at both the national and regional level, to restore travel funds for program monitoring, and to automate Program Information Reports. ACYF should be required and staffed to provide an annual report to Congress that provides extensive management data on the status of the Head Start program.[15]

To revitalize the federal leadership of Head Start, Congress should also establish within ACYF an internship program similar to the Society for Research in Child Development's Congressional Fellows program. Such fellowships should be made available to recent graduates of doctoral programs, in the hope that some interns might stay on to fill openings for permanent positions in the national and regional offices overseeing Head Start.

Once this new monitoring staff is in place, we recommend a nationwide review of all Head Start grantees. In the course of writing this book, we saw some wonderful Head Start centers, but we also observed some that were a discredit to the program's reputation. No grantee or delegate agency that is continually out of compliance with program standards should continue to receive Head Start funds. After 25 years, poor Head Start programs must be weeded out and new grantee agencies selected that can deliver better quality services.

ALLOCATE THE FULL COST OF QUALITY

Although the Head Start Expansion and Quality Improvement Act of 1990 attempted to address many of the above quality issues, the Bush administration is trying to block expenditures for quality improvements. While the reauthorization legislation provided that 25 percent of the 1993 increase be designated for quality improvements, the administration proposed that only $46 million, or 7 percent of its proposed increase for Head Start, be used to address quality. The rest of the money would be used for expansion.

Our preference would be to reverse the administration's priorities, placing more emphasis on quality than quantity until the expenditure per child reaches the amount necessary to provide a quality program. At the least, Congress should restore the $133 million increase for quality improvements that had been projected for 1993.

Based on a 1988 study by the General Accounting Office, the average cost of a full-day, high quality early childhood program accredited by the National Association for the Education of Young Children was $4,797 per child. Taking into account the more comprehensive health and social services required by the Head Start Performance Standards, the National Head Start Association estimates the cost of a high quality Head Start program at $5,400 per child; this estimate also allows sufficient funding for one-quarter of the children to be enrolled in full-day, full-year services. Interestingly, both of these estimates hover around $5,000 per child per year, roughly the sum expended for the Perry Preschool program.

Reaching the full price of full-quality Head Start would cost the federal government only $4,320 per child, since communities would have to come up with the other 20 percent in local match. Based on the 1991 Head Start expenditure of $3,159 per child, it would cost the federal government $696 million to close the gap between the current expenditure per child in Head Start and the amount necessary to provide a full-quality program for the current enrollment of nearly 600,000 children.* This should be accomplished by 1994, regardless of the amount appropriated for program expansion.

---

*We arrived at this estimate as follows: $4,320 − $3,159 = $1,161 × 600,000 children = $696 million. This estimate does not take into account inflation, which at an annual rate of 4 percent would cost the Head Start program nearly $80 million per year.

2. Recognize Head Start as a Full Partner in Welfare Reform

Our second priority is to recognize Head Start as a full partner in welfare reform. Twenty years ago, the nation almost enacted legislation that would have clearly adopted a two-generational approach to welfare reform. The Family Assistance Plan proposed by the Nixon administration would have offered quality child care regulated by federal standards to welfare recipients participating in employment and training programs. Head Start would have served as the model, if not the hub, for child care services.

Given President Nixon's veto of the Child Development Act of 1971, his commitment to protecting the quality of child care for any group *but* the children of welfare recipients is certainly questionable. However, there is little doubt that members of the Nixon administration—including Pat Moynihan, Elliot Richardson, and me—understood the importance of providing quality child care, not just baby-sitting, to keep already disadvantaged children from becoming the next generation of welfare recipients. Unfortunately, by the time federal welfare reform legislation was finally enacted in 1988, both the Bush administration and Congress seemed to have lost sight of the two-generational approach to welfare reform. The Family Support Act contains provisions for funding child care for participants in the Jobs Opportunities and Basic Skills (JOBS) program, but there are no federal standards to protect the quality of care. Similarly, the new Child Care and Development Block Grant program not only contains no standards, but also restricts the state's role in the protection of the quality of care. A sort of federal myopia has set in, where both the president and Congress endorse high quality Head Start programs but adopt an "anything goes" stance toward publicly funded child care.

There are multiple ironies in this situation. Head Start serves much the same population targeted by the Family Support Act: 49 percent of the parents of Head Start children are on AFDC, and, hence, may be candidates for the JOBS program. Furthermore, Head Start from its outset was designed as a two-generational program, promoting social competence for children and economic self-sufficiency for parents. At its best, Head Start has incorporated both a jobs and a services strategy in attacking poverty. AFDC families participating in Head Start should be the first to have access to JOBS-funded child care and employment and training services, but they frequently appear to be among the last.

Because JOBS child care funds have largely bypassed Head Start, many children eligible for Head Start may be consigned to low quality child care at the very time that both the administration and Congress are supporting a major expansion of Head Start. Furthermore, Head Start programs may miss out on resources for employment and training that are greatly needed by Head Start parents.

There are several barriers to fulfilling Head Start's promise as the natural partner in any welfare reform effort. The primary obstacle is the welfare system itself. President Nixon was right—welfare as currently configured *is* stigmatizing. Unfortunately, unlike the original Family Assistance Plan designed by Moynihan and others, the Family Support Act lacks the central provision that would have removed the stigma—namely, the negative income tax or guaranteed income that would have automatically supplemented the income of the poor who were already working, as well as provided incentives for those not employed to find jobs. Without this provision, AFDC recipients must still contend with an extensive, dehumanizing set of means tests and rules in order to obtain any assistance. Thus, perhaps it is not surprising that many Head Start leaders seem to keep their distance from programs that require extensive coordination with welfare departments. Indeed, in discussions with social service coordinators in the Head Start programs highlighted in this book, two of the coordinators seemed to have little or no knowledge of the JOBS program, and a third saw little benefit in the relationship that had been established. Only one of the programs we visited seemed to be actively engaged in a partnership with the JOBS program.

Given the basic flaws that remain in the nation's welfare system, and even in the programs designed to reform it, we hesitate to recommend that Head Start become too entwined with the delivery system for JOBS child care funds. But we do think that there are ways to enhance Head Start's capacity to empower more parents to work or obtain training. First, the program must offer full-day, full-year services if it is to help parents secure employment. Second, Head Start should improve its linkages with a broad range of job training programs instead of limiting its focus to the field of early childhood education.

OFFER FULL-DAY, FULL-YEAR SERVICES

Full-day services were the most frequently stated need by Head Start parents responding to a Silver Ribbon Panel survey, according to Joan Lombardi, project director for the panel. Yet, the percentage of full-day programs actually declined from one-third in 1972 to about 15 percent today.[16] Even those programs characterized as full-day often meet for less than a full working day or fewer than 12 months a year, and only 6 percent of Head Start children are in a nine-hour-day program.[17]

Currently configured as a half-day program, Head Start actually provides an incentive for parents *not* to participate in employment and training programs. According to Lombardi, a few parents actually said that they quit their jobs so their children could be in Head Start.[18] Additional evidence that Head Start can serve as a disincentive to employment comes from a Head Start Recruitment and Enrollment Study. While 40.3 percent of the parents on the waiting list for Head Start were employed, only 28.5 percent of the parents of the enrolled children were employed. The need for full-day child care was also the second most frequent reason for families dropping out of Head Start.[19]

The Administration for Children, Youth and Families certainly acknowledges that some Head Start families need access to full-day care. Recently, the ACYF charged with administering Head Start was placed under the same federal umbrella as the Family Support Administration charged with administering JOBS; this move could facilitate collaboration between the two programs. To that end, ACYF has funded 12 local projects to demonstrate how to develop linkages between Head Start and other programs such as JOBS.[20]

ACYF basically takes the position that Head Start programs should "wrap around" public funds from other child care programs to finance full-day services. While we strongly support collaborative efforts among early childhood programs, there are several problems with the wraparound concept. First, it implies that there are enough child care funds to go around, if only they were managed properly. In truth, placing a priority on using Child Care and Development Block Grant funds for Head Start children would only succeed in taking these dollars away from other children who may be just as needy but who are just slightly above the poverty line. Channeling JOBS child care funds to the children of welfare recipients enrolled in Head Start makes more sense, but most states are already running short of money for this program. No matter how we rearrange the current federal funds for child care, there are simply not enough of them.

Another concern is that there are many barriers to effective collaboration. Currently, there are more than five separate federal funding streams for child care, and each has a different set of eligibility and funding requirements. Furthermore, while Head Start provides advance funding, most federal funds for child care are only available on a reimbursement basis. State and local matching requirements also vary widely. As a result, mixing these various separate funds for early childhood is a complex managerial task at best. If the federal government truly expects Head Start to rely on other child care dollars, federal officials should take the lead in making it easier to do so.

In addition to addressing these administrative barriers to collaboration, federal officials should also make it more possible for Head Start grantees to use some of their expansion funds to supplement the quality of other early childhood programs already serving Head Start eligible children. As the Silver Ribbon Panel points out, this is a way to add parent involvement, health, and other services to child care centers and state prekindergarten programs that serve a population of children greatly in need of comprehensive services. It is also a way to address the space shortage that currently is an obstacle to Head Start expansion in some communities.

Yet another option is to obtain the funding necessary for full-day Head Start programs directly. Based on a last-minute addition to the Head Start Expansion and Quality Improvement Act in 1990, Head Start programs in theory already have the right to spend Head Start funds on extended day programs. However, Congress has yet to appropriate the funds necessary to finance full-day, full-year programs. As suggested earlier, an average $5,400 per child expenditure for Head Start would allow for one-quarter of the children to receive full-day services, about the percentage estimated to need full-day care by nonrelatives. Another possibility would be to amend the Family Support Act itself to establish a separate funding stream for Head Start extended-day programs. However, caution would be needed to protect Head Start's federal-to-local delivery system and its integrity as a comprehensive family support program. Head Start must not become just another "welfare" program.

BROADEN JOB SEARCH AND TRAINING STRATEGIES

As a program promoting maximum feasible parent participation, Head Start has long offered parents both training in early childhood education and job opportunities in the Head Start program itself. If Head Start is to be a full partner in welfare reform, however, the program needs access to a broader range of employment and training activities. Head Start parents should not be limited to job training in early childhood education.

The maximum feasible parent participation policy has served Head Start well. Thirty-five percent of Head Start staff are parents of current or former Head Start children. Head Start has also helped many parents receive professional training in early childhood education. As we noted in the 15th anniversary report, over 12,000 Head Start parents had received college training for credit through the Head Start program, and over 1,000 had received A.A. or B.A. degrees by 1980.[21] Of the 30,000 professional credentials awarded through the CDA program since its establishment in 1972, from one-third to one-half are estimated to have gone to Head Start parents.[22]

Despite this impressive record in promoting early childhood training, we agree with Howard University scholars Valora Washington and Ura Jean Oyemade that Head Start should broaden its approach to helping parents find suitable employment and training.[23] Head Start parents may well be interested in working in early childhood programs, but what about those parents who would prefer to develop other skills? Even at its best, early childhood is no ticket to financial security. Furthermore, job search and training efforts should not be limited to mothers, but should also reach out to the fathers of Head Start children.

We are not suggesting that Head Start itself offer job training programs in other fields, but rather that linkages between Head Start and the Job Training and Partnership Act and JOBS programs be improved so that Head Start parents have easy access to a fuller range of jobs and job training options.

Finally, through its PIR, Head Start should collect more complete information on how many parents enter employment or training programs as a result of their participation in Head Start. According to the National Head Start Association, about half of Head Start parents were engaged in either work or training programs in 1988—32 percent of Head Start parents were working full-time, and another 19 percent worked part-time, or were in education or training programs.[24] However, there is very little quantifiable information available on the extent to which Head Start has helped parents find jobs or appropriate training. According to one study by Abt Associates of Head Start graduates and their peers in 1978, 8 percent of Head Start parents indicated that Head Start had helped them find a job, and 9 percent said that the program had helped them further their educations.[25] Head Start should track changes in parents' employment and training status, and this data should help guide strategies for improving linkages between Head Start and employment and training programs.

3. Allow Head Start to Serve Infants and Toddlers

Almost from the outset of Head Start, there has been concern that the program started too late. Head Start's founders knew that a six-week or even one-year program directed at three- and four-year-olds could not inoculate a child against poverty. We started with that age group primarily because there was still widespread prejudice against any out-of-home program for infants, and because there was very little experience with programs for children below preschool age.

Soon after the initiation of Head Start, the Johnson administration created 36 new Parent and Child Centers to serve children from birth to age three. During the 1970s the Office of Child Development initiated a demonstration project called the Child and Family Resource Program, which offered comprehensive services to children from birth through age eight. The 1980 report on Head Start requested by President Carter noted that "it makes no sense to wait until a child is age three to make sure he or she has the proper nutrition."[26]

What was true in 1970 and 1980 is even more true today. First, Head Start is working with more dysfunctional families than it was in previous years. In a nation where infant and toddler deaths from totally preventable diseases are increasing, children need an earlier "head start" to ensure their very survival.[27] When families are afflicted by substance abuse, domestic violence, or child abuse, child victims literally may not be around to benefit from a Head Start program that does not begin until age three or four. Infants and toddlers of teenage parents, in particular, could benefit from Head Start services.

Second, Head Start must adjust to a society where the entrance of parents with young children into the workforce is the norm, and where welfare policies mandate that parents of children age three or over either work or enroll in training. Head Start's parent involvement component, in the sense of actively involving parents as classroom volunteers or as recipients of home visits, simply does not work as well when parents are expected to be employed full-time. In order to maintain this excellent component of Head Start, the program must reach out to parents of younger children who are more apt to have time to volunteer in the program and who may gain more from home visits because their patterns of parenting are just forming.

Thus, we support the Silver Ribbon Panel's recommendation that by the year 2000, Head Start should build the capacity to serve children under age three. Our specific recommendations include the following:

GIVE COMMUNITIES THE FLEXIBILITY TO SPEND EXPANSION DOLLARS ON INFANTS AND TODDLERS

Lest we be accused of expanding the target population for Head Start before the program has served all the eligible preschool population, we think it is important to point out that statistics indicating that Head Start serves only a third* of the eligible population can be misleading.

These statistics do not take into account the other programs serving poor preschool children. Much has changed since 1965, when Head Start was the only preschool program in many communities. Thirty-five states now offer some kind of prekindergarten program targeted at disadvantaged four-year-olds,[28] and a substantial portion of subsidized child care funds in many states also goes to the preschool age group. Summing up the status of publicly funded early childhood programs, Joan Lombardi, project director for the Silver Ribbon Panel, notes, "It has gotten to the point that if you are poor in this country, your children better be four years old, since that is when they will finally have priority for services."

No doubt fully aware that a large number of eligible four-year-olds are already served in other programs, the Bush administration has focused on four-year-olds as the target group for Head Start. Politicians like to narrow the size of a target group precisely so they can boast that they have served all of the "eligible" population.

Head Start advocates have been reluctant to address how many of the eligible four-year-olds are already served in other early childhood programs for fear of limiting funds for expansion. Yet, Head Start need not have a monopoly on services for preschool children

*The Congressional Research Service estimates that the program serves 28 percent of the eligible children. Other estimates range from one-fifth to one-third.

in order to make the case for new funding. It is time to identify systematically how many of the eligible four-year-olds are already served in other programs that have the potential to provide comprehensive services, precisely so that Head Start can be free to serve younger children.

What we are recommending is that each Head Start grantee, with the consent of its Policy Council, be allowed to decide how to spend its own expansion dollars. In those communities where there are already other programs serving a large portion of the four-year-olds, Head Start programs may prefer to target expansion dollars to infants and toddlers, particularly children of teen parents and those who are drug-exposed. Head Start programs should have the flexibility, based on a community needs assessment, to make their own decisions on which age groups to serve. Indeed without this flexibility, it is questionable why Head Start programs should bother to conduct community needs assessments at all.

Speaking of Head Start's mission for the 1990s, Bill Stone, who formerly headed the Community Action Program in Broward County, says, "We need to reinvent Head Start." Stone is very proud of the formalized Head Start program for preschool children, which is now located in Fort Lauderdale's public schools. But he thinks "we need an entire new Head Start program, more like the original model, for the younger children." Stone would employ more Head Start parents and paraprofessionals in this program for children from birth to age three, and find space in the community as available.

ALLOW HEAD START MORE DISCRETION IN PROGRAM OPTIONS

Closely related to the above recommendation is that Head Start be allowed more discretion in program options. During the 1970s, Head Start experimented with the Child and Family Resource

Program (CFRP) model, which offered a broad range of services to children from birth through age eight. Far from being limited to a classroom-based program, the CFRP offered such services as home visiting for infants, special services for developmentally delayed children, and even therapeutic services, such as crisis intervention and counseling, on an "as-needed" basis.

Unfortunately, despite favorable evaluations of the CFRP by both Abt Associates and the General Accounting Office, the Reagan administration terminated the CFRP program in 1983. The Reagan stance seemed to be keep Head Start alive, but dispense with what he regarded as "frills." Under the Bush administration, some of the old spirit of innovation in Head Start has been restored. With passage of legislation enacting the Comprehensive Child Development Centers in 1988, some demonstration funding was provided to establish multiservice centers for children from birth to age five. ACYF Commissioner Wade Horn has also established some Family Service Centers, which embody certain aspects of the CFRP programs.

However, what is still missing is the conception that the CFRP cafeteria model, offering families a range of service options, should be incorporated into the very essence of Head Start. Particularly with respect to services to children under age three, it is likely that not every family would want center-based services. For this age group, Head Start might want to emphasize its health, social service, and parent involvement components. Given the fact that children under age two have the lowest rates of immunization, just making sure that infants get innoculations would be a major service. In addition, Head Start might want to offer therapeutic services, more intensive but fewer hours per week, to families with drug-exposed infants and toddlers.

IMPLEMENT THE INFANT AND TODDLER PERFORMANCE STANDARDS

A major barrier to the expansion of Head Start services to younger children has been the failure to promulgate performance standards specific to this group. As the National Center for Clinical

Infant Programs (NCCIP) has noted, "the care of infants and toddlers must be regarded as a distinct kind of care, not as a scaled down version of the care of older children."[29] Without specific standards for infant care, even the commitment by Congress to ensure that every state has at least one Parent and Child Center serving infants and toddlers may achieve far less than it could.

Parent and Child Centers have been operating for more than two decades without any federal standards, thereby placing the most vulnerable age group of children at risk. ACYF has been struggling to agree upon and implement standards for at least five years. In 1986 the agency completed a first draft of the standards, and in 1990 it finally released proposed infant and toddler standards for public comment in the Federal Register.[30] Congress stated its intent in the last Head Start reauthorization act that the standards be implemented in a timely manner. Nevertheless, as of this writing, they have yet to be finalized and enacted.

The proposed rules would require that teachers in Parent and Child Centers have a CDA in the infant and toddler area or other certification in child development, and would also set standards for health screenings for infants. NCCIP has suggested some revisions in the proposed rules, such as easing up on the requirement that parents agree to spend half the program time at a Parent and Child Center in supervised parent-child interactions. NCCIP and other groups also consider the proposed one-to-five staff-child ratio insufficiently protective for infants as young as 13 months.

We recommend that ACYF incorporate the NCCIP suggestions and finalize the Infant and Toddler Performance Standards immediately so that Head Start can proceed with the expansion of quality services for this vulnerable age group.

4. Revamp Chapter 1 to Sustain Head Start Benefits in Elementary School

From the earliest evaluations of Head Start, it was clear that the program did not last long enough, and the most recent research confirms the same finding. It is hard to change a child's growth trajectory; a summer is certainly insufficient, and a program of one or two year's duration is not enough for the children at greatest risk. If more disadvantaged children who get a "head start" are to stay ahead, what is really needed is a plan for services that extend from birth through at least grade three.

In the section that follows, we are not recommending that Head Start actually provide the extra services for school-age children. Rather, we propose that the schools pick up two of the most important pieces of the Head Start model, parent involvement and comprehensive services, in order to sustain the gains made by Head Start children when they enter school. Furthermore, as explained more fully in a forthcoming book with Sally Styfco, we suggest that since Congress has already allocated the funds necessary to pay for this recommendation, it just needs to revamp an existing program.[31]

The recognition that Head Start did not last long enough led to the creation of Project Follow Through in 1967. Project Follow Through was intended to be a large-scale service delivery program that extended Head Start's comprehensive services through the early primary grades. In addition, Title I of the Elementary and Secondary Education Act (ESEA) was meant to provide federal funds to the nation's poorest school districts so they could improve the education delivered to low-income children from preschool through high school. With both of these programs in place, the nation would seem to have the necessary components for sustaining the progress made by Head Start through the school years.

Unfortunately, for different reasons, neither Follow Through nor Title I fulfilled this expectation. Follow Through never became a national program and now represents a tiny experiment in the Department of Education conducted in a mere 40 schools throughout the entire country. Although evaluations of individual Follow Through curriculum models indicate that some are quite successful, dissemination of their methods is barely funded, the program is far too small to make a difference, and the project has been threatened with termination so often that it is no longer taken seriously in educational and political circles. Furthermore, while the initial Follow Through model was meant to offer comprehensive services identical to those in Head Start, today the project operates primarily to demonstrate innovative curricula.

Unlike Follow Through, Title I (now Chapter 1) has grown tremendously and now exists in over 90 percent of the nation's school districts. Individual schools use their Chapter 1 allocations at their discretion, so that there is no coherent "program" that can be articulated much less systematically evaluated to determine how well it works. However, the basis for Chapter 1's growth and political support appears to be that it has become a funding source for local schools rather than a proven educational treatment.[32]

Chapter 1 lacks the essential components of a successful intervention program—comprehensive services, parent involvement, innovation, and evaluation. In fact, Chapter 1 was never meant to provide comprehensive services but rather to correct "educational deprivation." The primary Chapter 1 strategy has been to offer more instructional time to low-achieving students. But without the comprehensive services required to put a child in a position to benefit from extra instruction, attempts to drill children on academic skills are an empty exercise.

Chapter 1 has also flip-flopped on the issue of parent involvement. While initially the law that established Title I paid little attention to a role that parents should play, more recent legislation calls for an expanded role for parents without indicating the means for their involvement.[33]

After pouring billions of dollars into Chapter 1 for over two decades, Congress is finally demanding an outcome evaluation of the program. But one wonders if the evaluation studies come too late to instigate change in long-established programs. While there is not much data on the effectiveness of Chapter 1, policymakers have ignored the results that do exist, namely that participating students do not exhibit meaningful improvements in achievement levels.[34] With over $6 billion in annual funds, Chapter 1 has received three to four times the financial resources of Head Start and has yet to prove its worth empirically.

Another problem is that Chapter 1 funds are not targeted very effectively. Although its budget is huge, the money is apportioned in most school districts to serve students across school years, with

80 percent of the funds spent on preschool through grade six. In addition, more than half of the children served are "educationally deprived," meaning that they score poorly on achievement tests but are not necessarily poor.

Given the problems that have plagued both Follow Through and Chapter 1, it is heartening to see a new demonstration program designed to address the transition from Head Start into the elementary school. The Head Start Transition Project, based on legislation sponsored by Senator Edward Kennedy, is establishing its first demonstration sites in each state. Briefly, the Head Start Transition Project is designed to accomplish what Follow Through hoped to do, namely ease the transition for children from Head Start to kindergarten through grade three. When each Head Start child enters kindergarten, the child's parent, Head Start teacher, and kindergarten teacher will meet to discuss the child's transition. Both Head Start and the school will work with community agencies to ensure that comprehensive health and social services are available to the children and their families throughout the primary grades. Provisions are also built in to ensure parent involvement and program evaluation.

If the evaluation of the Head Start Transition Projects is favorable, we recommend that Congress consolidate both the Follow Through program and the new Transition Projects into a new Chapter 1 Transition Project. That is, the recommendation is to put aside the ineffectual educational model of Chapter 1 and adopt on a large scale the proven model of Head Start.

The current Head Start Transition Project is one attempt to move Head Start's valuable lessons into the school, but it is unlikely that the federal government will soon find the money to extend the program to all poor children. Chapter 1 already serves many of the nation's poorest children, but not very well. Moving the Transition Projects and Follow Through into Chapter 1 would create a program with enough resources to make a major difference in the lives of low-income children.

In order to ensure that every Head Start graduate has access to the proposed Chapter 1 Transition Projects, we recommend that at least half of the funds be reserved for Head Start–eligible children. Head Start, including expanded Parent and Child centers, and the Chapter 1 Transition Projects would then be two parts of a coherent federal policy to meet the needs of poor children from birth through grade three.

5. Raise the Income Eligibility Guidelines

When the Head Start Planning Committee was convened in 1965, several of us already were concerned about limiting Head Start to poor children. The idea of segregating children by family income seemed to have some of the same drawbacks as segregating children by race. Concerns about providing for at least a symbolic socioeconomic mix led to the provision that 10 percent of the children in Head Start could come from families over the federal poverty level. The 10 percent rule ended up being even more of a token effort than the Planning Committee realized. Today, only 5 percent of Head Start children are over the federal poverty level, and most of those are physically or mentally handicapped.

There are two problems with Head Start's rigid income guidelines. First, they arbitrarily exclude some children from the program who greatly need it. Second, Head Start children might benefit more from a program with a socioeconomic mix.

Our primary concern is that there are many families just above the federal poverty level who are still poor, and who may have no other access to the kind of comprehensive services that Head Start provides. It is heartbreaking to exclude children who have had no immunizations or physical health exams and who live in the poorest housing just because both their parents are working. Indeed, excluding such children from Head Start seems to be the worst kind of self-fulfilling prophecy: if the message is that you must quit your job or become a single parent in order to secure the services your children need, many parents will do so.

Using the federal poverty level as an admission criterion also discriminates against children who live in urban areas. While the federal poverty level may be a reasonable requirement for Head Start eligibility in rural Alabama, it is totally unrealistic in the urban Northeast. "You can be virtually homeless and still not be eligible for Head Start in this city," says Fran Collins, director of Head Start in Cambridge, Massachusetts.

Head Start currently has much more rigid income eligibility guidelines than nearly all other federal programs. Recognizing the inadequacy of the official poverty line as an index of poverty, Medicaid sets the eligibility limit at 133 percent of the poverty level, the Child Care Food Program at 130 percent, and WIC at 185 percent. Income eligibility for the Job Training and Partnership Act is adjusted for regional variations in living costs.

Thus, we support the National Head Start Association's recommendation that eligibility for Head Start be raised to match the Medicaid guidelines for young children (133 percent of the poverty level).[35] This would allow a child from a family of four with an income of $17,822 per year to be admitted to the program. We also recommend that a special working group of Head Start directors be convened to take into account regional variations in the cost of living for purposes of setting income guidelines.

The verdict on the importance of maintaining a socioeconomic mix among preschool children is less clear. Everything we know about modeling suggests that both poor and more affluent children might benefit from exposure to each other. Yet, children in Head Start also benefit from parental empowerment, and some low-income parents might be less apt to take an active or leadership role in a more economically mixed program.

Taking into account the uncertainties about the importance of a socioeconomic mix among preschool children and the realities of always limited Head Start dollars, Head Start should launch a demonstration project that experiments with admitting families on a sliding fee scale. The program should also sponsor research comparing the effects on poor children of preschool programs that are integrated across income levels with those that limit admission to poor children.

At the Crossroads

Underlying all of our recommendations is the conviction that it is time for Head Start to build on its status as the nation's laboratory for services for poor children from birth to age five. Head Start, the birthplace of comprehensive services in a family setting, should be the first place to experiment with quality programs for infants and toddlers, therapeutic services for drug-exposed children, and improvements on its own two-generational strategy for fighting poverty.

During the 1970s, Head Start did serve as a national laboratory, taking the lead on such efforts as Home Start, competency-based training in the form of the Child Development Associate program, and family support programs, such as the Child and Family Resource Program. Head Start also had the research, demonstration, and evaluation (RDE) budget to support these efforts. In fact, it might be said that we focused on these experimental programs almost to the exclusion of the expansion of the basic center-based program for preschool children; the latter was simply "not in the cards" in the first years after the Westinghouse report that nearly brought an end to the program.

The election of President Reagan, however, brought Head Start's national laboratory to a halt. Research, demonstration, and evaluation declined from 2.5 percent of the overall budget in 1974 to only .11 percent of the total budget in 1989.[36] Fortunately, under the Bush administration, research funds were almost back to their 1971 level of $4 million by 1991, and scheduled to rise to $7 million in 1992. Head Start is also once again promoting innovations, such as its new Substance Abuse Initiative, which attempts to provide guidance to grantees on how to work with children and families affected by drug or alcohol abuse.

Amid the calls for "full funding" for Head Start in the 1990s, therefore, Head Start now stands at a crossroads. How can the program expand to serve all the children and families who need it and, at the same time, renew its status as the pioneer and innovator in child and family programs?

Our position is that much of Head Start's agenda for the 1990s should consist of implementing what has been learned from earlier research and demonstration projects. We do not need more research to establish how vital it is to improve the quality of the program, or to offer full-day services. Nor is a demonstration project required to prove that Head Start should begin earlier for the most vulnerable infants and toddlers, or that its benefits would be more enduring if the intervention continued into elementary school. The importance of all of these proposed "new" directions for Head Start in the 1990s has been abundantly clear for years.

Research and demonstration projects are needed, however, on what the Silver Ribbon Panel called the "finer" points of Head Start programming. Research is needed to provide more information on the components of quality. For example, while we know that children benefit from having teachers trained in early childhood, how much training is enough? Although we know that Head Start has been successful in improving children's health, to what extent do improvements in children's health contribute to other successful outcomes, such as being in the right grade for the right age, or not winding up on welfare?

As discussed frequently in this book, research is also needed on how Head Start affects the whole family, not just the child directly enrolled in the program. What are the dynamics of Head Start that help some families obtain jobs and move to better neighborhoods, and how can the program broaden these effects to more of its participants?

Finally, much more effort should be expended in disseminating some of the lessons learned from Head Start to other early childhood programs. Head Start's health and parent involvement components, and its Performance Standards, should be used as a model for improving the nation's child care services. Federally funded child care, while targeted at disadvantaged children, does not begin to promote the kind of comprehensive family support services that have proved to be effective in Head Start.

Head Start is the nation's most successful educational and social experiment. It was a pioneer in providing comprehensive services in a family-centered context, and it continues to offer the only real two-generational assault on poverty. Over 11 million children are better off today because of Head Start—in some cases, dramatically better off. Yes, Head Start can be—and should be—improved. But our commitment to an ever-improving Head Start is based on the record of its services to children and families so far. Head Start has proved itself as the nation's laboratory for child and family programs that is most deserving of our support.

It's graduation day at the St. Peter's Head Start Center in Miami's Little Havana. Most of the children are newcomers to the United States; they have come from Nicaragua, El Salvador, Puerto Rico, and Colombia. They still speak Spanish, though after a year of Head Start, most of them are now fluent in English as well. The graduates' families, including aunts, uncles, and grandparents, fill the room. Camera bulbs flash; there are exclamations of approval as the children march down a white carpet that has been rolled out for the occasion. They climb up to the stage, where a large American flag covers the entire back wall. The children sing a traditional Hispanic song of leave-taking, "Adios, St. Peter." Then, with faces full of hope, they conclude with "The World Is a Rainbow."

Notes

Chapter 1
High Hopes

1. Edmund Gordon and Carol Lopate, "Head Start: A Comprehensive Report," Typescript, October 30, 1968, p. 50.
2. This and subsequent comments in Chapter 1 by Sargent Shriver were made in an interview with Susan Muenchow, October 12, 1990.
3. The President's Panel on Mental Retardation, *Report of the Task Force on Prevention, Clinical Services and Residential Care* (Washington, D.C.: Public Health Service, 1963), pp. 13–14.
4. Susan W. Gray, "Children from Three to Ten: The Early Training Project," in *A Report on Longitudinal Evaluations of Preschool Programs*, ed. Sally Ryan, vol. 1, *Longitudinal Evaluations*, DHEW Publication no. (OHD) 74-24 (Washington, D.C.: Department of Health, Education and Welfare, 1974).
5. Ibid.
6. Robert Cooke, interview with Susan Muenchow, March 1, 1991.
7. This and subsequent comments by Cooke are from interview with Muenchow.
8. Polly Greenberg, "Head Start—Part of a Multi-Pronged Anti-Poverty Effort for Children and Their Families . . . Before the Beginning: A Participant's View," *Young Children* 45 (6 [September 1990]).
9. Jule Sugarman, "The Early Administrators," in *Project Head Start: A Legacy of the War on Poverty*, ed. Edward Zigler and Jeanette Valentine (New York: The Free Press, 1979), p. 116.

10. Sargent Shriver, "Speech to Public Relations Society," *Public Relations Journal*, January 1967, p. 11.
11. Joseph McVicker Hunt, *Intelligence and Experience* (New York: The Ronald Press Company, 1961).
12. Ibid., p. 168.
13. Ibid., p. 274.
14. Ibid., p. 277.
15. David R. Caruso, Janine J. Taylor, and Douglas K. Detterman, "Intelligence Research and Intelligent Policy," in *How and How Much Can Intelligence Be Increased?*, ed. D. K. Detterman and R. J. Sternberg (Norwood, N.J.: Ablex, 1982).
16. Maya Pines, "How Three-year-olds Teach Themselves to Read—and Love It," *Harper's Magazine*, May 1963, pp. 58–64.
17. "Early Learning Right in the Crib," *Life*, March 31, 1967, pp. 40–47.
18. C. Windle, "Prognosis of Mental Subnormals," *American Journal of Mental Deficiency* 66 (5 [1962]).
19. Edward Zigler, "Familial Mental Retardation: A Continuing Dilemma," *Science* 155 (3760 [January 20, 1967]): 292–98; Edward Zigler and Jacques DeLabry, "Concept-Switching in Middle-Class, Lower-Class, and Retarded Children," *Journal of Abnormal and Social Psychology* 65: 267–73.
20. Cooke, interview with Muenchow.
21. Bruno Bettelheim, Testimony on the Comprehensive Preschool and Education and Child Day-Care Act of 1969, House Select Subcommittee on Education of the Committee on Education and Labor, p. 541.
22. The President's Panel on Mental Retardation, *Report of the Task Force on Prevention, Clinical Services and Residential Care*, (Washington, D.C.: Public Health Service, 1963), p. 15.
23. Urie Bronfenbrenner, interview with Susan Muenchow, December 17, 1991.
24. The Panel of Experts was chaired by Dr. Robert Cooke; "Recommendations for a Head Start Program by a Panel of Experts," February 19, 1965 (Washington, D.C.: U.S. Department of Health, Education and Welfare, Office of Child Development; now available from the Administration for Children, Youth and Families, Office of Human Development, Department of Health and Human Services, Washington, D.C.).
25. Jule Sugarman, telephone interview with Susan Muenchow, February 13, 1991.
26. Liz Carpenter, interview by Joe B. Frantz, May 15, 1969, University of Texas Oral History Project, Lyndon Baines Johnson Library, AC 74-193, tape 2, pp. 31–32.
27. Lyndon B. Johnson, Note on "Presidential Report to the Nation on

Poverty," in *Public Papers of the Presidents of the United States: Lyndon B. Johnson (1963–69)*, February 17, 1965, p. 201.

28. Daniel P. Moynihan, *Maximum Feasible Misunderstanding: Community Action and the War on Poverty* (New York: The Free Press, 1969), p. 28.

29. Lyndon B. Johnson, Remarks upon receiving the Second Report of the President's Committee on Mental Retardation, in *Public Papers of the Presidents*, September 24, 1968, entry 493, p. 972.

30. Jule Sugarman, interview with Susan Muenchow, September 21, 1990.

31. Leon Eisenberg and C. Keith Conners, "The Effect of Head Start on the Developmental Process" (Paper presented at the Joseph P. Kennedy, Jr., Foundation Scientific Symposium on Mental Retardation, Boston, April 11, 1966).

32. Sargent Shriver, Testimony during Hearings before the Subcommittee on the War on Poverty Program of the Committee of Education and Labor, House of Representatives (Washington, D.C.: March 8–10 and 15–16, 1966), p. 155; 1966 Amendments to the Economic Opportunity Act of 1964.

33. Lyndon B. Johnson, Remarks on Head Start, in *Public Papers of the Presidents*, May 18, 1965, entry 259, p. 556.

34. Ibid.

CHAPTER 2
Miracle Workers

1. Jule Sugarman, interview by Stephen Goodell, March 14, 1969, University of Texas Oral History Project, Lyndon Baines Johnson Library, AC 73-45, p. 14.

2. Jule Sugarman, interview with Susan Muenchow, September 21, 1990.

3. Jule Sugarman, Address at the Founding Fathers and Early Directors Forum, National Head Start Association, Seventeenth Annual National Head Start Association Training Conference, San Antonio, Texas, March 30, 1990.

4. Julius Richmond, interview with Susan Muenchow, December 16, 1990.

5. Julius Richmond, interview by Michael Gillette, October 5, 1981, University of Texas Oral History Project, Lyndon Baines Johnson Library, pp. 13–14.

6. Sargent Shriver, interview with Susan Muenchow, October 12, 1990.

7. Richmond, interview with Muenchow.

8. Sylvia Pechman, telephone interview with Susan Muenchow, October 16, 1990.

9. Edmund Gordon and Carol Lopate, "Head Start: A Comprehensive Report," Typescript, October 30, 1968, p. 57.

10. Jean Yavis Jones and Jan Fowler, *The Head Start Program—History, Legislation, Issues and Funding*, Congressional Research Service Report no. 82-93 EPW (Education and Public Welfare Division), Library of Congress, January 17, 1979, updated May 10, 1982, p. 7.

11. Ibid.

12. Shriver, interview with Muenchow.

13. Robert Cooke, interview with Susan Muenchow, March 1, 1991.

14. Richmond, interview by Gillette, p. 49.

15. Richmond, interview with Muenchow.

16. Gordon and Lopate, *Head Start*, p. 42.

17. Sugarman, interview by Goodell, p. 18.

18. Julius Richmond, Address at Founding Fathers and Early Directors Forum, National Head Start Association, Seventeenth Annual National Head Start Association Training Conference, San Antonio, Tex., March 30, 1990.

19. "Recommendations for a Head Start Program by Panel of Experts," February 19, 1965 (Washington, D.C.: U.S. Department of Health, Education and Welfare, Office of Child Development, p. 4; now available from the Administration for Children, Youth and Families, Office of Human Development, Department of Health and Human Services, Washington, D.C.).

20. Cooke, interview with Muenchow.

21. Gordon and Lopate, *Head Start*, p. 34.

22. Frances Degen Horowitz, Correspondence with Edward Zigler, October 15, 1990.

23. James L. Hymes, "The Founders," in *Project Head Start: A Legacy of the War on Poverty*, ed. Edward Zigler and Jeanette Valentine (New York: The Free Press, 1979), p. 97.

24. Eveline Omwake, "Assessment of the Head Start Preschool Education Effort," in *Project Head Start*, ed. Zigler and Valentine, p. 222.

25. Gordon and Lopate, *Head Start*, p. 56.

26. Gordon and Lopate, *Head Start*, p. 60.

27. Gordon and Lopate, *Head Start*, p. 48.

28. Barbara Carter, "The Great Society: A Man with a Problem," *The Reporter*, May 20, 1965, pp. 32–33.

29. Jeannette Galambos Stone, Head Start observation notes, May 6 and 7, and June 3 and 4, 1987.

30. "Recommendations for a Head Start Program," p. 7.

31. Sugarman, interview with Muenchow.

32. Richmond, interview with Muenchow.

33. Edmund Gordon, interview with Susan Muenchow, August 1990.
34. Edward Zigler, "The Nature-Nurture Issue Reconsidered," in *Social-Cultural Aspects of Mental Retardation*, ed. H. Carl Haywood, Proceedings of the Peabody-NIMH Conference (Appleton-Century-Crofts, 1970).
35. Lyndon B. Johnson, Remarks on Announcing Plans to Extend Project Head Start, in *Public Papers of the Presidents of the United States: Lyndon B. Johnson (1963–69)*, August 31, 1965, p. 466.
36. Gordon, interview with Muenchow.

CHAPTER 3
On the Defensive

1. Max Wolff and Annie Stein, "Study I: Six Months Later, A Comparison of Children Who Had Head Start, Summer 1965, with Their Classmates in Kindergarten" (A Case Study of Kindergartens in Four Public Elementary Schools, New York City). (Washington, D.C.: Research and Evaluation Office, Project Head Start, Office of Economic Opportunity, 1966).
2. "Not Enough Head Start?" *Newsweek*, November 7, 1966, p. 100.
3. "Dispute Over Value of Head Start," *New York Times*, April 20, 1969.
4. Edward Zigler and Earl C. Butterfield, "Motivational Aspects of Changes in IQ Test Performance of Culturally Deprived Nursery School Children," *Child Development* 39 (1 [March 1968]): pp. 1–14.
5. Ibid.
6. James S. Coleman et al., *Equality of Educational Opportunity* (Washington, D.C.: U.S. Department of Health, Education and Welfare, 1966).
7. James S. Coleman and T. Hoffer, *Public and Private High Schools: The Impact of Communities* (New York: Basic Books, 1987).
8. Daniel P. Moynihan, "On the Present Discontent" (Address at the Convocation for the 140th Anniversary of the School of Education, State University of New York, September 22, 1984).
9. Sheldon H. White, "The National Impact Study of Head Start," in *Compensatory Education: A National Debate*, ed. Jerome Hellmuth, vol. 3, *Disadvantaged Child* (New York: Brunner/Mazel, 1970).
10. Walter Williams and John W. Evans, "The Politics of Evaluation: The Case of Head Start," *Annals of the American Academy of Political and Social Science* 385 (1969): 118–32.
11. Ibid.
12. John Evans, telephone interview with Susan Muenchow, November 26, 1990.

13. Marshall S. Smith and Joan S. Bissell, "Report Analysis: The Impact of Head Start," *Harvard Educational Review* 40 (1 [Winter 1970]).

14. Ibid.

15. Edmund Gordon, interview with Susan Muenchow, August 8, 1990.

16. Williams and Evans, "Politics of Evaluation."

17. Ibid.

18. Jule Sugarman, interview with Susan Muenchow, September 21, 1990.

19. Gordon, interview with Muenchow.

20. Sugarman, interview with Muenchow.

21. Williams and Evans, "Politics of Evaluation."

22. Office of the White House Press Secretary, "Executive Order 11452 Establishing the Council for Urban Affairs," January 23, 1969. The Nixon Project, National Archives and Records Administration, Alexandria, Va.

23. John D. Ehrlichman, Notes of meetings with the president, Spring 1969 (undated), White House Special Files, Box 3 [of 4], The Nixon Project, National Archives and Records Administration, Alexandria, Va.

24. Daniel P. Moynihan, interview with Susan Muenchow, July 11, 1991.

25. Evans, interview with Muenchow.

26. Richard Blumenthal, Memorandum to Daniel P. Moynihan, March 1969, White House Central Files, Box 1 [of 4], Ex FG6-12 (3/19/69–4/14/69), Subject Files, Council for Urban Affairs, The Nixon Project, National Archives and Records Administration, Alexandria, Va.

27. "Dispute Over Value of Head Start," *New York Times*, April 2, 1969.

28. Richard Nixon, Message to Congress, in *Public Papers of the Presidents of the United States: Richard M. Nixon (1969–74)*, February 19, 1969.

29. Daniel P. Moynihan, *The Politics of a Guaranteed Income* (New York: Random House, 1973), p. 150.

30. Nixon, message to Congress, *Public Papers*.

31. Richard Nixon, Message to the Congress Transmitting Report Relating to the Head Start Program, in *Public Papers of the Presidents*, February 19, 1969.

32. Moynihan, interview with Muenchow.

33. Daniel P. Moynihan, *Maximum Feasible Misunderstanding: Community Action and the War on Poverty* (New York: The Free Press, 1969), p. 99.

34. Chester Finn, telephone interview with Susan Muenchow, November 29, 1990.

35. John D. Ehrlichman, Memorandum for the president re: Head Start, March 19, 1969, The Nixon Project, National Archives and Records Administration, Alexandria, Va.

36. Evans, interview with Muenchow.

37. Victor G. Cicirelli, *The Impact of Head Start: An Evaluation of the Effects of Head Start on Children's Cognitive and Affective Development* (Athens, Ohio: Ohio University, and New York: Westinghouse Learning Corporation, 1969).

38. "Finch Criticizes Head Start Study," *New York Times*, April 25, 1969, p. 22.

39. Smith and Bissell, "Report Analysis."

40. Donald T. Campbell and Albert Erlebacher, "How Regression Artifacts in Quasi-Experiemental Evaluations Can Make Compensatory Education Look Harmful," in *Disadvantaged Child*, ed. J. Hellmuth, vol. 3, *Compensatory Education: A National Debate* (New York: Brunner/Mazel, 1970), pp. 185–200.

41. Victor G. Cicirelli, "Relevance of the Regression Artifact Problem to the Westinghouse-Ohio Evaluation of Head Start: A Reply to Campbell and Erlebacher," in *Disadvantaged Child*, ed. J. Hellmuth, vol. 3, *Compensatory Education: A National Debate* (New York: Brunner/Mazel, 1970), pp. 211–15.

42. Donald T. Campbel and Albert Erlebacher, "Reply to the Replies," in *Disadvantaged Child*, pp. 221–25.

43. Daniel P. Moynihan, *Politics of a Guaranteed Income*, p. 151.

44. William Fillmore, interview with Susan Muenchow, February 20, 1992.

45. Arthur R. Jensen, "How Much Can We Boost IQ and Scholastic Achievement?" *Harvard Educational Review* 39 (1 [Winter 1969]): 1–123.

46. Ibid., p. 80.

47. Richard Nixon, Statement announcing the establishment of the Office of Child Development, in *Public Papers of the Presidents*, April 9, 1969.

48. John D. Ehrlichman, Notes of meetings with the president, May 22, 1969, White House Special Files, Box 1 [of 4], The Nixon Project, National Archives and Records Administration, Alexandria, Va.

CHAPTER 4

My First Crisis

1. Elliot Richardson, *The Creative Balance: Government, Politics, and the Individual in America's Third Century* (New York: Holt, Rinehart and Winston, 1976).

2. Robert Patricelli, telephone interview with Susan Muenchow, August 7, 1990.

3. Daniel P. Moynihan, *The Politics of a Guaranteed Income* (New York: Random House, 1973), p. 131.

4. Richard Nixon, "Special Message to the Congress on Education Reform," in *Public Papers of the Presidents of the United States: Richard M. Nixon (1969–74)*, March 3, 1970.

5. Stephen Hess, *Organizing the Presidency* (Washington, D.C.: Brookings, 1976), p. 122.

6. Office of Management and Budget staff, Executive Office of the President, May 16, 1991.

7. Donald Rumsfeld, Memorandum for John Ehrlichman and George Shultz on the Report of the Subcommittee of the Whole of the Urban Affairs and Rural Affairs Councils to examine the problems attending Federal Grant Programs, Planning Assistance Programs, and Regional Commissions, July 15, 1970, The Nixon Project, National Archives and Records Administration, Alexandria, Va.

8. Elliot Richardson, interview with Susan Muenchow, September 21, 1990.

9. "New Head Start Chief Hits Report Nixon Used," *Washington Evening Star*, June 27, 1970.

10. "Provocative Child Agency Head," *New York Times*, June 27, 1970.

11. "Smooth Run for Head Start Pledged," *Washington Daily News*, November 24, 1970, p. 7.

CHAPTER 5
Maximum Feasible Parent Participation

1. Panel of Experts chaired by Dr. Robert Cooke, "Improving the Opportunities and Achievements of the Children of the Poor," February 19, 1965 (Washington, D.C.: U.S. Department of Health, Education and Welfare, Office of Child Devlopment, now available from the Administration for Children and Families, U.S. Department of Health and Human Services, Washington, D.C.).

2. Midco Educational Associates, Denver, Colo., *Perspectives on Parent Participation in Project Head Start*, Document no. HEW-OS-72-45 (Washington, D.C.: Department of Health, Education and Welfare, Office of Child Development, 1972).

3. Urie Bronfenbrenner, interview with Susan Muenchow, December 17, 1991.

4. Urie Bronfenbrenner, "Head Start, A Retrospective View: The Founders," in *Project Head Start: A Legacy of the War on Poverty*, ed.

Edward Zigler and Jeanette Valentine (New York: The Free Press, 1979).

5. Valora Washington and Ura Jean Oyemade, *Project Head Start: Past, Present and Future Trends in the Context of Family Needs* (New York and London: Garland Publishing, 1987), p. 75.

6. Polly Greenberg, *The Devil Has Slippery Shoes: A Biased Biography of the Child Development Group of Mississippi* (Washington, D.C.: Youth Policy Institute, 1990), p. 3.

7. Ibid., p. 780.

8. Bessie Draper, interview with Susan Muenchow, October 1990.

9. Office of Economic Opportunity, *Head Start Child Development Program: A Manual of Policies and Instructions* (Manual 6108), September 1967.

10. Office of Child Development, *Project Head Start: Parent Involvement 10A—A Workbook of Training Tips for Head Start Staff* (Washington, D.C.: GPO, 1969).

11. Draper, interview with Muenchow.

12. Ibid.

13. Kenton Williams, telephone interview with Susan Muenchow, January 30, 1991.

14. Draper, interview with Muenchow.

15. Jerome Bruner, *The Relevance of Education* (New York: W. W. Norton, 1971), p. 153.

16. CSR, Incorporated, Region V Head Start Training and Technical Assistance Resource Center, *Head Start Success Stories*, January 1990.

17. Rossie Drummond Kelley, interview with Susan Muenchow, October 11, 1990.

18. Frankie Brundage King, interview with Susan Muenchow, February 21, 1991.

19. Faith Lamb Parker, Chaya S. Piotrkowski, and Lenore Peay, "Head Start as a Social Support for Mothers: The Psychological Benefits of Involvement," *American Journal of Orthopsychiatry* 57 (2 [April 1987]).

20. Robert K. Leik, Mary Anne Chalkley, and Nancy Peterson, "Policy Implictions of Involving Parents in Head Start," in *The Reconstruction of Family Policy*, ed. E. Anderson and R. Hula (Westport, Conn.: Greenwood Press, forthcoming).

21. Ibid.

22. Penelope K. Trickett, "Career Development in Head Start," in *Project Head Start*, ed. Zigler and Valentine.

23. Silver Ribbon Panel, National Head Start Association, *Head Start: The Nation's Pride, A Nation's Challenge*, p. 4.

24. Washington and Oyemade, *Project Head Start*, p. 66.
25. Sheila Smith, "Two-Generational Program Models: A New Intervention Strategy," *Social Policy Report* 5 (1 [Spring 1991]).
26. Sen. Orrin G. Hatch, Letter to Nancy Spears, Education Committee Chair, National Head Start Association, December 3, 1984.
27. Nancy Spears, interview with Susan Muenchow, February 21, 1991.

CHAPTER 6
Head Start Meets Child Care

1. Jack Duncan, interview with Susan Muenchow, May 7, 1991.
2. Ibid.
3. "Comprehensive Preschool Education and Child Day-Care Act of 1969," Hearings before the Select Subcommittee on Education of the Committee on Education and Labor, House of Representatives, 91st Congress, First and Second Sessions (Washington, D.C.: GPO, 1970), p. 842.
4. Ibid.
5. John Brademas, interview with Susan Muenchow, October 19, 1990.
6. "Comprehensive Preschool Education and Child Day-Care Act of 1969," p. 29.
7. Brademas, interview with Muenchow.
8. Family Assistance Act of 1970, H.R. 16311, Hearings before the Committee on Rules, House of Representatives, 91st Congress, Second Session, April 7, 1970.
9. Richard Nixon, Remarks on his proposed welfare reform bill, as cited in House of Representatives, Committee on Education and Labor, "Report on the Comprehensive Child Development Act Together with Minority and Additional Views," Report no. 92-1570, October 11, 1972, p. 8.
10. Elizabeth Shelton, "Raising Kids, Not Computers," *Washington Post*, May 3, 1970.
11. Roger Boger, *Heterogeneous versus Homogeneous Social Class Groupings of Preschool Children in Head Start Classrooms* (Washington, D.C.: Office of Economic Opportunity, 1969).
12. Thelma G. Alper, H. T. Blane, and Barbra K. Abrams, "Reactions of Middle and Lower Class Children to Finger Paints," *Journal of Abnormal and Social Psychology* 51 (1955): 439–48.
13. "Irrational Backlash," *New York Times*, August 30, 1970.
14. Calvin Tomkins, "A Sense of Urgency," *The New Yorker*, May 27, 1989, pp. 48–74.

15. These and subsequent comments by Marian Wright Edelman were made, unless otherwise noted, in an interview with Susan Muenchow, October 10, 1990.

16. Day Care and Child Development Council of America, "Industry–Day Care Conference," *Voice for Children* 3 (4 [May 1970]): 7.

17. John Brademas, Opening statement at Hearings on Comprehensive Preschool Education and Child Day-Care Act of 1969, p. 8.

18. House of Representatives, Committee on Education and Labor, "Report on the Comprehensive Child Development Act Together with Minority and Additional Views," Report no. 92-1570, October 11, 1972, p. 6.

19. *Congressional Record*, House of Representatives, September 30, 1971, p. 34287.

20. Brademas, interview with Muenchow.

21. Duncan, interview with Muenchow.

22. Walter Mondale, Statement in the *Congressional Record*, U.S. Senate, December 9, 1970.

23. Hearings on the Child Development Act of 1971, U.S. Senate, May 25, 1971, p. 523.

24. Brademas, interview with Muenchow.

25. *Congressional Record*, The Senate, December 9, 1970.

26. Kevin P. Phillips, "The Day-Care Trap," *Washington Post*, May 20, 1971, p. A19.

27. Letter from Secretary of Health, Education and Welfare to Sen. Walter Mondale, June 15, 1971 (reprinted in Hearings Before the Committee on Finance, U.S. Senate, 92nd Congress, on S. 2003, Child Care Provisions of H.R. 1 and Title VI of Printed Amendment 318 to H.R.1, September 22–24, 1971 [Washington, D.C.: GPO], pp. 100–103).

28. Statement of Stephen Kurzman, assistant secretary for legislation, Department of Health, Education and Welfare; accompanied by Dr. Edward Zigler, director, Office of Child Development, Department of Health, Education and Welfare, Hearings on the Comprehensive Child Development Act of 1971, U.S. Senate, Subcommittee on Employment, Manpower and Poverty, and Subcommittee on Children and Youth of the Committee on Labor and Public Welfare, June 16, 1971, pp. 760–61.

29. Brademas, interview with Muenchow.

30. Orval Hansen, Statement in *The Congressional Record*, House of Representatives, September 30, 1971, p. 34288.

31. Brademas, interview with Muenchow.

32. John D. Ehrlichman, Notes of meetings with the president, November 15, 1971, White House Special Files, Box 6, 8/3/71–12/31/71, The Nixon Project, National Archives and Records Administration, Arlington, Va.

33. John D. Ehrlichman, Notes of meetings with the president, December 8, 1971, White House Special Files, Box 6, 8/3/71–12/31/71, The Nixon Project, National Archives and Records Administration, Alexandria, Va.

34. James Kilpatrick, as cited in the House of Representatives, "Committee on Education and Labor, Report on the Comprehensive Child Development Act Together with Minority and Additional Views," Report no. 92-1570, October 11, 1972, p. 45.

35. Duncan, interview with Muenchow.

36. Brademas, interview with Muenchow.

CHAPTER 7
Keeping the Experiment Alive

1. Donald Campbell, "Reforms as Experiments," *American Psychologist* 24 (1969): 409–29.

2. Carolyn Harmon and Edward J. Hanley, "Administrative Aspects of the Head Start Program," in *Project Head Start: A Legacy of the War on Poverty*, ed. Edward Zigler and Jeanette Valentine (New York: The Free Press, 1979).

3. Ibid.

4. Ibid.

5. Jeanette Valentine, "Program Development in Head Start: A Multifaceted Approach to Meeting the Needs of Families and Children," in *Project Head Start*, ed. Zigler and Valentine.

6. Ibid.

7. Dennis Deloria, Craig Coelen, and Richard Ruopp, *National Home Start Evaluation: Interim Report V, Executive Summary* High/Scope Education Research Foundation, Abt Associates, October 15, 1974.

8. Ibid.

9. Milton E. Akers and Marilyn M. Smith, "Final Report: Feasibility Study for Child Development Project," September 1, 1971, submitted to Office of Child Development.

10. Penelope K. Trickett, "Career Development in Head Start," in *Project Head Start*, ed. Zigler and Valentine.

11. Edward Zigler and Victoria Seitz, "Head Start as a National Laboratory," *Annals of the American Academy of Political and Social Science* 461 (1982): 81–90.

12. Stephen L. Schlossman, "The Parent Education Game: The Politics of Child Psychology in the 1970s," *Teacher's College Record* 79 (1978): 788–808.

13. Comptroller General of the United States, *Report to the Congress:*

Early Childhood and Family Development Programs Improve the Quality of Life for Low-Income Families, Document no. (HRD) 79-40 (Washington, D.C.: U.S. General Accounting Office, February 6, 1979).

14. Urie Bronfenbrenner, *A Report on Longitudinal Evaluations of Preschool Programs*, ed. Sally Ryan, vol. 2, *Is Early Intervention Effective?*, DHEW Publication no. (OHD) 74-25 (Washington, D.C.: Department of Health, Education and Welfare, 1974).

15. Sally Ryan, "Overview," in *A Report on Longitudinal Evaluations of Preschool Programs*, ed. Sally Ryan, vol. 1, *Longitudinal Evaluations*, DHEW Publication no. (OHD) 74-24 (Washington, D.C.: Department of Health, Education and Welfare, 1974).

16. Willa D. Abelson, "Head Start Graduates in School: Studies in New Haven, Connecticut," in *A Report on Longitudinal Evaluations of Preschool Programs*, vol. 1, *Longitudinal Evaluations*.

17. Bernard B. Brown and Edith H. Grotberg, "Head Start: A Successful Experiment," *Extrait: Courier* 30 (1980): 337.

CHAPTER 8
The Carter Surprise

1. Jim Parham, Memorandum to Frank Raines on the Cornell study, June 9, 1977, Box ED-1, Jimmy Carter Library, National Archives and Records Administration, Atlanta, Ga.

2. Ada J. Mann, Adele Harrell, and Maure Hurt, Jr., *A Review of Head Start Research Since 1969 and An Annotated Bibliography* (Washington, D.C.: Social Research Group, The George Washington University, May 5, 1977).

3. Jule Sugarman, Presentation at the Founding Fathers and Early Directors Forum, National Head Start Association, Seventeenth Annual National Head Start Association Training Conference, San Antonio, Tex., March 30, 1990.

4. Edmund Gordon and Carol Lopate, "Head Start: A Comprehensive Report," Typescript, October 30, 1968, p. 59.

5. Ibid., p. 5.

6. Richard E. Orton, "Head Start, A Retrospective View: The Founders," in *Project Head Start: A Legacy of the War on Poverty*, ed. Edward Zigler and Jeanette Valentine (New York: The Free Press, 1979), p. 130.

7. Richard E. Orton, Presentation at the Founding Fathers and Early Directors Forum, National Head Start Association, Seventeenth National

Head Start Association Training Conference, San Antonio, Tex., March 30, 1990.

8. These and subsequent comments from Harley Frankel were made in an interview with Susan Muenchow, September 12, 1990.

9. This and subsequent comments by Caspar Weinberger were made in a telephone interview with Susan Muenchow, November 28, 1990.

10. Sylvia Pechman, telephone interview with Susan Muenchow, October 16, 1990.

11. *NEA Reporter*, June 1976.

12. Terry Herndon, Letter to the president, March 29, 1977, Jimmy Carter Library, National Archives and Records Administration, Atlanta, Ga.

13. Committee on Governmental Affairs, U.S. Senate, Legislative History of Public Law 96-88, Department of Education Organization Act, part I (Washington, D.C.: GPO, 1980), p. 13.

14. Decision memorandum from the vice president, Bert Lance, Joe Califano, and Stu Eizenstat to the president on Reorganization of Federal Education Activities, June 22, 1977, Jimmy Carter Library, National Archives and Records Administration, Atlanta, Ga.

15. James McIntyre, Memorandum for the president, President's Reorganization Project, Reorganization of Education Programs, November 23, 1977, Jimmy Carter Library, National Archives and Records Administration, Atlanta, Ga.

16. Ibid., p. 9.

17. Ibid., appendix C, p. 7.

18. Ibid., appendix A, p. 29.

19. James T. McIntrye, Memorandum for the president, "Next Steps on Education Reorganization," Decision memo returned from president, January 9, 1978, Jimmy Carter Library, National Archives and Records Administration, Atlanta, Ga.

20. Mailgram to Ms. Patricia Gwaltney, deputy associate director, President's Reorganization Project, March 22, 1978. James T. McIntyre Collection, Box 36, Memoranda to the President, 4/3/78–4/20/78, Jimmy Carter Library, National Archives and Records Administration, Atlanta, Ga.

21. Marian Wright Edelman, interview with Susan Muenchow, October 10, 1990.

22. James T. McIntyre and Stuart Eizenstat, Memorandum for the president on the Department of Education, April 12, 1978, Jimmy Carter Library, National Archives and Records Administration, Atlanta, Ga.

23. Frankel, interview with Muenchow.

24. Stuart Eizenstat, interview with Susan Muenchow, May 28, 1991.

25. James T. McIntyre, Memorandum for the president on Including Head Start in the Department of Education, April 14, 1978, James T. McIntyre Collection, Box 36, Memoranda to the President, 4/3/78–4/20/78, Jimmy Carter Library, National Archives and Records Administration, Atlanta, Ga.

26. Bill Smith, Office of the Vice President, Memorandum for Stuart Eizenstat on the President's Request for Calls to Marian Wright Edelman and Coretta Scott King on Head Start, May 8, 1978, Jimmy Carter Library, National Archives and Records Administration, Atlanta, Ga.

27. Ibid.

28. Frankel, interview with Susan Muenchow.

29. Blandina Cardenas Ramirez, interview with Susan Muenchow, September 18, 1991.

30. Peggy Pizzo, interview with Susan Muenchow, May 8, 1991.

31. Ibid.

CHAPTER 9
Surviving the Reagan Years

1. Peggy Pizzo, interview with Susan Muenchow, May 7, 1991.

2. Lawrence Schweinhart and David Weikart, "Young Children Grow Up: The Effects of the Perry Preschool Program on Youths Through Age 15," *Monographs of the High/Scope Educational Research Foundation* 7 (1980).

3. Harley Frankel, interview with Susan Muenchow, September 12, 1990.

4. *Head Start in the 1980's: A Report Requested by the President of the United States* (Washington, D.C.: Office of Human Development Services, Administration for Children, Youth and Families, September 1980).

5. Dorothy Gilliam, "Scrooge 1981," as cited in *The Congressional Record—Senate*, December 15, 1981, S. 15330.

6. John Busa, interview with Susan Muenchow, May 9, 1991.

7. Administration for Children, Youth and Families, Office of Human Development Services, Department of Health and Human Services, "Head Start: Directions for the Next Three Years" (draft report), October 22, 1981.

8. Ibid., p. 14.

9. Ibid., p. 15.

10. Henlay Foster, interview with Susan Muenchow, May 9, 1991.

11. Clennie Murphy, interview with Susan Muenchow, September 18, 1990.

12. Jim Robinson, telephone interview with Susan Muenchow, March 13, 1991.

13. Nancy Spears, interview with Susan Muenchow, February 21, 1991.

14. Sen. Orrin Hatch, correspondence to Nancy Spears, National Head Start Association, December 3, 1984.

15. Spears, interview with Muenchow.

16. Ronald Reagan, Message to Thirteenth Annual Head Start Training Conference on Child and Family Development Training, February 3, 1986.

17. Ruth McKey, Larry Condelli, Harriet Ganson, Barbara Barrett, Catherine McConkey, and Margaret Plantz, *The Impact of Head Start on Children, Families and Communities: Head Start Synthesis Project*, DHHS Publication no. (OHDS) 85-31193 (Washington, D.C.: GPO, 1985).

18. Irving Lazar and R. B. Darlington, *Lasting Effects of Early Education, Monographs of the Society for Research in Child Development* 47 (195 [1982]): 2–3.

19. John Berrueta-Clement, Lawrence Schweinhart, W. Steven Barnett, Anne Epstein, and David Weikart, *Changed Lives: The Effects of the Perry Preschool Program on Youths Through Age 19. Monographs of the High/Scope Educational Research Foundation* 8 (1984).

20. Carol D. Copple, Marvin G. Cline, and Allen N. Smith, *Path to the Future: Long-Term Effects of Head Start in the Philadelphia School District* (Washington, D.C.: U.S. Department of Health and Human Services, Office of Human Development Services, Administration for Children, Youth and Families, Head Start Bureau, September 1987).

21. McKey et al., *The Impact of Head Start*.

22. Judith Chafel, "Funding Head Start: What Are the Issues?" *American Journal of Orthopsychiatry* 62 (1 [January 1992]): 9–21.

23. Berrueta-Clement et al., *Changed Lives*.

24. Urie Bronfenbrenner, *The Experimental Ecology of Human Development* (Cambridge, Mass.: Harvard University Press, 1979).

25. Faith Lamb Parker, Chaya S. Piotrowski, and L. Peay, "Head Start as a Social Support for Mothers: The Psychological Effects of Involvement," *American Journal of Orthopsychiatry* 57: 220–33.

26. Victoria Seitz, Laurie K. Rosenbaum, and Nancy Apfel, "Long-Term Effects of Family Support Intervention: A Ten-Year Follow-Up," *Child Development* 56: 376–91.

27. George Bush, "Leadership on the Issues," Campaign document, October 12, 1987.

CHAPTER 10
Head Start: The Next Generation

1. Connie Leslie with Pat Wingert, Howard Manley, and Sue Hutchinson, "Everybody Likes Head Start," *Newsweek*, February 20, 1989, pp. 49–50.

2. Lawrence Schweinhart, "How Much Do Good Early Childhood Programs Cost?" Forthcoming.

3. Julie Rovner, "Head Start Is One Program Everyone Wants to Help," *Congressional Quarterly* 48 (16 [April 21, 1990]): 1191–95.

4. Silver Ribbon Panel, National Head Start Association, *Head Start: The Nation's Pride, A Nation's Challenge, Recommendations for Head Start in the 1990's*, p. 17.

5. This and subsequent comments by Fran Collins were made in an interview with Susan Muenchow, December 13, 1990.

6. Joanne P. Brady and Irene F. Goodman. *Lessons Learned: Head Start's Experience with State Activities*. Forthcoming.

7. R. Kusserow, *Dysfunctional Families in the Head Start Program: Meeting the Challenge*, no. OAI-09–89-01000. (Washington, D.C.: U.S. Department of Health and Human Services, 1989).

8. This and subsequent comments by Don Bolce were made in an interview with Susan Muenchow, September 1990.

9. David Chavkin and Peggy Pizzo, "Head Start and Medicaid: A New Marriage for the 1990s," National Head Start Association, Spring 1991, pp. 53–57.

10. Silver Ribbon Panel, p. 22.

11. Ibid., p. 23.

12. *Head Start in the 1980's: A Report Requested by the President of the United States* (Washington, D.C.: U.S. Department of Health and Human Services, September 1980).

13. Ibid., p. 27.

14. Silver Ribbon Panel, p. 24.

15. Ibid., p. 40.

16. *Head Start in the 1980's*, p. 32.

17. Silver Ribbon Panel, p. 26.

18. Joan Lombardi, Presentation to Regional Administrators Meeting, Washington, D.C., September 18, 1990.

19. Charles Gershenson, Head Start paper comments to Marlys Gustafson, November 10, 1987.

20. Sheila Smith, "Two-Generation Program Models: A New Intervention Strategy," *Social Policy Report* 5 (1 [Spring 1991]): 5.

21. *Head Start in the 1980's*, p. 12.

22. Bolce, interview with Muenchow.
23. Valora Washington and Ura Jean Oyemade, *Project Head Start: Past, Present, and Future Trends in the Context of Family Needs* (New York and London: Garland Publishing, 1987).
24. Silver Ribbon Panel, p. 26.
25. *A National Survey of Head Start Graduates and Their Peers*, ED152422 (Cambridge, Mass.: Abt Associates, 1978).
26. *Head Start in the 1980's*, p. 36.
27. Peggy Pizzo, "Family-Centered Head Start for Infants and Toddlers: A Renewed Direction for Project Head Start," *Young Children* 45 (6 [September 1990]): 30–35.
28. Silver Ribbon Panel, p. 13.
29. Eleanor Szanton, National Center for Clinical Infant Programs, "Memo to Day Care Committee on Performance Standards for Head Start," August 3, 1990.
30. U.S. Department of Health and Human Services, Office of Human Development Services, Administration for Children, Youth and Families, "Program Performance Standards for Head Start Programs Serving Infants, Toddlers and Pregnant Women," 45 CFR, part 1307, Proposed Rules, *The Federal Register* 55 (118 [June 19, 1990]).
31. Edward Zigler and Sally Styfco, "Strength in Unity," in *Head Start and Beyond: A National Plan for Extended Childhood Intervention*, ed. Edward Zigler (New Haven: Yale University Press, forthcoming).
32. L. F. Carter, "The Sustaining Effects Study of Compensatory and Elementary Education," *Educational Researcher* 13 (1984): 4–13.
33. Edward Zigler and Sally Styfco, "Strength in Unity: Consolidating Federal Education Programs for Young Children." Forthcoming.
34. C. G. Arroyo and Edward Zigler, "America's Title I/Chapter 1 Programs: Why the Promise Has Not Been Met," in *Head Start and Beyond: A National Plan for Extended Childhood Intervention;* T. W. Fagan and C. A. Heid, "Chapter 1 Program Improvement: Opportunities and Practice," *Phi Delta Kappan* 72 (1991): 582–85; U.S. House of Representatives, *Opportunities for Success: Cost-Effective Programs for Children*, no. 101-1000 (Washington, D.C.: GPO, 1990).
35. National Head Start Association, "Head Start Income Guidelines Are Out of Touch with Poverty," Press release, December 5, 1991.
36. Silver Ribbon Panel, p. 33.

Index